THE BETA ISRAEL (FALASHA) IN ETHIOPIA

STEVEN KAPLAN

The Beta Israel (Falasha) in Ethiopia

From Earliest Times to the Twentieth Century

NEW YORK UNIVERSITY PRESS

NEW YORK AND LONDON

NEW YORK UNIVERSITY PRESS
New York and London

Library of Congress Cataloging-in-Publication Data
Kaplan, Steven.
The Beta Israel (Falasha) in Ethiopia : from earliest times to the
twentieth century / Steven Kaplan.
p. cm.
Includes bibliographical references and index.
ISBN 0-8147-4625-X
1. Falashas—History. 2. Ethiopia—Ethnic relations. I. Title.
DS135.E75K35 1992
963'.004924—dc20   92-1175
CIP

New York University Press books are printed on acid-free paper,
and their binding materials are chosen for strength and durability.

Manufactured in the United States of America

c 10 9 8 7 6 5 4 3 2 1

For Booshun and Yona

Contents

Acknowledgments

This book, which marks the culmination of almost a decade's research on the history of the Beta Israel, could never have been written without the support and assistance of countless individuals and institutions. While it is impossible to list all of those on four continents who have in one way or another helped me in my work, I must at least attempt to acknowledge some of the most important.

Since making *aliyah* in 1977 I have been affiliated with the Hebrew University of Jerusalem and more specifically with the departments of African History and Comparative Religion. My colleagues at the university have been unstinting in their encouragement of my work. Particular mention must be made of Professors Nehemiah Levtzion and Michel Abitbol, who were directors of the Ben Zvi Institute for the Study of Oriental Jewish Communities during the period from 1983–1989 when I headed its research project on Ethiopian Jewry. In the face of the increasing politicization of research on the Beta Israel, they continued to maintain a policy that made academic excellence and scholarly integrity the Institute's sole priorities. In a similar fashion, the Harry S. Truman Research Institute for the Advancement of Peace under the guidance of Professors Zvi Schiffrin, Ben-Ami Shillony, and Naomi Chazan supported my work long before research on Ethiopian history and culture became fashionable and continued to encourage my interest in basic research when more contemporary work may have earned more attention.

During the 1989–90 academic year when most of this book was written, I was on sabbatical and received the generous support of a University Teacher's Fellowship from the National Endowment for the Humanities. My family and I lived at the Center for the Study of World Religions at Harvard University and were truly made to feel completely at home. At the same time, I was also fortunate to be a visiting scholar at the African Studies Center of Boston University. The staff and scholars there provided me with a warm and stimulating environment that contributed immeasurably to my progress during the year. The Hill Monastic Manuscript Library of St. John's University in Collegeville, Minnesota, and the Frobenius Institute in Frankfurt, Germany, also kindly hosted me for short visits and generously made the resources of their libraries available to me.

Edward Ullendorff, Getatchew Haile, Kay Kaufman Shelemay, James McCann, Irene Eber, and Chaim Rosen all generously commented on portions of my manuscript. Their comments and criticisms have enabled me to correct many of the deficiencies of earlier drafts. They, of course, bear no responsibility for those that may remain in the final version. An earlier version of Chapter 6 appeared in *Jewish Social Studies* 49 (Winter 1987), pp. 27–42, and an earlier version of Chapter 7 was published in *Paideuma* 36 (1990), pp. 67–77. I wish to thank the editors of both journals for permission to include revised versions of these articles in this book.

Norma Schneider assisted throughout all stages in the preparation of this book from the presentation of the original proposal to the submission of the final manuscript. For many years I had hoped to work with Norma on a book, and I trust that the experience was as rewarding for her as it has been for me. I hope less time will pass before we begin work on our next project.

The eighteen months during which this book was written involved a period of great personal and political upheaval. Certainly when I began writing, I had no idea that the final pages of the manuscript would be completed in a new home with a gas mask at my side. More than once, I impatiently waited for the computer to "save" a portion of the text, so that I could heed the warnings of the air-raid sirens and enter my sealed room. That I was able to retain my focus and continue my work was due in large part to the incredible support I received from many dear friends including Vivienne Burstein, David Satran, Mindy Milberg, Kay Shelemay, Diane Baxter, Linda Aronson, Sally Zanger, and Irit Averbuch. Although rarely the primary topic of our many conversations, this book could not have been written without the reassurance and affirmation they offered.

Finally, I wish to thank my children, Booshun and Yona, and dedicate this book to them. Their patience, love, and humor have taught me more than I ever knew there was to learn.

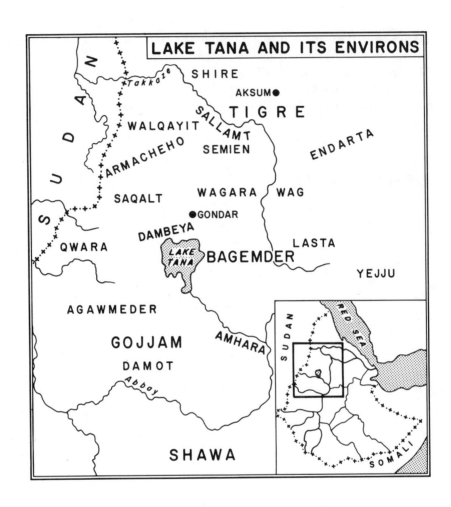

THE BETA ISRAEL (FALASHA) IN ETHIOPIA

Introduction

Despite the existence of a vast and ever-expanding literature on the Beta Israel (Falasha) of Ethiopia, no book-length scholarly study of their history has yet been published. Major works on their literature and religion have generally offered only brief surveys of their history, and most of the standard books in Ethiopian and Jewish history have dealt at best only briefly with their particular story. Thus, while recent events have focused attention on the Beta Israel to an unprecedented degree, much of their history remains only dimly understood. This book seeks to offer a partial remedy to this problem by tracing the history of Jews and Jewish influences in Ethiopia from earliest times until the twentieth century.

The starting point of this book probably needs no explanation. Anyone with even a passing familiarity with the Beta Israel will have noticed the extent to which interest in their origins has dominated discussions of their historical, cultural, and even national identity. While most of these discussions have been singularly uninformed, and the dearth of sources places the topic itself more in the realm of prehistory than history, no study of the Beta Israel would be complete without a detailed examination of the evidence for and the impact of early Jewish influences upon Ethiopian culture. Although there is little reason to assume that a direct link exists between the Beta Israel and these early elements, the milieu they helped create is an essential ingredient for any understanding of later events.

This early history is, therefore, discussed in some detail in Chapter 1. Chapter 2 is concerned with events from the fourth to thirteenth century, a vast period during which we have no reliable sources on Jews in Ethiopia. Although much of what is presented in this chapter is of necessity very tentative, in this case at least an overcautious approach appears to be a necessary corrective to the bulk of previous speculation. In the next chapter, we begin recounting the history of the Beta Israel in earnest and examine the circumstances that led to the transformation of loosely affiliated groups in northwest Ethiopia into a clearly defined ethnic-religious entity known as the Falasha. Chapter 5 considers the causes and consequences of the wars between the Falasha and the Christian rulers of Ethiopia. In Chapter 6, we describe the events and forces that changed the Beta Israel from a highly valued group of artisans and builders to a despised semi-caste group. The final two chapters examine the impact of Protestant missionary activity and the great famine of 1888–1892. In the conclusions, we consider the significance of this book for the study of both Judaism and Christianity in Ethiopia.

The decision to limit this study to the period prior to the twentieth century may require more explanation than its starting point. Interest in the more recent history of the Beta Israel is clearly considerable and probably exceeds that which exists for most of the periods examined in this book. Unquestionably, events that took place after 1900 including the activities of the Jewish counter-missionary Ya'acov (Jacques) Faitlovitch, the Emperor Haile Sellassie's policies of modernization, Christianization, and Amharization, the Italian Fascist conquest of Ethiopia, and the growing relationship of the Beta Israel with World Jewry that culminated in the massive *aliyah* (immigration) movement of the 1980s and 1990s, are all richly deserving of detailed study. Nevertheless, it was decided to exclude them from this work. Despite the abundance of written and oral documentation of these events, in almost every case even the most preliminary research has yet to be undertaken. Thus any attempt to extend this volume to include events up to and including the last decades of the twentieth century would have involved a vast amount of preliminary spadework and identification of sources for each of these modern topics. The completion of this volume with its analysis of earlier periods would have been delayed by at least several years.

Even more important, the history of the Beta Israel in the twentieth century differs substantially from that of any earlier period. As we shall discuss in greater detail below, prior to the twentieth century, the history of the Jews of Ethiopia is the story of their life *in Ethiopia*. Events outside that country and, in particular, developments among other Jewish communities had virtually no impact on their condition. From the twentieth century onward, however, the history of the Beta Israel became increasingly entwined with that of Jews in the Diaspora and Israel. While the Ethiopian context rarely ceased to be decisive, numerous external variables came increasingly into play. Accordingly, I have decided that rather than delving into areas foreign to me both with regard to their period and region, I would end this volume on the eve of Ethiopian Jewry's entry into World Jewish history. It is to be hoped that in the future a later volume or volumes will take up the challenge of exploring this fascinating theme.

Problems of Sources

In part at least, the dearth of historical studies on the Beta Israel may be attributed to the peculiar nature of the available sources. Although the Beta Israel have for many centuries been literate and possess a significant *corpus* of religious literature, none of the texts which have reached us to date are historical in character. Indeed, serious questions must be raised as to whether the Beta Israel themselves ever wrote history. Given the lack of internal written sources, scholars of Beta Israel history have had little choice but to turn to two alternative forms of documentation: external written materials and oral traditions collected from both Beta Israel and Christian Ethiopian informants.

Well into the 1970s almost all attempts to trace the history of the Beta Israel rested exclusively on written sources. The problems these posed for scholars were considerable. Reliable mentions of the Beta Israel or their ancestors only appear in these sources from the fourteenth century onward. Even then, none of the texts written prior to the middle of the nineteenth century is concerned with the Beta Israel per se. Instead, they offer passing references in the context of discussing the miracles of a holy man, the military exploits of a king, the fate of the Jews in exile, and so on. Thus, the historical record, rather then offering a clearly defined chronologically linked narrative, provides a disjointed series of episodes, each of which is presented not for its inherent importance to the Beta Israel but for its usefulness in illustrating one or another of the themes of real interest to the author. To these already substantial difficulties must be added the fact that the three languages of the greatest importance for this subject—Ge'ez, Portuguese, and Medieval Hebrew—are not among the most commonly known or most widely translated tongues on earth.

Previous Research

Not surprisingly in light of these difficulties, the best attempts to reconstruct Beta Israel history on the basis of written sources have been both brief and cautious. Most notable among these is almost certainly the American scholar Robert L. Hess's article, which appeared in two formats in the 1960s.[1] Balanced and judicious, this essay has long provided a useful starting point for any serious student of Beta Israel history. Its main faults, which are two-fold, are closely linked to each other. Unable to consult either the Ge'ez or Portuguese contemporary sources in the original, Hess relies far too much on later works, in particular the eighteenth-century Scottish explorer James Bruce. Not only does this mislead him on occasion in matters of fact, but it also tends to strongly color the general tone of his article. While avoiding the highly strident tone of some authors, Hess generally presents a gloomy picture of Beta Israel history. Wars, persecutions, and forced conversions appear to be the dominant note of their history in Ethiopia. In part, no doubt, this is the result of a widespread tendency that has continued to this day, to emphasize the downtrodden condition of the Beta Israel (usually referred to as their "plight"), and to overemphasize the extent of their isolation from their Christian neighbors. To some extent, however, it may be attributed to Hess's inability to consult a number of Ge'ez, particularly hagiographic sources, which offer a far more nuanced and overall more positive image of the Beta Israel's position.

Whatever the faults of Hess's essays, these appear relatively minor when compared with many of the more recent attempts to portray the history of the Beta Israel. Ignorant of either the necessary source languages or Ethiopian history (and often both), a number of recent authors have sought to reconstruct Beta Israel history by synthesizing the existing written sources. By far the most ambitious of these is David Kessler's

The Falashas: The Forgotten Jews of Ethiopia.[2] As I have discussed this book and some of its shortcomings in some detail elsewhere, these need not detain us for too long here.[3] Although clearly the product of considerable time and effort, Kessler's book suffers from a number of basic faults. Unable to consult the requisite source languages (and, in this case, Hebrew must be added as well), he relies uncritically on later texts, principally Bruce, and in some cases upon questionable secondary works. Moreover, unguided by a basic familiarity with Ethiopian history and culture, he is prone to misinterpretations and misreadings, many of which stem from an unnatural attempt to squeeze the history of the Beta Israel into his own concepts of Diaspora Jewish history.

Although published in 1982, Kessler's book is at its best representative of scholarly opinion from a decade earlier. During the 1970s considerable progress was made in our understanding of the Beta Israel, largely as a result of work by two American scholars: Kay Kaufman Shelemay and James Arthur Quirin.[4] Based primarily on oral sources collected in Ethiopia between the years 1973 to 1975, the works of Shelemay and Quirin represent a turning point in the reconstruction of Beta Israel history and culture. Not only did their pioneering fieldwork enable them to fill in many of the gaps left by the haphazard record of the external written sources, they also achieved something of a revolution in our understanding of the origins and genesis of Beta Israel culture.

Shelemay, an ethnomusicologist trained at the University of Michigan, focused her attention primarily upon the Beta Israel liturgy. Through a multidisciplinary approach combining both oral and written sources and a detailed comparison with liturgical materials from the Ethiopian Orthodox Church, she was able to demonstrate that the Beta Israel's religious system far from deriving from an archaic Jewish source is, in the main, an outgrowth of the Christian Ethiopian tradition. She dated it, moreover, no earlier than the fourteenth or fifteenth century and traced its origins to contact in that period with Ethiopian Christian monks. Originally submitted as a Ph.D dissertation in 1977, Shelemay's work was eventually published in her award-winning book, *Music, Ritual, and Falasha History*. It is a truly impressive book and will long remain a basic text for anyone seriously interested in the Beta Israel. Although it does perhaps minimize the evidence for continued change in Beta Israel tradition after the fifteenth century, this is a comparatively minor fault when weighed against its overwhelming contribution.[5] Of

greater immediate relevance to our present effort, it remains, its historical contribution notwithstanding, primarily an ethnomusicological study.
Thus, while its discussions of history are among the most precise and
balanced published to date, in the end they take up a relatively small
portion of her book and invite rather than preclude more detailed study.

The basic core of such a study is indeed found in James Quirin's
dissertation, "The Beta Israel (Felasha) in Ethiopian History: Caste Formation and Culture Change, 1270–1868." Submitted to the University
of Minnesota in 1977, Quirin's thesis represents the first in-depth study
of a major period in Beta Israel history and is a seminal contribution to
our understanding of their story. Unfortunately, publication of this work
has been long delayed and its importance even in scholarly circles has
not been fully appreciated. Certainly, had it not existed, the present
book would have had a greatly different form. Moreover, it was only
when serious questions began to arise concerning its timely publication
as a book that I began to seriously consider writing this volume.

Obviously, two works seeking to describe the history of the same
people and using many of the same sources will share many themes in
common. However, in the forms familiar to me, the two works can be
said to differ in several significant ways. First, there is the matter of
chronology. As I have already noted, the present volume commences
with the question of early Jewish influences in Ethiopia. Thus, it only
begins to overlap with Quirin's study from Chapter 3 onward. In a
similar fashion, I have decided to conclude my story not in 1868 with
the death of the Emperor Tewodros II, but to devote substantial attention to the activities of the Protestant missionaries from 1860 to 1888
and the disastrous famine that struck Ethiopia from 1888 to 1892.
Second, and perhaps more significant, although the two studies share
many of the same sources, they differ appreciably in their emphasis.
While Quirin, quite naturally has emphasized his knowledge of Amharic
and his trailblazing work in the collection of oral traditions, my own
work depends to a far greater extent upon written sources, particularly
those in Ge'ez. At times this has led to only minor shifts in interpretation, in other cases it has produced substantial differences of opinion.

Perhaps most noteworthy among the latter, I differ from Quirin with
regard to both the origin and extent of political centralization among
the Beta Israel. While oral traditions appear to collapse most regional
distinctions and recount many events as episodes in the history of the

Beta Israel as a single people, written sources provide a record of regional divisions and differences in almost every period. Thus while the available sources do not often allow us to reconstruct a complete picture, it often appears that we are dealing with a number of distinct regional histories rather than one history. This is particularly true for the period prior to the sixteenth century. Although it has often been assumed that there existed throughout this period a "Falasha" kingdom whose roots stretched deep into the distant past, my own work argues for the gradual coalescence of a relatively centralized political group only toward the end of this period and in one region.

Another significant difference between this study and that of Quirin is that while I, primarily on the basis of my studies of Beta Israel literature and other written sources, tend to emphasize the ongoing evolution of Beta Israel culture after the crucial events of the fifteenth century, Quirin (and here he is largely in agreement with Shelemay) tends to concentrate on this one period. Here again, I would argue that both authors have been somewhat misled by the tendency of the oral traditions to trace virtually all significant features in Beta Israel society to the culture heroes Abba Sabra and Ṣagga Amlak.

Third, and finally, while Quirin's study displays a deep concern with comparative and theoretical issues and draws heavily on the social sciences, my own study is basically a narrative history in the humanities tradition.

The Beta Israel in Their Ethiopian Context

These differences notwithstanding, the present study can be said to be closely aligned to those of Shelemay and Quirin in a number of ways. Most important, this book, like their earlier studies, is guided by the view that the history of the Beta Israel can only be understood when analyzed in the context of Ethiopian history in general. Studies of the Beta Israel can be crudely divided between those that have sought to understand them as Ethiopians and those that have viewed them primarily as Jews. In the former category, besides the recent works of Shelemay and Quirin, belong among others the writings of Ullendorff, Strelcyn, and to a lesser extent Leslau. Proponents of an approach emphasizing their Jewish identity have included Wurmbrand, Halévy, Faitlovitch, and in some respects Aešcoly.[6]

The present work unabashedly belongs to the former group. In attempting to situate the Beta Israel in the larger context of Ethiopian history and culture it is not my intention to raise questions concerning either their *halachic* or legal status as Jews or their rights to immigrate to and be accepted as equal citizens in Israel. This book is about their past, not their present or future. Accordingly, every attempt has been made to avoid the tendency to take their current situation or their history as it developed in the twentieth century as the starting points for an investigation of earlier periods. Much of what has been popularly written about the Beta Israel has contained more than a hint of determinism and historicism and has portrayed their story as an inevitable recapitulation of that of other Diaspora Jewish communities. "Exile" and "Return" are only the most recent additions to a series of key terms such as "persecution," "martyrdom," and "Anti-Semitism," which have been intended to liken their history to that of other Jewish groups.[7] In writing this book, I have attempted to take the events, themes, and categories of Ethiopian history as my starting point.

My intention to place the history of the Beta Israel firmly within its Ethiopian context should in the final analysis be hardly surprising. Indeed, in a paradoxical fashion it accords well with some of the most important trends in the evolution of post World War II *Jewish* historiography, and in particular with the growing realization that the best works in Jewish history locate their subject firmly within the broader framework of national and regional developments.[8] More significantly, however, I have attempted to demonstrate that we must turn to the Ethiopian milieu even in order to formulate the categories through which this history is to be understood. As I shall demonstrate repeatedly below, attempts to reconstruct the history of the Beta Israel on the basis of external ideas of "Jews" and "Judaism" versus "Christians" and "Christianity" obscure far more than they illuminate. Indeed, only when we leave such imported concepts behind can we begin to forge a history based on the sources rather than imposed upon them.

Beta Israel, Falasha, Ethiopian Jews?[9]

Closely connected to the consideration of the Beta Israel in their Ethiopian context and to the entire issue of the categories to be used in reconstructing their history is the vexed question of what name or names to use in identifying them. As is already apparent, we have chosen whenever possible to use the term "Beta Israel" rather than either "Falasha" or "Ethiopian Jews." Several considerations have led to this decision.

To this day, the Jews of Ethiopia are most familiar to the reading public under the name "Falasha." Indeed, prior to the 1980s it is difficult to find any substantial piece of work that uses any other term to describe them. In recent years, however, members of the community itself have objected to the term. In particular, they have argued that since the arrival of a large portion of their population in Israel, their continued identification by what they view as a derogatory Ethiopian name is no longer appropriate. These views are certainly deserving of respect, and without question Ethiopian Jews in Israel have as much right as any group to choose the name under which they wish to be known. Nonetheless, the question remains open as to whether these recent expressions of their preference should dictate the manner in which they are referred to in historical writings. At this point, however, yet another factor must be considered. Crucial to the argument of this book is the claim that the Falasha are in a cultural sense the product of events that took place in Ethiopia between the fourteenth and sixteenth century. Even the term itself does not appear to have been specifically applied to Judaized groups prior to the sixteenth century. To refer to groups from earlier periods as Falasha is clearly anachronistic and presumes a degree of continuity that the research of this book does not support. In the final analysis, therefore, the general use of this term has been rejected on both historical and "political" grounds.

In contrast to Falasha, the term Ethiopian Jews (Hebrew: Yehudē Etiopiya) is today universally accepted as the designation preferred by members of the community. In Israel today and in the popular Jewish press, they rarely if ever are referred to by any other term. Historically, however, the term is extremely problematic. In medieval Ethiopia, for example, *Ayhud* (Jews) was a derogatory term used by authors to identify those they viewed as Christian heretics. Rarely, if ever, can it be shown to designate Jews, in the more universally accepted sense of the term. To use this term, therefore, would not only distort the historical record, but would also imply a similarity between the contents of Ethiopian "Jewishness" and "normative" Judaism that is not supported by the sources. As with the aforementioned anachronistic usage of the term

Falasha it would imply a linkage, which the argument of this book in no way supports. Moreover, it must be remembered that prior to the second half of the nineteenth century the Beta Israel did not commonly refer to themselves as Jews. Indeed, there are few clearer witnesses to the dramatic changes they have undergone in the past century and particularly the past two decades than the development of an almost unanimous preference for a term so far removed from the Ethiopian context.

Finally, we turn to the term "Beta Israel." Here too, several difficulties are apparent. First, it must be admitted that the name is not readily recognized and is easily confused with that of other groups, most notably the Bene Israel of India. Second, in the Ethiopian context the designation (Beta) Israel was not limited to those popularly known as Falasha. Indeed, in most contexts the term "Esra'élawiyān" is most likely to be a reference to a member of the imperial dynasty, allegedly descended from King Solomon, than to an "Ethiopian Jew." [10] Third, it is virtually impossible to indicate when this term came into common use. These caveats notwithstanding, several considerations strongly recommend the use of this term. Not only is it the name by which the community in Ethiopia most commonly referred to itself, but it also carries none of the political-polemical weight of either Falasha or Ethiopian Jews. Its relative neutrality, therefore, as well as its clear authenticity have led us to choose this as the most common name used throughout this book.

Against Relevance

It is impossible to conclude the introduction to this book without saying at least a few more words about its alleged relevance to the circumstances of the Beta Israel today. The Beta Israel's desire to come to Israel and the recognition of their Jewishness by that country's rabbinical and political leaders were both well established before I began my research on their history. Nothing that appears in this book will have any impact on those decisions, nor should it. Governmental policy and rabbinic *halacha* are based upon considerations far removed from those of the historian. Indeed, in light of the changes undergone by the Beta Israel in the past two decades, almost any discussion of their identity in previous periods is open to charges of anachronism.

These considerations notwithstanding, for several years I hesitated to express in print (and particularly in Hebrew) my views on the cultural identity of the Beta Israel. In this manner, I hoped to avoid being embroiled in a pointless controversy and to prevent the misuse of my findings by those with little genuine interest in either the Beta Israel or their history. Both my own experience and that of other writers had demonstrated that "pro-Ethiopian" organizations had little concern for the niceties of academic freedom when their most cherished myths were being challenged.[11] In the end, the continued delay in the publication of Quirin's thesis, coupled with the realization that the immigration and absorption of Ethiopian Jews in Israel involved a long-term process due to continue for many years, moved me in June 1989 to begin this book. In it I sought to present a synthesis of all my previous research on the Beta Israel. By the time the writing of this book had been completed in early 1991, its "relevance" had yet again been transformed. Not only had the *aliyah* movement from Ethiopia been renewed, but also large-scale immigration from the Soviet Union and other former Communist countries had presented Israel with an unexpected challenge. Most significantly, the arrival of immigrants from the Eastern bloc clearly revealed that the question of "Jewishness" according to Israeli Law and rabbinic *halacha* was not solely or even primarily confined to the Ethiopians. Indeed, the conflict between differing definitions and understandings of what constitutes Jewish identity is one that Israel and the communities of the Diaspora will continue to ponder for many years. In light of this more general controversy there appears even less reason than before to fear that my findings will in any way affect the Ethiopians as they come forward to press their legitimate claims to be completely recognized by the Israeli state and World Jewry on an equal basis. Indeed, it is my hope that in time this book will provide a record of their history that they can point to with pride, and add to on the basis of their own traditions.

1

Ethiopian Jews: Obscure Beginnings

Anyone with even a passing interest in the Beta Israel will have noted the extent to which the question of their origins has dominated the study of this people. Although much of their modern history remains shrouded in obscurity and a first-rate ethnography of the group has yet to be published, almost everyone who has written about Ethiopian Jewry has felt compelled to weigh in with his or her contribution to the "Falasha origins" debate. Politicians, journalists, rabbis, and political activists have all succumbed to the temptation to play historian and have attempted to unravel this intriguing riddle. In many cases, their results have been both presented and accepted with a seriousness far beyond what they merit.

There are without doubt a number of sociological, psychological, and historical factors that explain the continuing obsession with the origins question. Few people can resist a good mystery, and many have probably been enticed by the possibility of being the first person to present a complete solution to this fascinating problem. It is doubtful, however, if this issue would have received so much attention were it not for the longstanding controversy concerning the precise relationship of the Beta Israel to the rest of World Jewry. For more than a century, the question of the Beta Israel's Jewishness and of the best policy to pursue on their behalf has occupied a variety of Jewish organizations. Moreover, neither the decision of the Israeli Parliament to recognize the Beta Israel as Jews under Israel's "Law of Return" nor the recent immigration of close to forty thousand Ethiopian Jews to Israel has ended the controversy concerning their precise status under Jewish religious law. The fine points regarding this aspect of their Jewish identity still remain unresolved and are the subject of much bitter debate both within and outside the Ethiopian community in Israel.[1]

As a result of this situation, the question of Beta Israel origins has long been invested with an aura of relevance rarely accorded to problems in ancient history. Not surprisingly, only a small proportion of those drawn to this subject have possessed the skills necessary to pass an informed judgment on the matter. Many have not even succeeded in correctly defining the problem under discussion and have confused the question of origins with various other issues such as *halachic* status, standing under Israeli law, and the Beta Israel's own self-image.[2] Thus we find ultraorthodox rabbinical sources citing with evident approval the opinions of secular historians and linguists; scholarly works quoting rabbinical opinions as if they were definitive *historical* documents; and the Beta Israel's deep attachment to their Israelite identity presented as proof of their origins. Clearly some clarification is long overdue.

In this chapter an attempt will be made to review the existing primary sources and scientific theories concerning the origins of the Beta Israel. The question of their *halachic* and legal status will not concern us here or anywhere else in this book. Nor will their self-image be of immediate interest to us in this chapter, although the community's own traditions about its origins will, of course, be considered alongside other sources on this subject. The question we are seeking to answer in this chapter is not the emotive, "Are the Beta Israel Jews?" Rather, we shall give attention to a series of specific historical inquiries: When did Jews or Judaism reach Ethiopia? From where did it/they come? Are the Beta Israel descendants of Jews or merely a group shaped by Jewish influences?

Aksum

The search for the origins of Ethiopian Jewry begins in the ancient kingdom of Aksum. Aksum (the name applies to both the kingdom that ruled over the Tigrean plateau in northern Ethiopia and to the urban concentration that formed its largest area of settlement) is the earliest cradle of Ethiopian civilization. As a matter of course, any discussion of the manner in which Jews or Judaism reached Ethiopia must be set against the general context of what is known about the history and cultural development of the Aksumite kingdom.[3]

The origins of the Aksumite state have yet to be completely unraveled by scholars. There is, for example, no clear consensus as to when the transition from the pre-Aksumite to Aksumite period occurred or about the subdivisions within each period. Nevertheless, the major internal processes and external influences that led to the rise of a highly developed civilization and political structure in northern Ethiopia appear sufficiently clear to enable us to reconstruct the most important trends.[4] Roughly speaking, the pre-Aksumite period can be said to begin around the fifth century B.C. Already at the outset of this period, there is clear archaeological evidence of a strong South Arabian influence on the northern part of the Ethiopian highlands and the predominantly Agaw peoples of the region.[5] At Yeha, the most famous of pre-Aksumite sites, researchers have uncovered a temple from the fifth or fourth century that displays marked similarities to contemporary South Arabian buildings, as well as a number of inscriptions written in a South Arabian language and in a South Arabian syllabary.[6] Similar indications of the impact of South Arabian immigrants are also found in the religious beliefs and social-political organization of this period. Indeed, so powerful does this South Arabian influence appear at first glance that some scholars have depicted pre-Aksumite civilization as little more than a reflection of influences that arrived from across the Red Sea.[7] More recently, however, greater emphasis has been placed upon "the original aspects of this culture, which represents a synthesis of various influences and which, when it draws its inspiration from south Arabian forms, shows that it is superior to its models."[8]

Whatever the original character of this civilization, by the third century B.C. we are clearly dealing less with external influences and more with indigenous developments, which grow out of this earlier foundation. The language of local inscriptions, for example, is less and less like the original South Arabian language.[9] Political terminology also appears less directly connected to South Arabian models. At the same time, cultural and trading ties seem to have developed with the Nile valley, particularly the Nubian kingdom of Meroë.

During the first century of the Christian Era a variety of factors, including a favorable climate, easily protected natural boundaries, proximity to sources of agricultural and natural products, and the decline of the South Arabian kingdoms, enabled the rulers of Aksum to gain control over much of the international trade in the Red Sea area and establish a powerful and highly organized kingdom. During much of the next seven centuries their influence was felt not only throughout northern Ethiopia (see map), but also to the north as far as Meroë and across the Red Sea into large parts of South Arabia. In the third century, Aksum enjoyed so great a reputation that the Persian prophet Mani considered it one of the four greatest kingdoms in the world.[10]

The name Aksum appears for the first time toward the end of the first century in a commercial guide known as the *Periplus Maris Erythraei* (Circumnavigation of the Erythrean Sea). Adulis, which served as its trading outlet and is said by the author of the *Periplus* to be five-days journey from Aksum, is already mentioned by Pliny around the year 60 A.D.[11] In part, at least, Aksumite culture can be clearly seen to preserve the heritage of the earlier pre-Aksumite period. "Certain features of the language and writing, a religious emblem, the name of a god [Astar] . . . architectural and agricultural traditions . . . show that in the early centuries of our era an ancient heritage was still alive."[12] In many respects, however, a new form of civilization can be seen to have developed, which was far more rooted in the indigenous culture. By the second century A.D., for example, a distinctive Ethiopic script, consonantal in form, had appeared. At first it is employed only in short inscriptions, but over time it comes to be used in longer texts. Finally, between the fourth and sixth centuries, it becomes the language of the newly established Ethiopian Church and is used as the language of scripture.[13] During this period, South Arabian and Greek were also used, with the latter probably the primary language of international trade and diplomacy. Already at the end of the first century, Zoscales, the first Ethiopian king mentioned by name, is said to have known Greek.[14]

In a similar fashion both the architecture and the pottery of Aksum show significant differences from that of earlier periods. Religion too appears to have changed dramatically. Only Astar of the South Arabian gods survives in Aksumite belief. The other pre-Aksumite deities are replaced by a triad of indigenous divinities, Mahrem, Baher, and Medr.[15] In the fourth century an even more dramatic change occurs with the conversion to Christianity of the Aksumite king Ezana.[16] His conversion, which completely transformed the cultural basis of the Ethiopian monarchy, is perhaps the most revolutionary event in the history of ancient

Ethiopia. It marks the beginning of a cultural-political tradition that survived for over 1600 years. Yet even before this crucial transformation another earlier religious tradition, that of Jews and Judaism, had succeeded in striking roots in Aksumite culture.

Jews and Jewish Influences

In contrast to the rich archaeological and epigraphic evidence of the South Arabian impact on Aksumite civilization, the proofs of Jewish influences are almost all indirect. None of the contemporary sources offers unequivocal testimony for a Jewish presence in the kingdom. Yet, as we shall demonstrate below, there can be little question that prior to the introduction of Christianity in the third and fourth centuries, Judaism had had a considerable impact on Aksumite culture.

According to some Ethiopian traditions, half the population of Aksum was Jewish prior to the advent of Christianity. While there can be little doubt that this is a considerable exaggeration, the overwhelming impact of biblical and Hebraic patterns on early Ethiopian culture is undeniable. Indeed, well into the twentieth century, much of Ethiopia remained embedded in "attitudes, beliefs, and a general quality of life ... forcefully reminiscent of the Old Testament world."[17] The full range of this biblical-Hebraic molding has been described and analyzed in detail by several of this generation's leading Ethiopianists, and there is, therefore, no need to fully explore this phenomenon in this chapter.[18] A brief consideration of some of its key elements is, however, necessary both for an understanding of Jewish influences on Aksumite culture and for a proper evaluation of the Beta Israel in their proper context. For, as we shall stress repeatedly, an intelligent analysis of the history and culture of the Beta Israel must take as its starting point the fact that biblical practices and an Israelite self-identity are the common heritage of both Jews and Christians in Ethiopia.

No church anywhere in the world has remained as faithful to the letter and spirit of the Old Testament as the Ethiopian Orthodox Church. Numerous biblical customs have survived in the practice of Ethiopian Christians. Thus, for example, male children are circumcised on the eighth day after birth.[19] The Saturday Sabbath long held sway in Ethiopia and figured prominently in the ritual, liturgy, theological literature, and even politics of the Church.[20] Traditional Ethiopian dietary laws conform closely to those of the Old Testament,[21] and the three-fold

division of churches in Ethiopia clearly replicates the architectural structure of the Temple in Jerusalem.[22] On the literary level, the biblical ethos
of Ethiopian Christian culture is epitomized in the country's national
epic *Kebra Nagast* (The glory of kings), which depicts the rulers of
Ethiopia as direct descendants of Menelik I, the putative son of King
Solomon and the Queen of Sheba.[23]

The presence of these and other biblical forms in the dominant Christian culture of Ethiopia raises a number of serious issues of direct
relevance to the history of the Beta Israel. In particular, the mutual
dependence and clear similarities between Ethiopian Christianity and
Ethiopian Judaism will concern us throughout much of this book. Of
more immediate concern, however, is the question of whether these
biblical characteristics taken by themselves constitute unambiguous proof
of a Jewish presence in Aksum.

Although the terms "biblical" and "Jewish" are frequently used inter-
changeably in discussions of Ethiopian culture, it is at times crucial that
they be distinguished. By far the most articulate proponent of this point
with regard to the question of "Jewish influences" in Ethiopia is the
French scholar, Maxime Rodinson. Rodinson argues that Ethiopian culture has been shaped far more by the imitation of the Old Testament
than by direct Jewish influences. Indeed he contends, in agreement with
the nineteenth-century German scholar, August Dillmann, that many of
Ethiopian Christianity's biblical characteristics were not introduced in
the Aksumite period, but only in the reign of the fifteenth-century reforming king Zar'a Ya'eqob.[24] Ethiopian Christianity is, therefore, in his
opinion merely one more example, albeit an extreme one, of the common Christian practice of adopting biblical names, customs, symbols,
and even genealogies.

Given the weight of their contributions to the subject, Rodinson and
Dillmann's arguments deserve to be treated with the utmost seriousness.
Above all, they serve as a valuable warning against a simplistic approach
that ignores both cultural influences and historical developments. In the
final analysis, however, their approach does not appear to satisfactorily
explain all the available data. Of particular significance in this context
are the numerous Jewish-Aramaic loanwords in the Ge'ez (Ethiopic)
version of the Bible. As is well known, the Ge'ez version of the Old
Testament, which was translated between the fourth and sixth centuries,
is based upon a Greek (or at least primarily Greek) *Vorlage*.[25] As one
might expect, this resulted in a fair number of Greek terms entering

Ethiopic at an early date. More surprising, however, is the presence of a significant number of works dealing with religious concepts and practices that derive from Jewish-Aramaic or Hebrew. Words such as *meṣwat* (alms), *tabot* (Ark), and *ṭa'ot* (idol) are all distinctively Jewish in either form or content.[26] Similarly, in Ethiopic the name for the sixth day *'arb*, does not follow the system of naming for the other days of the week: First (Sunday), Second (Monday), Third (Tuesday), etc. The name *'arb* (Friday) does not mean "sixth," but "eve" or "evening" and refers to the eve of the Jewish Sabbath![27] As H. J. Polotsky has observed, "It seems hardly possible that the Aramaic words should have been introduced by Syriac speaking missionaries. . . . None of these words is distinctively Christian in meaning. What they denote belongs to the Jewish leaven in Christianity."[28] In other words, in the view of Polotsky and most other scholars, such loanwords could only have been introduced to Ethiopia prior to the introduction of Christianity and the translation of the Bible. "The Hebraic-Jewish elements were part of indigenous Aksumite culture adopted into Ethiopian Christianity."[29] With regard to the loanwords, moreover, these are almost certainly the product of direct contact with Jews and/or Judaism and cannot be explained as an example of *imitatio Veteris Testamenti*. Thus, the linguistic evidence would seem to clearly indicate that Jewish influences in Ethiopia were, at least in part, both early, i.e., Aksumite, and direct.

Additional support for this view can be gleaned from the Ge'ez versions of several Old Testament and Apocryphal books. Although in general agreement that the Greek version is the primary source for most of these texts, scholars have produced numerous examples of the Ge'ez version's direct dependence upon either a Hebrew or Aramaic *Vorlage*.[30] While the precise circumstances under which such Hebrew-Ethiopic or Aramaic-Ethiopic elements entered the text cannot be determined, and some may even date to later recensions, much of this material would seem to be associated with the original Ethiopic translations.[31]

On the basis of the cultural elements, loanwords, and textual evidence cited above, it appears possible to offer some clear suggestions concerning the earliest Jewish influences on Ethiopian culture. The first carriers of Judaism reached Ethiopia between the rise of the Aksumite kingdom at the beginning of the Common Era and conversion to Christianity of King Ezana in the fourth century. They used Aramaic for religious purposes and probably brought with them texts in that language and perhaps Hebrew. Given the predominantly literary and linguistic evidence for their presence, there appears to be no reason to assume that they were particularly numerous. A relatively small number of texts and individuals dwelling in the cultural, economic, and political center could have had a considerable impact. Initially they settled in the Aksum region and mingled with their pagan and later Christian neighbors. Thus, their influence was diffused throughout Ethiopian culture in its formative period. By the time Christianity took hold in the fourth century, many of the originally Hebraic-Jewish elements had been adopted by much of the indigenous population and were no longer viewed as foreign characteristics. Nor were they perceived as in conflict with the acceptance of Christianity.

Although this summary accounts satisfactorily for most of the material presented above, it leaves unanswered a number of crucial questions concerning the arrival of Judaism in Ethiopia. In particular, it offers no insight into either the provenance of the Jewish influences that reached the Aksumite kingdom or the manner in which they reached Ethiopia. In fact, both these questions have been hotly debated by scholars for more than a century and at least half a dozen theories have been proposed in an attempt to answer them. The exposition and evaluation of these theories will occupy us for most of the remainder of this chapter.

Ethiopia and the Bible

The Land of Cush. We begin our search for the source(s) of the Jewish elements in Aksumite culture with a consideration of the land known to biblical writers as "Cush." The Hebrew Bible contains some fifty references to Cush or Cushites, most of which are translated in the Septuagint as "Ethiopia." Since the ancient Greeks used the term "Ethiopia" to designate any southern land inhabited by people with "burnt-faces," this appears to be a generally satisfactory rendering of the Hebrew term. Unfortunately, some scholars ignore this usage and seriously confuse matters by simplistically identifying ancient Cush/Ethiopia with present-day Ethiopia.[32] This misreading not only distorts the intention of the biblical (and later Greek) authors, but also, when applied to the question of Beta Israel origins, produces connections and loci of Jewish settlement where none existed. We shall have cause, therefore, at several points in our discussion to return to this issue.

In the Hebrew Bible, the term Cush refers to a number of different locations. In some cases, particularly the genealogical table in Genesis 10:6–10, it is extremely difficult to understand the passages' intent.[33] In others, most notably Esther 1:1 ("From India to Cush"), it seems to mean simply the ends of the earth. In most instances, however, the term "Cush" is used to designate the "Nubian kingdom which was situated along the Nile, south of Egypt."[34] Such references are especially common in the eighth and seventh centuries B.C., when the twenty-fifth or "Ethiopian" (i.e., Nubian) dynasty ruled Egypt and its kings played a major role in the international politics of the period.[35]

As the references cited above and many others indicate, already in the pre-exilic period the ancient Israelites were familiar with the land of Cush and its people and enjoyed, albeit primarily on an indirect basis, certain connections with that distant land. Several verses appear to even offer some support for the claim of a Jewish presence, either individual or communal in the region. Isaiah 18:1–2, which speaks of papyrus boats sailing beyond the rivers of Cush, may well be based upon information from eyewitnesses.[36] Isaiah 11:11, Psalm 87:4, and Zephaniah 3:10 all seem to indicate that a diaspora community existed in Cush,[37] and there appears to be no reasonable basis for rejecting this assumption. Nevertheless, caution must be exercised concerning the significance of these alleged communities on several levels. It must be stressed, for example, that the biblical claims of an Israelite presence in Cush receive no support from the substantial archaeological work undertaken in the region.[38] At the least this could appear to indicate that the Israelite cultural impact was extremely limited. Moreover, and perhaps even more important, on both chronological and geographical grounds none of these references can be said to shed any light on the manner in which Jewish influences reached Aksum. All of them significantly predate both the crystallization of Judaism and the emergence of civilization in the Aksum region.[39] Most of them are clearly concerned with a Nubian rather than an Aksumite milieu. Accordingly, even if we concede the existence of an Israelite diaspora in some regions south of Egypt, it is difficult to conceive of it as the primary source for the Hebraic-biblical characteristics that entered Ethiopian culture.

Solomon and Sheba. Of all the explanations offered for the biblical influences on Ethiopian culture and the origins of the Beta Israel, none has captured the imagination as much as the tradition that associates them with King Solomon and the mysterious Queen of Sheba. The reservations of historians (and, more recently, the Beta Israel themselves) notwithstanding, this story appears to claim pride of place in any account of their origins, history, and culture.[40]

The story of the Queen of Sheba first appears in two slightly different biblical versions: 1 Kings 10:1–13 and 2 Chronicles 9:1–12.[41] In both places the text offers only the sparsest of narratives: The Queen of Sheba, having heard of Solomon's greatness travelled to Jerusalem to test him with difficult questions. Solomon won her over not only by answering her questions, but also through the evidence of his well managed court, his palace, and the Temple. The Queen blessed God and gave Solomon gifts of gold, spices, and precious stones. After Solomon reciprocated, the Queen returned to her land.

As is often the case, the very brevity of the biblical narrative seems to have encouraged the development of a series of legendary elaborations on the story. Muslim, Jewish, Medieval Christian, and, of course, Ethiopian sources have added vivid details to the concise and circumspect biblical story.[42] Although each of these traditions provides its own particular twists and variations to the story, the Ethiopian version is unique in several respects. Not only is it the lengthiest and most elaborate of the Sheba legends, but also it differs significantly from the others in purpose and function. If elsewhere the primary focus of the story is Solomon's wisdom and miraculous powers, the Ethiopian text is concerned with the Queen, her son through Solomon, Menelik, and the transfer of the mantle of God's chosen people to the Ethiopians. If elsewhere the Sheba legend represents a minor topic within a vast corpus of legendary material, in Ethiopia it stands at the heart of the country's religio-political traditions.

The classic formulation of the Solomon and Sheba legend is found in a book known as the *Kebra Nagast* (The glory of kings).[43] This work, which is justly recognized as the Ethiopian national epic, was probably first composed some time between the sixth and ninth centuries A.D.[44] In the fourteenth century, it received its definitive form and served as the "charter legend" for a new dynasty of kings, who based their legitimacy on a claim of descent from King Solomon and the Queen of Sheba.[45]

According to the *Kebra Nagast*, the Queen of Sheba, known as Makeda, travelled from Aksum to visit King Solomon in Jerusalem. During her stay, Solomon not only dazzled her with his wisdom, but also tricked her by a clever ruse into having sexual relations with him. The Queen conceived a son, whom she bore upon her return to Aksum. When he reached maturity, this son, Menelik, journeyed to Jerusalem to meet his father. At the completion of Menelik's visit, Solomon commanded that the first-born sons of the priests and elders of Israel accompany him to Aksum. Before setting out, however, Menelik and his companions led by Azariah, the son of the High Priest, stole the Ark of the Covenant from the Temple. Thus, the glory of Zion passed from Jerusalem and the Children of Israel to the new Zion, Aksum, and the new Israel, the Ethiopian people.

The story is engaging, at points even amusing. Yet its occasional lightness of tone should not lead one to underestimate its centrality for an understanding of the thought-world of traditional Ethiopia. Whatever the initial intent of the earliest compilers of the *Kebra Nagast,* the Solomon-Sheba legend eventually became the basic metaphor for legitimacy and authority within Ethiopian culture. Far from being the sole possession of a small ruling elite, the story was transformed into a crucial element in the genealogies of numerous regional and ethnic groups.[46] Not least among these were the Beta Israel.

The eighteenth-century Scottish explorer James Bruce was the first author to state that the Beta Israel traced their origins to Solomon and Sheba.

The account they give of themselves, which is supported only by tradition, is, that they came with Menilek from Jerusalem, so that they perfectly agree with the Abyssinians in the story of the queen of Saba. . . . They agree also, in every particular, with the Abyssinians, about the remaining part of the story, the birth and inauguration of Menilek, who was their first king; also the coming of Azarias, and twelve elders from the twelve tribes, and other doctors of the law, whose posterity they deny have ever apostatised to Christianity, as the Abyssinians pretend they did at the conversion.[47]

A little more than half a century later in 1830 the Anglican missionary Samuel Gobat brought a similar account, noting, however, that it was not the only Beta Israel story concerning their origins.

They do not know of what tribe they are; nor have they any adequate idea as to the period when their ancestors settled in Abyssinia. Some say that it was with Menelic, the son of Solomon; others believe that they settled in Abyssinia after the destruction of Jerusalem by the Romans.[48]

Two decades later the French cleric and explorer Antoine d'Abbadie received a similar confusion of traditions from the mouth of the learned

Beta Israel monk and High Priest, Abba Yeshaq: "Nous sommes venus avec Salamon. . . . Nous sommes venus après Jérémie le prophète. Nous ne comptons pas l'année de l'arrivée de Min Ylik. Nous vînmes sous Solomon."[49]

The obvious contradictions in these last two testimonies notwithstanding, there can be little question that the claim of a connection to Solomon and Sheba lay at the heart of a, perhaps *the,* major Beta Israel tradition concerning their origins. Many later authors, including twentieth-century ethnologists and linguists have stated unequivocally that this version was reported to them by their Beta Israel informants.[50] Indeed, only in the past decade do the Beta Israel appear to have begun to distance themselves from this legend.[51]

Yet, despite the evidence of these testimonies, there would appear to be no basis for accepting the Solomon and Sheba legend as an historical explanation for either the Jewish elements in Ethiopian culture or the origins of the Beta Israel. From a chronological point of view, the *Kebra Nagast* presents a number of insurmountable difficulties. The reign of Solomon is generally dated to the tenth century B.C., at least five centuries before the first glimmerings of Aksumite civilization. On a similar basis, many of the major features of the Jewish impact on Ethiopian culture, both among the Christians and the Beta Israel, clearly date from a period long after Solomon's time.[52] Indeed, to this day most scholars continue to view the Queen of Sheba as a visitor from South Arabia.[53] Thus while the Solomon and Sheba story is certainly a major element of the biblical molding of Ethiopian civilization, and a careful analysis of its numerous versions and levels of meaning a fruitful direction for research, it offers little by way of an historical explanation for the origins of the Beta Israel.

The Lost Tribe of Dan. In 1973 when the Sephardi Chief Rabbi of Israel, Ovadiah Yosef, publicly declared the Beta Israel to be Jews according to *halacha,* he stated that they were descendants of the lost tribe of Dan.[54] In ascribing this lineage to the Beta Israel he invoked a tradition that in different forms can be traced back through Jewish sources for over five hundred, perhaps even more than a thousand years. In a later section, we shall examine some texts that discuss this tradition to see what, if any, information they contain concerning the history of the Beta Israel. For the moment we shall be concerned exclusively with the alleged Danite connection. The earliest source for a tradition connecting the Jews of Ethiopia with the tribe of Dan is probably the mysterious ninth century figure Eldad Ha-Dani. Eldad himself claimed to be from the tribe of Dan (hence the name Ha-Dani), which lived along with Naftali, Gad, Asher, and the "sons of Moses" "beyond the rivers of Cush."[55] To this day scholars remain uncertain about his origins and motives. While some have dismissed him as a hoax, others have viewed him as a Karaite, Arabian, or even Ethiopian Jew.[56] Abraham Epstein, who almost one hundred years ago published what remains a definitive study of *Sefer Eldad*, cast grave doubt on Eldad's Ethiopian origins.[57] More recently, Ullendorff has argued that

His language reveals no trace of Ethiopic nor does his narrative betray any first-hand knowledge of Abyssinia. He shows, however, more than a casual acquaintance with Arabia, and his Hebrew offers some evidence of an Arabic substratum. It is therefore likely that he was a Jew from South Arabia.[58]

Modern scholarly opinion notwithstanding, many of Eldad's Jewish contemporaries viewed him as an authentic representative of the lost tribes and accepted his claim of Danites and other tribes living in distant lands.[59]

Eldad's narrative, while highly influential, does not at any point unequivocally link the tribe of Dan to the Jews of Ethiopia. The first source to explicitly make this connection is a letter from the noted rabbi and talmudic scholar Obadiah of Bertinoro.[60] In a letter to his father written on August 15, 1488, Obadiah reports on the Jews who live in the land of "Prester John," including two he met in Egypt. After briefly discussing their religious practices, he notes, "And they say that they belong to the tribe of Dan."[61] This statement is significant not merely for its clarity, but also because it is unique in stating that the Ethiopians themselves put forward a claim to a Danite origin.

The most important sources for the Beta Israel-Danite connection are without question two *responsa* of the sixteenth-century Egyptian talmudic scholar and halachic authority, David Ben Abi Zimra, the Radbaz.[62] Writing in the first half of the sixteenth century in response to questions concerning the halachic status of Beta Israel brought to Egypt as slaves, the Radbaz twice affirmed their Jewishness and Danite origin. "Those [Jews] that come from the land of Cush are without doubt from the tribe of Dan."[63] Such was the authority of the Radbaz that his ruling established a halachic precedent that has retained its validity to this day. Thus beginning with his student Rabbi Ya'acov Castro (1525–1610) and continuing more recently with Rabbi Ovadiah Yosef and Israeli Supreme Court Justice Menachem Elon, Jewish authorities have cited the Radbaz and affirmed the Danite lineage of the Beta Israel.[64]

As with the Solomon and Sheba legend, the tradition associating the Beta Israel with the tribe of Dan is long established and may even have a basis in their own oral history. Once again, however, it appears to be seriously deficient as an historical explanation of their origins. External evidence for a Danite presence in Ethiopia is, of course, completely lacking. Nor do any of the sources that put forward this claim attempt to offer a plausible explanation as to how the Danites may have reached that country. Even within the context of rabbinic and *halachic* opinion, the Beta Israel-Danite connection is not universally accepted. Several important rabbinical authorities have dismissed this alleged tribal affiliation as erroneous, and Jewish tradition offers little support for a Danite migration to Ethiopia.[65] On the basis of all of these difficulties, there appears to be little if any basis for accepting the idea of a link to the tribe of Dan as the solution to the riddle of the origins of the Beta Israel.[66]

As we have seen above, none of the solutions examined thus far offers an adequate explanation of either the origins of the Beta Israel or the presence of biblical-Hebraic elements in Ethiopian culture. In fact, both the Danite and Solomon-Sheba accounts must be viewed primarily as mythic or legendary tales of greater interest for their symbolic meaning than for the direct insight they offer into these historical problems. The suggestion of the existence of a Jewish presence in ancient Cush, while plausible, does not appear to move us markedly closer to a resolution of these issues. Not surprisingly, none of these theories enjoys strong support among the leading scholars in the field. These appear to be divided between proponents of an Egyptian origin for Ethiopian Judaism on the one hand and supporters of a South Arabian source on the other. It is to the first of these positions that we now turn our attention.

Egypt. No feature of recent scholarship on the Beta Israel is more indicative of the current state of research than the numerous attempts to press the claim that Egypt was the primary source of Jewish influences on Ethiopian culture. This theory, which in the past was espoused by, among others, the outstanding Italian Ethiopianist Ignazio Guidi and the respected scholar and second President of Israel Itzhak Ben Zvi has long been rejected by most scholars.[67] Recent advocates of this position have brought little that is new to the debate and have usually failed to either contend with or overcome the numerous objections presented to this theory in the past.[68]

The argument for an Egyptian origin for the Beta Israel can be briefly summarized as follows.[69]

Egypt, as is well known, was already in pre-exilic times the site of a diaspora Jewish community. In the Second Temple period (586 B.C.–70 A.D.) this community thrived and represented one of the premier centers of Hellenistic Judaism. The Greek translation of the Hebrew Bible, the Septuagint, which served as the basis for the Ge'ez version was the product of Egyptian, particularly Alexandrian Jewry. Given the geographical proximity of Egypt to Ethiopia, it seems reasonable to suggest that Jews following the path of the Nile could have made their way to its sources in Ethiopia. Significantly, perhaps, the traditional areas of Beta Israel settlement were in regions near the source of the Blue Nile. Certain cultural phenomena would also appear to link Egyptian and Ethiopian Jewry. Of particular interest in this respect is the Jewish military garrison that existed between the seventh- and fifth-century B.C. on the island of Elephantine, near present-day Aswan. The religious practice of this community was in several ways similar to that of the Beta Israel, most notably in its inclusion of a sacrificial cult conducted by priests. Finally, it should also be noted that some of the Beta Israel's own traditions mention Egypt as their country of origin.[70]

At least with regard to some of its minor points, the Egyptian theory can be shown to be based on misunderstandings. Thus, for example, the fact that the Ge'ez version of the Old Testament is based primarily on a Greek *Vorlage* is of limited significance once it is recalled that it is almost certainly the product of Christian translators.[71] As we have noted above, it is not the Greek but rather the Aramaic and Hebrew that appear to reveal a distinctively Jewish element. In a similar fashion, while the hypothesis of a Nile route would appear at first glance to explain the Beta Israel's presence in the Lake Tana region,[72] it completely ignores the fact that the Nile, from Egypt to Ethiopia, has never been navigable. It does not, moreover, account for the strong Jewish influences that were felt in the Aksumite region. Are these to be seen as the product of a different stream of Judaism?

Of even greater concern are the questions that must be raised concerning the alleged ties between Elephantine and Ethiopia, which lie at the core of most arguments for an Egyptian origin for the Beta Israel.[73] The

Jewish community at Elephantine was established some time in the seventh century B.C. and survived for approximately two hundred and fifty years. The site it occupied, an island in the Nile at the first cataract, the traditional southern border of Egypt, was of considerable strategic importance throughout its history. The Elephantine garrison came to the attention of scholars at the beginning of the twentieth century with the discovery and subsequent publication of a large collection of Aramaic papyri, which detailed the essentials of the community's life.[74] Unfortunately, no external sources on the Jews of Elephantine have been discovered to date and our knowledge of the community's history and religious life remain incomplete.

Since there is no direct evidence of an association between the Jews of Elephantine and those of Ethiopia, proponents of this theory have relied upon the indirect evidence of geographical proximity and shared religious practice to support their case. With regard to the former, relatively little attempt has been made to develop a detailed migration theory. Since even the most diehard diffusionists have recognized that cultural parallels do not themselves prove contact, the silence of scholars on this matter is more than a little troubling. While we would certainly not claim that either the eight-hundred mile overland journey from Elephantine to Aksum or the two-thousand (!) mile journey via the Nile to the Lake Tana region are impossible endeavors, further discussion of such matters as route, timing, and motive would be welcome.

In this context, it is particularly distressing to note the tendency of some authors to minimize the difficulties they confront not by a more detailed explanation of their theories, but by the geographical equivalent of a shell game. Elephantine island was, as we have noted, located near the traditional border of Egypt and Nubia. To speak of it as being located on the border of Egypt and the [modern] Sudan is both inaccurate (by almost two hundred miles) and misleading.[75] In a similar fashion, while it is certainly correct to locate Elephantine on the border of what the Greeks called "Ethiopia," that is, the area south of ancient Egypt, too casual a use of this term is merely confusing. Thus, while it may well be that some residents of Elephantine knew an Ethiopian language and that certain garrisons revolted and fled to Ethiopia, neither report should be taken to refer to Aksum or Ethiopia in its present connotation.[76]

Turning to the issue of a shared religious culture, here too, considerable difficulties can be shown to exist. To begin with, it is not at all clear precisely how one can demonstrate an historical link between a little known group that disappeared long before the Christian Era and a community whose religious system can only be documented beginning in the fifteenth century.[77] These difficulties aside, it must be admitted that an Elephantine connection could explain some features of Beta Israel culture. The Elephantine and Beta Israel communities are almost unique among Jewish groups in their practice of a sacrificial ritual outside the Land of Israel. Even here, however, it must be admitted that important differences also exist. While the Jews of Elephantine performed their sacrifices in a Temple, the Beta Israel *masgid* (house of worship) was used primarily for prayer. Sacrifices were performed in the open air.[78] In fact, when a careful comparison is made between the religious life of the two communities, differences can be shown to greatly outweigh similarities. The attitudes toward the Sabbath presented by the two communities are, for example, a study of contrast. Although the Elephantine papyri contain no explicit mention of Sabbath observance in that community, one can easily concede Porten's claim that the local Jews were aware of and commemorated the day in some way.[79] The Sabbath, he concludes, "appears to have been honored more in the breach than in the observance [at Elephantine]."[80] Nothing could be further from the custom of the Beta Israel among whom the Sabbath is accorded tremendous respect and celebrated with great rigor.[81] Moreover, the Sabbath observance of the Beta Israel differs substantially from that of the Elephantine Jews not only in degree, but also in kind. The Beta Israel's rules concerning the Sabbath, as well as many other features of their religious life, are strongly influenced by the *Book of Jubilees,* a work composed in the middle of the second century B.C., long after the Elephantine community had ceased to exist.[82] Thus, the Sabbath as observed in Elephantine can scarcely be said to have resembled that of the Ethiopians.

Nor is this the only major difference between the two communities. The Aramaic texts found at Elephantine are in a dialect quite different from that of the Aramaic loanwords in Ge'ez, and accordingly this colony could not have been a source for these linguistic influences.[83] Supporters of the Elephantine origins of Ethiopian Judaism have generally preferred to ignore the clear evidence of religious syncretism in the Egyptian community's life. While there can be little question that Yahu (Yahweh), the God of Heaven, was the primary focus of religious attention for the Jewish garrison, proof also exists that other gods were rendered homage as well. "There is evidence for this devotion [to the gods] on both the individual and communal level."[84] Particularly striking in this context is the decision of the Jewish leader Jedaniah b. Gemariah to distribute a portion of the monies collected for YHW to the deities Anathbethel and Eshembethel.[85] Needless to say, neither of these gods nor any gods like them are found among the Jewish influences that reached Ethiopia.

Finally, a word must be said about the religious literature of the Ethiopian Jews. No copy of the Pentateuch was found at Elephantine,[86] nor is it likely that the community possessed one. It is hardly likely that the Jews of Elephantine would have appealed to Jerusalem for help in rebuilding their temple and renewing their sacrifices had they been aware of King Josiah's reform (ca. 622 B.C.) and the Deutronomic prohibition of sacrifice outside of Jerusalem.[87] Similarly, while they may have possessed some portions of the Bible, it must be noted that even the Torah, the first part of the Hebrew Bible to be canonized, did not formally receive that status until the time of Josiah.[88] Thus, whatever the literary sources for the religious life of the Elephantine Jews, they could scarcely have been the same as the Orit (Torah)-centered Beta Israel. The situation with regard to the later biblical books, as well as the apocryphal literature, is even more striking. None of these works could have been in the possession of the Elephantine Jews, and they must, therefore, have reached the Beta Israel through other channels.

We, therefore, see that despite the efforts of a number of recent authors to argue to the contrary, clear differences exist between the practice of the Jews of Elephantine and those of Ethiopia. Nothing in the recently published literature provides any reason to dissent from Ullendorff's succinct summary of the subject published more than twenty years ago:

Such aspects of Elephantine religious life as emerge from the papyri are in sharp contrast to the entire cast of religious expression among the Falashas in particular and the Judaizing trends of the Abyssinian Church in general. This estimate remains true even when the fullest allowances are made for the inevitable deficiencies in our knowledge of the Elephantine community.[89]

South Arabia. In contrast to proponents of the Egyptian theory, who are concerned almost exclusively with the Beta Israel and rest their case primarily on alleged similarities in religious practice, scholars who support a South Arabian origin generally begin with the larger question of Jewish influences on Ethiopian culture and base their arguments on geographical proximity and the long history of contacts between both sides of the Red Sea. In the first part of this chapter we briefly discussed the earliest period of these contacts and noted that over time a characteristic Ethiopian culture, similar but not identical to that of South Arabia, emerged in the Aksum area. The development of a distinctive Ethiopian civilization was neither the result of nor a cause for a complete break with South Arabia. In fact, commercial, military, and political ties between the Red Sea neighbors remained strong, at least until the rise of Islam in the seventh century.[90] Given the clear indications of a Jewish presence in the Arabian peninsula throughout most of this period, it is difficult to preclude the possibility that Jewish immigrants reached Ethiopia from this direction.

Precisely how early Jews reached South Arabia and from what date their impact could have been felt in Ethiopia remains the subject of some controversy. Maxime Rodinson, for example, has questioned whether prior to the late fourth century Judaism was sufficiently entrenched in the Arabian peninsula to have also influenced Ethiopia.[91] Ullendorff has argued that a strong Jewish presence existed in the peninsula from the first century A.D. onward.[92] To a considerable degree, one's verdict in this dispute will depend on just how strong one feels the Jewish influence in South Arabia must have been for it to be felt in Ethiopia as well. Certainly, there can be little argument concerning the fact of an early Jewish presence in the Arabian peninsula.

Although the biblical text's numerous references to "Arav" or "Aravim" reveals no great wealth of knowledge about the Arabian peninsula, later literature is more informative. Jewish soldiers were apparently among the ten thousand troops that Aelius Gallus took to South Arabia around the year 25 B.C.[93] More significantly, the great sage Rabbi Akiba is said to have travelled far into Arabia, where he encountered a Cushite (black, Ethiopian) king of the Arabs.[94] The report is noteworthy not only because it indicates that an Ethiopian ruler reigned over part of South Arabia ca. 130, but also because the journey itself must be viewed as evidence of a sizeable Jewish community in the region. Only such a presence would justify the undertaking of such a lengthy and difficult journey.[95] While some Jews may, as some traditions claim, have reached Arabia in the First Temple period, they most probably arrived after the destruction of the Second Temple in 70 A.D. Thus there was an important Jewish presence in South Arabia throughout most of the period of its contacts with Aksum. Some Jews, although almost certainly not an organized community, were probably among the South Arabian colonists and merchants who came to Ethiopia. Others may have had contact with citizens of Aksum who crossed the Red Sea during various periods. Certainly, a strong case exists for accepting the view of many scholars that South Arabia was the primary source of Jewish influences on Ethiopian civilization.[96]

As we have demonstrated above, a number of factors would appear to indicate that many of the biblical/Hebraic elements were in place prior to the introduction of Christianity in the fourth century. This, of course, would not preclude the strengthening of these elements during a later period, either as the result of a growing familiarity with biblical literature or as a consequence of later contacts. Several authors have suggested, for example, that Jews may have reached Ethiopia as prisoners of war in the sixth century following the Aksumite victory over the Judaized Arabian king Joseph Du Nuwas.[97] Although no firm evidence exists in support of this supposition, neither can it be dismissed out of hand. It appears unlikely, however, that this could have marked the earliest Jewish contact with Ethiopia. In a similar fashion, while the Arabian peninsula is most probably the earliest and most important source of Jewish influences, our limited sources make it impossible to completely rule out the possibility of later and secondary influences from other sources.

Finally, we must close this chapter with some words of caution. As we have attempted to demonstrate, the most probable source for the biblical-Hebraic molding of early Ethiopian civilization involves elements that reached Aksum from South Arabia in the second and third centuries A.D. This claim leaves open for the moment a question that is crucial to the continuation of our discussion: Are the Beta Israel the descendants of those who brought Judaism to Ethiopia or are they simply one of the groups that emerged through their influence? As we shall attempt to show in the remaining chapters, despite the vociferous views of their political allies and the learned pronouncements of rabbinical authorities, it would be simplistic to depict the Beta Israel as direct descendants of Jewish immigrants to Ethiopia. It is, moreover, even more problematic to claim that their religious system as it existed in the late nineteenth and early twentieth centuries was based on ancient Jewish practice. Immigration, intermarriage, acculturation, and major religious upheavals all played a part in the formation of the people known as the Beta Israel or Falasha.

2

Speculation and Legend

The Establishment of the Church in Aksum

Given the success and influence Hebraic elements enjoyed in the Aksum region, a Judaized faith may eventually have had a chance of becoming the dominant religion in the region. Certainly, this is what happened briefly in parts of South Arabia during the sixth century. However, while Aksumite culture was still in its infancy, the religious map of the country was transformed by its ruler's acceptance of Christianity. Throughout all its subsequent history the development of Judaism in Ethiopia was conditioned by the presence in the country of a politically dominant Christian element. It is with this element, therefore, that we continue our story.

While various legends seek to trace the introduction of Christianity to Ethiopia to the Apostolic period, scholars are virtually unanimous in viewing the arrival of the Syrian brothers Frumentius and Aedesius in the fourth century as the turning point in the Aksumite kingdom's religious history.[1] The story of their activities, which appears with minor variations in both Ethiopic and non-Ethiopic sources, offers a vivid picture of the process whereby Christianity entered Ethiopia.

Arriving in Ethiopia as refugees from a plundered ship, the two Syrians became important officials in the court of the Ethiopian king.

When this monarch died, his queen asked the brothers to assist in governing until her infant son was old enough to rule the kingdom himself. During this period, Frumentius took advantage of his position to seek out and support Christian merchants residing in Aksum. When the prince had grown up and assumed the throne, the two Syrians left Ethiopia: Aedesius returning home to Tyre and Frumentius travelling to Alexandria, where he met the Egyptian Bishop Athanasius. Apprised of the fact that Ethiopian Christians lacked both bishops and priests, Athanasius appointed Frumentius as the first bishop to Ethiopia. Frumentius then returned to Ethiopia and preached Christianity throughout the country.[2]

Corroboration for this episode is found in a letter from the Emperor Constantius to the Aksumite rulers Ezana and Shaizana in which the Arian emperor advises them that Frumentius' consecration by the anti-Arian Athanasius was not valid and suggests that they return him to Egypt to be reconsecrated by the Arian Bishop George of Cappadocia.[3] Since one of these rulers is the same Ezana whose inscriptions testify to his conversion from paganism to Christianity, the establishment of the Church in Ethiopia is unusually well documented.

The newly converted Aksumite king, Ezana, found himself in a difficult position. On the one hand, he did not wish to startle or offend the bulk of his subjects who remained loyal to their previous faiths. On the other hand, he sought to present himself in as favorable a light as possible to the influential Christian minority, which lived close to the capital, engaged in trade, and had extensive external contacts. He was thus forced to steer a middle path between proponents of the new religion and traditionalists. To the foreign community he portrayed himself as a devout Christian ruler, commencing a Greek inscription, "In the faith of God and the power of the Father, and the Son, and the Holy Ghost."[4] In a Ge'ez inscription written at the same time, however, the king attempts to present himself in a manner acceptable to his non-Christian subjects. In this text, he refers to God as the "Lord of Heaven," a designation that would certainly have been understood by the bulk of the population as a reference to a traditional God such as Astar.[5] Indeed, as late as the seventh century, the Christian translator of the *Ecclesiasticus* (Ben Sira) refers to God as "Astar" in at least two places.[6] Thus Ezana was able to present his new beliefs in terms compatible with the traditional cosmology.[7]

In light of the circumstances of his conversion and given the limited resources commanded by the Church during the next few decades, it is unlikely that Ezana's decision was the cause of any immediate change in the fortunes of the Judaized residents of Aksum. Initially the number of local Christians was probably small and their faith only vaguely articulated. Active persecution or discrimination, as has been suggested by Rathjens and Wurmbrand, appears therefore highly unlikely.[8] Moreover, the lack of both trained clergy and books in Ge'ez must have been major obstacles to the spread of Christianity. For many years the impact of the new religion was probably limited to the royal court and the resident foreign merchants. Taddesse Tamrat suggests that for more than a century after Ezana's conversion "the effective sphere of influence of the Church was limited to a narrow corridor between Adulis and Aksum along the main caravan routes."[9]

Of course, even without the use of coercion Christianity enjoyed a number of advantages that helped it attract converts. As the religion of the kingdom's political and commercial elite it almost certainly benefitted from its association with power and wealth. In addition, the manner and timing of its entry also enhanced its chances for success. Not only did Christianity spread from the top-down, that is, from ruler to ruled, it also came to Ethiopia comparatively early in the process of state formation and thus had an excellent opportunity for becoming an integral part of the country's political institutions and ritual. In the course of time, almost certainly by the sixth century, Ethiopia had become not merely a state ruled by Christians, but a Christian state; one in which the organizing principles and basis for legitimacy were rooted in Christianity. Membership in the ruling elite and participation in most governing institutions was also limited exclusively to Christians. This too would have worked to draw people, including local and immigrant Jews into the Church. These converts were almost certainly the primary carriers of the Hebraic elements in Ethiopian Christianity.[10]

It is difficult to know for how long the Judaized groups in the Aksumite population lived peacefully alongside their Christian and pagan neighbors. Fourth-century Aksum appears to have provided fertile ground for a variety of religious identities, none of which necessarily conformed to idealized notions of "normative" Judaism or Christianity. Syncretism was probably the rule rather than the exception, and it is probably best to view the different faiths as closely related rather than clearly defined units.[11] The elements held in common may well have outweighed those that differentiated between the various groups.

The fortunes of the young Church took a dramatic turn for the better toward the end of the fifth century with the arrival of two groups of Syrian missionaries, one known as the Ṣadqan and the other as the Nine Saints. Although the precise reasons for their coming to Ethiopia cannot be determined, several authors have suggested that they were monophys-ites fleeing persecution.[12] Taddesse conjectures that their arrival was part of a carefully planned program supported by Aksum and Alexan-dria.[13] Whatever their motives, these foreign monks were zealous mis-sionaries, who significantly expanded the area under Christian influ-ence.[14] In addition to their missionary activities, they were probably also responsible for major advances in the translation of the Bible and other religious books into Ge'ez. Although some translations must have been made shortly after the introduction of Christianity, and small portions may have even been translated by Judaized members of the population, it appears likely that only with the arrival of these missionaries would there have been sufficient trained clergy to complete the project.[15] As was indicated in the previous chapter, both the vocabulary and versions used by the translators reveal access to Hebrew and Aramaic sources. There is, therefore, every reason to assume that they were assisted in their work by Jews or those influenced by Judaism in Aksum.[16] Conse-quently, this would appear to be further evidence for both a continued Jewish presence in Aksum and for cordial rather than hostile relations with the surrounding population.

Kaleb and Du Nuwas

The missionary, educational, and literary advances of the late fifth cen-tury all contributed to the growing self-confidence and self-awareness of the developing Church. If we wish to search for a true turning point in relations between the Judaized population of Aksum and their Christian neighbors, however, the logical starting point is the reign of the early sixth-century Ethiopian Emperor Ella-Asbeha, better known as Kaleb. There are a variety of sources that would seem to indicate that Kaleb's reign saw significant changes both in the character of church-state rela-tions in Aksum and in the monarchy's attitude toward the Jews. Most of this information is concerned either directly or indirectly with Kaleb's war in 525 against the Judaized king of the Hiymarites, Yusuf Du Nuwas.

In the first quarter of the sixth century the struggle for supremacy in South Arabia between Judaism and Christianity took the form of a series of persecutions, martyrdoms, and military struggles, which eventually involved not only the local population but also Byzantium and Ethiopia.[17] Events began to move toward a climax ca. 520, when the king of the Himyarites, who had converted to Judaism and taken the name Yusuf, massacred the Christians in the important South Arabian city of Najran. The task of avenging the martyrs and restoring the Christian position in the region fell to the Ethiopian ruler Kaleb. In the year 525 Kaleb led a military expedition to South Arabia, which defeated and killed the Judaized Himyarite ruler, and established Ethiopian sovereignty over the area. Before returning to Aksum, Kaleb established a new law code and engaged in a variety of building projects including the construction of a number of churches.

Even on the basis of this brief summary of this period it is possible to suggest that these events could easily have led to a deterioration of relations between Jews and Christians in Aksum. A more detailed examination reveals numerous additional reasons to assume that this was in fact the case. Du Nuwas, for example, may well have taken the name Yusuf as part of a semi-messianic program, which also included a state run along biblical lines.[18] Kaleb, for his part, was the first Ethiopian ruler to assume a biblical name. His choice, moreover, of the name of a progenitor of the Davidic house was probably deliberate. Thus, the two biblically named protagonists confronted each other.

Yusuf the Jewish king of Himyar who scoffs at the claims of one who was for him only a Cushite pretender, not a genuine Israelite; Caleb who claims descent from Israel in the flesh, as the lineal descendant of Solomon's first-born and also from Israel in the spirit, as the Christian king of the New Zion.[19]

Kaleb was, however, both an Israelite and a devout Christian. Even if one discounts some of the hagiographic excess of our sources, it is abundantly clear that Christianity was not merely a political tool for Kaleb. His expedition to South Arabia had the clear character of a crusade; his policies of evangelization, legislation, and church building all witness his programmatic approach to his faith; his destruction of idols, pagan temples, and synagogues all bespeak a major transformation of policy. "The former broad tolerance and moderate protection of Christians changed into active propagation of Christianity, which had been proclaimed as the state religion."[20]

As several authors have noted, Kaleb's program of simultaneously exalting his Israelite descent while pursuing vehemently anti-Jewish policies is precisely the same seemingly contradictory combination of themes one finds in the *Kebra Nagast*.[21] Indeed, this combination has led at least one author to argue rather convincingly that this quintessential Ethiopian work originated in the time of Kaleb.[22] In fact, as we shall see in later chapters, the opposition between bad Jews and good Israelites is one that recurs throughout the history of Ethiopia in general and the Beta Israel in particular.

On the basis of the information presented above, it is difficult to escape the conclusion that the first quarter of the sixth century must have been an especially trying time for the most Judaized groups in the Aksumite kingdom. The extreme politicization of religious identity in South Arabia may well have made itself felt by a hardening of distinctions in Aksum as well. The hitherto vague differentiation between Judaized groups and the growing number of Old Testament oriented Christians may have become far sharper. Even if they were not subject to overt persecution (and it must be remembered that in the early *seventh* century Ethiopia enjoyed a reputation for religious tolerance),[23] the position of the former could not have been an easy one. Precisely how they responded is not recorded, although several tantalizing clues permit us to engage in some informed if very tentative speculation and suggest that they began to migrate away from Aksum to more peripheral areas to the southwest.

As is well known, during most of their recorded history the Beta Israel resided in the regions around Lake Tana including Wagara, Ṣallamt, and the Semien mountains. Exactly how they came to be in these regions remains a mystery. Almost certainly their presence must be the result of the migration of Jews or Jewish influences from the Aksum region. In this context it is interesting to note some of the earliest references to the Semien region. In 525 the Greek traveller Cosmas Indicopleustes (Sailor of the Indian Sea) visited Ethiopia. Among the valuable information he recorded was an inscription by an unknown king found in the city of Adulis. Known as the *Monumentum Adulitanum,* this text makes mention of the king's victories across the Nile against a number of peoples

including the Athagaus, Kalaa, and Semena.[24] The last of these are said
to reside in inhospitable mountains covered with deep snow. Cosmas
comments, "As for the Semenai, where he says there are snow and ice, it
is to that country the King of the Axomites expatriates anyone whom he
has sentenced to be banished."[25] Thus, writing at precisely the time of
Kaleb's expedition against Du Nuwas, Cosmas is familiar with the Semien, in later periods an important area of Beta Israel settlement, as a
region of exile and banishment. Might not this have been the fate of
some of the Judaized residents of Aksum during the time of Kaleb's
campaign against their coreligionists in South Arabia?

Some support for this admittedly speculative suggestion may be found
in the enigmatic phrase, "Ba-zāyā t'alelaya falāš" ("At this point the
Falash[a] were separated"), which appears in a medieval Ethiopian document.[26] While the use of the name "Falasha" certainly dates this text
to the fifteenth or sixteenth century, the tradition of a Jewish group
separating itself or being separated from the bulk of the population may
be an ancient one. Certainly the text itself introduces this phrase almost
immediately after a mention of Menelik I, which would at least hint that
it refers to the Aksumite period.

Finally, one last piece may be added to this picture. According to
many Ethiopian traditions, Kaleb abdicated, became a monk, and was
succeeded by his son Gabra Masqal. Gabra Masqal's rise to power was
not, however, unopposed. According to some sources, his path to the
throne was almost blocked by his brother, Beta Israel.[27] The appearance
of this name (the designation used by the Falasha to refer to themselves)
in precisely the period in which we have suggested that the Aksumite
Jews "were separated" is truly a remarkable coincidence and may be
much more than that. The departure of the Aksumite Jews (should we
already say Beta Israel?) may have been provoked by a combination of
religious and political rivalry. The growing animosity between Judaism
and Christianity in the kingdom might possibly have also been expressed
in the struggle of rival political leaders for the throne.[28] Beta Israel, the
defeated head of the Judaized group, would than have departed with his
followers to a less hospitable region such as the Semien.

In the final analysis, it may never be possible to completely reconstruct the impact of events in the sixth century on the Jews of Aksum.
As we have suggested above, it appears probable that at least some of
them left the Aksum region for more isolated and peripheral regions.

This move may have been part of larger politico-religious conflicts in Aksum at the time, or it may have been a relatively isolated occurrence. What is clear is that in either case the departure from Aksum must have had major consequences for those who left.

First, although settlement in the Semien and other regions beyond the Takkaze river would not have placed the exile beyond the political borders of the Aksumite kingdom, it would have seriously limited their contact with the political and cultural center of the Ethiopian state. Thus, for example, if their migration preceded Kaleb's victory over Du Nuwas, it is doubtful if they would have come into contact with any of the Judaized prisoners brought from South Arabia at that time. In the longer term, residence in such peripheral regions would have greatly limited their access to the religious and intellectual elites active in Aksum. Literary works translated from Greek to Ge'ez would have reached them slowly if at all. Overall literacy must have declined and may even have disappeared.

From a social point of view, such a migration would have greatly increased contact with the predominantly Agaw population of the region. Even during the period when they were concentrated around Aksum the Jewish part of the population was probably not distinguishable on either a racial or ethnic basis. Rather, the relatively small number of Jewish immigrants who reached Aksum from South Arabia had almost certainly assimilated members of the surrounding population through conversion and intermarriage. These processes of intermarriage and acculturation appear to have continued in the predominantly Agaw regions as well. While a significant portion of the Agaw accepted Christianity, others probably embraced a more Judaized faith.[29] While this process cannot be documented in any detail, it is noteworthy that throughout their recorded history the Beta Israel appear closely associated with the Agaw both geographically and linguistically.

In closing, one final consequence of the departure from Aksum must be considered. Thus far in this book our attempts to reconstruct the earliest history of Jews and Judaism in Ethiopia have depended far more on our knowledge of Aksumite history than on any specific data concerning its Jews. Working on the basis of hints and indirect proofs we have tried to suggest the manner in which Jewish influences reached Ethiopia and what their impact may have been. However tentative our suggestions may have been to this point, they appear solidly based in comparison to our knowledge of Judaism in Ethiopia during the next few centuries. In part at least, this may be due, as we have indicated, to the departure of portions of the Jewish population from Aksum. Even more important, however, is the decline of the kingdom itself.

The Decline of Aksum

The reign of Kaleb and his conquest on behalf of the Christian world of South Arabia mark the apex of Aksumite power, prestige, and international fame. Although his successors soon lost control of South Arabia to one of their own generals, many Ethiopian traditions view the middle of the sixth century as a prosperous period that saw important developments in the evolution of both church and state.[30] By the end of the century, however, Aksum had begun a long period of decline that would eventually culminate in its abandonment and destruction. No one cause would appear to explain the fall of Aksum. Rather, a variety of political, economic, social, and ecological factors combined to undermine the fragile base upon which Ethiopian civilization had risen.

In the last quarter of the sixth century the Sassanid Persians seriously challenged Ethiopian control of South Arabia, and by the turn of the century that region had been removed from the Aksumite sphere of influence.[31] From a political perspective the withdrawal from South Arabia marked the end of Aksum's brief period as a major player on the international stage. Economically, the Persians posed a major threat to Byzantine and Aksumite control of the Red Sea trade. After 602 Aksum's access to export markets and freedom of navigation were considerably weakened. Finally, between 702 and 715, the Arabs eliminated the Aksumite fleet and destroyed Adulis.[32] This change in trading patterns, which left Aksum isolated and landlocked, was a major blow to the economic basis of Aksumite political power. At the same time, the rulers of Aksum were encountering ever-increasing difficulties in retaining control over the hinterland regions on which they depended for export items such as wood, ivory, cattle, and gold. In the north the Beja, a powerful pastoralist people, gained control of much of the coastal plain which today comprises modern Eritrea.[33] To the West, areas beyond the Takkaze river, which had long been conquered and incorporated into the kingdom, regained their independence and cut off the Aksumites from the main goldbearing districts.[34] The gold content of

Aksumite coins declines steadily throughout this period, being eventually replaced by copper and in some cases silver.[35]

Deprived of the wealth generated by trade, the Aksumites were increasingly forced to intensive agriculture as a means of feeding their sizeable population. Soil erosion and a decline in rainfall subsequently produced a further deterioration of the region's economic base.[36] Eventually, a large portion of the population abandoned the region in favor of more fertile lands further south. Within a few generations the cluster of towns and villages that had previously formed metropolitan Aksum had virtually disappeared.[37] By 800 A.D. Aksum had probably completely lost its economic and political hegemony, retaining only some ritual and symbolic functions.

The decline of Aksum did not immediately result in either the disappearance of its kings or the waning of Christian influence in the highlands of Ethiopia. Numerous traditions appear to indicate that from the seventh century onward the center of gravity of the Christian kingdom moved southward. Although it is impossible to follow this expansion of the kingdom and church in any detail, both Arabic and Ethiopian sources portray the ninth century as a time of military campaigns, church building, and evangelization as far south as the Amhara region.[38] Thus, Aksumite culture survived and even spread into regions not under its influence during its heyday. With regard to the internal history of Ethiopia, the period from the seventh to twelfth century remains one of the most obscure and least understood. Hardly any contemporary sources have survived and those that have are frequently fragmentary and/or legendary in character. Nonetheless, much of this material can be examined with some profit, if only to recognize the limits of our knowledge and the hazards involved in building too far-reaching an historical reconstruction on such shaky foundations.

The obscurity that characterizes much of Ethiopian history from the seventh century onward is only multiplied when we turn to the more specific question of Jews or Judaism during this period. Even the indirect sources of the kind used to make the tentative reconstructions suggested thus far in this book are, for the most part, lacking. We are forced, therefore, to rely on semi-legendary accounts of extremely limited historical value. Among the most important of these are the traveller's reports of Eldad Ha-Dani and Benjamin of Tudela, the letters of Prester John, and the traditions concerning Queen Gudit (Yodit/Judith). While the hard data to be gained from these documents are at best minimal, this has not prevented some scholars from drawing upon them to support major theses with important implications for our understanding of the Beta Israel. Thus, much of our discussion in the remainder of this chapter will of necessity be devoted to a critical reevaluation of these sources and a considerable rethinking of some of the more grandiose reconstructions that claim to be based upon them.

Eldad Ha-Dani

As we noted in our earlier discussion of the alleged Danite origins of the Beta Israel, Eldad Ha-Dani was a mysterious Jewish traveller who visited several Jewish communities toward the end of the ninth century. Although some rabbinic authorities viewed Eldad as an authentic representative of the "Lost Tribes," scholars have cast grave doubts upon the view that he came from Ethiopia. Far more complex, however, is the question of whether Eldad's narrative contains any authentic information concerning the Jews of Ethiopia. While Aešcoly, Ullendorff, and Beckingham tend to answer in the negative,[39] Baron, Borchadt, Conti Rossini, and Kobishchanov are only a few of the scholars who view *Sefer Eldad* as the earliest known reference to the Falasha.[40] Even if we ignore for the moment the latter group's anachronistic use of the relatively late term "Falasha," Eldad's book is problematic as a historical-geographic work. His broad familiarity with *aggadic* literature enabled him to construct a narrative of considerable literary interest. It is difficult, however, to determine where the legendary material ends and the "kernel of truth" (if any) begins. Borchadt appears to have the highest opinion of Eldad's reliability and identifies the "rivers of Cush" with the Takkaze and Abay, the "sea" Eldad travelled on with Lake Tana, and the "Romornos" with the Oromo (Galla).[41] Conti Rossini, in a typically learned analysis of the sources, offers a similarly detailed explanation of places mentioned by Eldad.[42] Significantly, perhaps, at no point do he and Borchadt appear to be in agreement. Aešcoly, while generally skeptical of their positive evaluation of Eldad's references to Ethiopia, finds the Romornos/Oromo connection reasonable.[43] Unfortunately, the reading "Romornos" is quite problematic, and, in any event, the Oromo did not enter Ethiopia prior to the sixteenth century.[44]

More important than any of Eldad's specific identifications, of course, is the general portrait he offers of Jewish life "beyond the rivers of Cush." Here too, serious questions must be raised. As one recent survey has shown, his *halachot* (religious laws) display only the most casual resemblance to those of the Beta Israel.[45] His portrayal of a Jewish kingdom should also not be accepted uncritically. In the next chapter of this book we will analyze the evidence for the existence of a Jewish "kingdom" in Ethiopia in some detail. There we shall argue that such a kingdom, if it existed at all, was a comparatively late phenomenon; a claim of crucial importance for our understanding of the trajectory of Beta Israel history. On face value, Eldad's ninth-century testimony would appear to contradict this claim, but, when critically assessed, his witness appears to be open to serious question. First, it must be remembered that Eldad reveals little, if any, firsthand knowledge of Ethiopia. In addition, it should be noted that a description of an independent kingdom was one of the most common themes in legendary accounts of the lost tribes. This idea, for example, recurs in the *Letters of Prester John,* a medieval (originally) Christian corpus that shares many motifs with Eldad's writings.[46] Thus Eldad's depiction of a kingdom, even if it is assumed to refer in some way to the Jews of Ethiopia, should not be given too much credence.

His aim was probably to raise the spirits of the Jews by giving them news of tribes of Israel who lived in freedom. . . . The report of the existence of such Jewish kingdoms undoubtedly encouraged and comforted Eldad's hearers, by contradicting the Christian contention that Jewish independence had ceased after the destruction of the Second Temple.[47]

These reports were not, however, necessarily based on fact, and receive no clear support from the Ge'ez or Arabic sources of the period.

Queen Yodit

As the result of a rather remarkable coincidence, Eldad Ha-Dani's appearance in the Jewish world occurred at approximately the same time as the activities in Ethiopia of the similarly named Haḍani Dan'el.[48] In three inscriptions dating from the end of the ninth century, Dan'el offers some insight into the turbulent political conditions of the period. In the first two he reports on victorious campaigns against the Baria and Walqayit, who threatened the Ethiopian kingdom from the north and west respectively. In the third and most significant text Dan'el describes the manner in which he subjugated the Aksumite king and reduced him to vassal status.[49] It appears, therefore, that while a king continued to reign in the name of the ancient Aksumite dynasty, real power rested with the *ḥaḍ-ani*, who resided further south.[50] This was not the last time in Ethiopian history that a warlord gained precedence over the imperial house. Thus, by the outset of the tenth century, little of the formal structure of the Aksumite kingdom appears to have survived. The king, as we have just noted, had apparently lost most of his power to the *ḥaḍani*. The political and economic center of the kingdom had deteriorated and shifted southward as a result of the Beja's incursions and Muslim control of the Red Sea. During the tenth century, moreover, the church was seriously weakened when over fifty years passed without the consecration of a new Bishop from Egypt.[51] While each of these elements contributed its share to the decline and turmoil characterizing the final period of Aksumite history, none of them has captured the place in Ethiopian tradition accorded the legendary Queen Yodit.

Although we lack any authentic internal sources from tenth-century Ethiopia, the overthrow of the country's Christian rulers by a powerful non-Christian queen appears well substantiated from external sources. *The History of the Patriarchs of the Egyptian Church* reports, for example, that during the reign of the Patriarch Philotheus (989–1004),

The king of al-Habesh sent to the king of Nubia, a youth whose name was Girgis (George), and made known to him how the Lord had chastened him, he and the inhabitants of his land. It was that a woman, a queen of Bani al-Hamwiyah had revolted against him and against his country.[52]

Ibn Haukal (943–77) in a reference that would appear to date these important events somewhat earlier notes:

The country of the *habasha* has been ruled by a woman for many years now: she has killed the king of *habasha* who was titled Haḍani. Until today she rules with complete independence on her own country and the frontier areas of the territory of the Haḍani in the southern part of [the country of] the *habasha*.[53]

For many years scholars have sought to determine the identity of the queen and the region from which she came. Conti Rossini, with characteristic perspicacity, suggested that the queen was probably of Damoti (Sidama) origin, a view that has been echoed by several scholars in recent years.[54] This identification has considerable merit, since it is in agreement with both a southern locale and well-documented traditions of female rulers in the Sidama region.[55] Nevertheless, of far greater relevance to our immediate purposes are the numerous attempts to depict the queen as the beautiful and powerful Queen Yodit (Judith), ruler of the Falasha.

Although certainly not the originator of the Judith legend, James Bruce appears most responsible for its dissemination into both scholarly and popular Western writings. In his *Travels to Discover the Source of the Nile,* he describes how the beautiful Judith, also known as Esther and Sa'at (Fire) set out to destroy Christianity and eliminate the Solomonic line. Taking advantage of the weakness of the Aksumites, she massacred most of the royal house and established a Jewish dynasty which ruled for many generations.[56] Here, as elsewhere, Bruce's reliability as a historian should not be exaggerated.[57] Once proclaimed, however, the legend of a Jewish queen proved difficult to shake. Ignazio Guidi, after correcting the queen's origin to Bani-al Yahoudya, accepted her Jewishness, as did Basset and Rathjens.[58] Moreover, although Conti Rossini demonstrated as early as 1921 that significant reasons exist for rejecting the queen's alleged Jewish identity, many recent authors continue to offer vivid descriptions of the Falasha queen's conquest of Aksum.[59]

Despite the Judith legend's popularity and its prominent position in the traditions of both Jews and Christians to this day, there appear to be several good reasons for rejecting the depiction of the tenth-century queen of the Bani al-Hamwiyah as a Falasha. Although some Ethiopic sources do portray Yodit as a Jewess, these generally identify her as a convert rather than the product of a well-entrenched indigenous religious community.[60] The material recorded by Bruce, which contains the earliest complete account of the legend, must be considered suspect on several grounds. In general, the story he presents appears to have been heavily shaped by events after the tenth century including later battles between the Christian kingdom and the Beta Israel and the sixteenth-century Muslim conquest of Ethiopia by Ahmad Gragn.[61] More specifically, Bruce's claim that Judith intented to extirpate the Solomonic line is highly questionable in light of contemporary evidence that her primary adversary was the *hadani,* who had already sharply curtailed the Aksumite king's power. Bruce's depiction of Judith as a Jewess also leaves unanswered the question of why her five successors all had "barbarous [i.e., pagan] names" (to use his term), and how they came to pass power on to the militantly Christian kings of Lasta.[62] Thus, while Bruce may well, in this case, have only been faithfully transmitting the traditions he collected, serious doubts must exist concerning their reliability.

The suggestion that the Falasha queen Yodit, putative conqueror of Aksum, is in fact the pagan queen of the Sidama, vanquisher of the *ḥaḍani*, is not as startling as it might appear at first glance. By transforming the queen from a pagan to a Jewess and her primary area of activity from the south to Aksum, Christian tradition neatly places her within the primary categories of Ethiopian political-religious discourse. On some levels, the Judith traditions can be said to mirror the themes of the *Kebra Nagast*. Both the Queen of Sheba and Judith are depicted as converts to Judaism. However, while the former is credited with a crucial role in the establishment of the Solomonic dynasty in Aksum, the latter is said to have conquered the city and deposed its legitimate rulers. In both stories, the opposition between evil Jews and good Israelites figures prominently, with the tenth-century Judith in particular being identified by later traditions with the "Falasha" (Jews), medieval enemies of the Solomonic (Israelite) kings.[63] For the Beta Israel the identification of Yodit as one of their own rulers not only places her in the context of their later wars against the Christians and thus gives their struggle a greater antiquity, but also allows them to claim a rare, albeit temporary, victory. Thus, the Judith traditions much like the *Kebra Nagast* are most valuable to the historian when read not at the level of a simple historical narrative, but as a symbolic statement concerning the interconnections and tensions between religion, legitimacy, and political power in Ethiopia.

The Zagwe Dynasty (1137–1270)

The identity and activities of the Queen of the Bani al-Hamwiyah's successors are even more of a mystery than her own. While they may have exerted political control over some parts of the Ethiopian highlands, there appears to be no reason to assume that they ruled effectively over all Ethiopia. Judaized groups living in peripheral areas such as Semien were probably relatively unaffected by the political upheavals happening around them. Christianity continued to survive and even consolidated its position in the regions of Lasta and Amhara. In the former region in particular the local, predominantly Agaw population not only converted, but also participated "actively in the economic, administrative, political and military affairs of the state."[64] In the course of time they took over the political leadership of the country and established a new dynasty known as the Zagwe.[65]

Although we still lack an authoritative history of the Zagwe, research conducted during the past century enables us to reconstruct a fairly accurate picture of the main themes of their history. Rather paradoxically, the Zagwe are depicted in Ethiopian hagiographies and chronicles as an illegitimate (i.e., non-Solomonic) dynasty, whose individual rulers were frequently saintly figures. Despite the attempts of some early authors to claim that they were Jews, it is today generally accepted that the Zagwe were committed Christians who both preserved and strengthened the religious traditions they inherited. The most concrete expression of their religious devotion came in the form of rock-hewn churches, particularly those in their capital city of Lalibala.[66] Built, according to tradition, by the early thirteenth-century ruler of the same name, Lalibala represents a deliberate attempt to rival Aksum as a replacement for the Holy City of Jerusalem.[67] Significantly, the eleven churches of Lalibala focus almost exclusively on New Testament and Christian figures, events, and values, an indication perhaps that the Zagwe were less committed to Hebraic elements than their "Israelite" Aksumite predecessors.

Although undoubtedly the most powerful rulers in Ethiopia for close to 135 years, the Zagwe's control of many parts of the country was extremely limited.[68] In Tigre province and the Aksum region many local rulers and church officials questioned their legitimacy and challenged their authority. To the south in Shawa and Amhara, the Zagwe's inability to protect the population and control the lucrative trade routes that passed through the region dealt them a crippling blow. To the best of our knowledge, the Zagwe did not exert effective control over the Semien, Dambeya, and Wagara regions, whose population probably included important Judaized groups.[69] The few hagiographic sources on this period (all probably composed decades or even centuries after the fact) make no mention of Jews or Judaism in Ethiopia, and the remaining sources both internal and external offer only the barest of hints on the subject.

Certainly the most reliable of these sources is a fifteenth- or sixteenth-century manuscript of the *Book of Isaiah* which in a colophon reports that "in the days of the Zagwe kings there came out of the country of Aden a man, a Jew called Joseph. . . . And he settled in the country of Elawz in land of Amhara."[70] Whether this Joseph was a lone immigrant or part of a larger process is impossible to determine. He was almost certainly not the only Adenite to make the journey, and perhaps not the only Jew. There is, however, no basis to conclude, as has one author, that "the Zagwe kings welcomed Jewish immigrants from Yemen."[71] More important, it is unclear what, if any, relevance such immigration would have had for indigenous Jewish groups. Joseph is said to have settled in Amhara well south of the Lake Tana region. His family, moreover, converted to Christianity after several generations. (The aforementioned manuscript represents their gift to a church.) Thus, while the story of the Adenite Jew who settled in Ethiopia is one of our earliest explicit references to Jews in the country, it is difficult to see any connection to the history of the Beta Israel.

While the story of Joseph from Aden is of limited value because of its geographical focus, the weakness of the *Letters of Prester John*'s lies in their heavily legendary character. For as Beckingham has commented, "From the very first mention of Prester John most of what we are told about him could not possibly be true, and most of the little that could conceivably be true is inconsistent."[72] The name of Prester John first appears in 1145 in a German chronicle describing him as a pious Christian king reigning in the Far East. During different periods his kingdom was identified with India, China, Central Asia, and, particularly in later years, Ethiopia. From about 1165 onward letters began to circulate that purported to be copies of Prester John's correspondence with various Christian European leaders. So popular were these texts that versions in Latin, Romance, Teutonic, Slavonic, and even Hebrew were soon extant. Although frequently referred to as "forgeries," the letters generally make little effort to convince the reader of their authenticity, and were probably recognized by many readers for what they were: works of fiction.[73] Moreover, while they may contain some kernel of truth, on the whole they share much more in common with the previously discussed work of Eldad Ha-Dani.[74] One of the themes shared with *Sefer Eldad* is the claim of the existence of a Jewish kingdom beyond a great river. While some authors have sought to see in such references a veiled description of the Jews of Ethiopia, this is far from certain.[75] Although in later years the connection between the figure of Prester John and Ethiopia solidified, and references to Jews in the land of Prester John were usually intended to depict the Beta Israel, this is certainly not the case in this period. Not only may the imaginary author of the letter(s) not have been an Ethiopian ruler, the description of the Jews in his kingdom may be little more than the presentation of a familiar legendary motif. Any historical connection between these texts and the Jews of Ethiopia must, therefore, be viewed as extremely tenuous.

The third and final source from the Zagwe period that may be concerned with the Jews of Ethiopia is *Sefer Ha-massa'ot* (*The Book of Travels*) of Benjamin of Tudela. Benjamin of Tudela (Toledo) was the greatest medieval Jewish traveller.[76] His journeys began sometime between 1159 and 1167 and concluded with his return to Spain in 1172/3. His book is an invaluable account of the Mediterranean basin and the Middle East in the second half of the twelfth century.

In what is for our purposes a crucial passage Benjamin reports that in the area of the Red Sea and Indian Ocean there is

India which is on the mainland which is called Aden and it is Eden which is in Thelasar [cf. 2 Kg 19:12]. And there are high mountains there and there are Israelites there and the Gentile yoke is not upon them. And they have cities and towers in the tops of the mountains and they go down to the plain-country called Lubia [or Nubia] which is ruled by Edomites [Christians].

Largely on the basis of the similarity between this description and the later wars of the mountain-dwelling Beta Israel against the Christian rulers of Ethiopia, many authors have argued that Benjamin's text represents an early reference to the Jews of Ethiopia.[77] In fact, the passage in question is extremely problematic. Benjamin himself did not visit the region and thus his report is at best an attempt to faithfully recount what he had been told by others. The confused reporting of several crucial names including Eden, Nubia, and others, which appear in sharply variant readings in different manuscripts, make it extremely difficult to decide with any certainty precisely what region is being discussed. Finally, we must also consider Benjamin's propensity to tailor his descriptions to suit the "truth" of the Bible.[78]

In light of all of the above it is difficult to reach any conclusion with a great deal of confidence. While some commentators believe that the reference to Aden indicates a Red Sea locale, they place the Jews at the Arabian not the Ethiopian side of the water.[79] Others accept the Ethiopian setting, but believe the people in question to be the Beja not the

Falasha.[80] If the Jews of Ethiopia are in fact being discussed, it is curious that Benjamin does not mention that they are black.[81] Nor is there any external support for the view that the Beta Israel were both mountain dwellers and at war with the Christian (Zagwe) in this period. Perhaps most important, at a later point in the same passage Benjamin discusses the "Cushites who have a king and they call him Sultan El-Habesh," but does not appear to connect this relatively clear reference to Ethiopia with the aforementioned Jews. On balance, therefore, while Benjamin's report may indeed have been influenced by the presence of Judaized groups in Ethiopia during the period of Zagwe rule, it is difficult to accept the view that his is a clear reliable reference to the Beta Israel.

Summary

As we noted at the outset of this chapter, it is virtually impossible to construct a detailed history of the Jews of Ethiopia for the period from the sixth to thirteenth century. While the sources that concern the Emperor Kaleb's war in South Arabia enable us to offer some hypotheses concerning the fate of some of the Judaized groups in Aksum, even these must be treated with considerable caution. At best they would seem to offer us a possible explanation for the manner in which elements of a Judaized faith began to reach peoples and areas outside of Aksum. The situation with regard to later periods is even less promising. The decline of Aksum and the movement of some of its Jewish elements to peripheral areas have left us with a complete dearth of historical sources on Ethiopian Judaism during this period. Despite the credence given his reports by rabbinic authorities and some scholars, Eldad Ha-Dani does not appear to have had any firsthand knowledge concerning Jews or Judaism in Ethiopia. In a similar fashion, later traditions notwithstanding, the queen who conquered Aksum or at least defeated the *ḥaḍani* does not appear to have been a Jewess, either by birth or through conversion. Nor do any of the sources concerning Ethiopia in the Zagwe period appear to offer firm evidence concerning the Beta Israel.

Lest the summary offered above appear too pessimistic and hypercritical of the sources, it is useful to close with a few more positive comments. There is every reason to believe, in light of the evidence of both earlier and later periods, that the Hebraic elements that entered pre-Christian Aksumite culture survived not only in the Ethiopian church, but among other groups as well. As we have seen, it is possible to combine the existing sources, however limited they may be, in such a way as to support the suggestion that some Judaized groups departed Aksum in the sixth century and settled in the area around Lake Tana and the Semien mountains. Whatever one's verdict on this hypothesis, beginning with the late thirteenth and early fourteenth century we enter a new period not only in the history of the Beta Israel, but in the country at large. The hitherto obscure references and legendary sources are gradually replaced by a collection of historical documents that enable us to both locate the Beta Israel and trace their development. We are, in other words, able for the first time to truly write their history. It is to this all important period that we now turn our attention.

3

From Ayhud to Falasha: The Invention of a Tradition

The Rise of the Solomonic Dynasty

The Zagwe dynasty ruled Ethiopia for nearly one hundred fifty years from 1137 to 1270. Almost from the outset their rule was a troubled one, as various problems served to weaken and eventually to completely undermine them. Although the Zagwe rulers were apparently devout Christians and presided over a major revival of the church, their enemies, including the nobility of Tigre province and the clergy of the Aksumite region, dismissed them as usurpers who had seized the throne of the legitimate Aksumite "Solomonic" rulers. The Zagwe sought to counter such claims by wooing the clergy of other regions and engaging in a massive program of church building in their home province of Lasta.[1] Their efforts were, however, significantly weakened by the internal dissension that plagued them throughout their history. Rarely do the Zagwe appear to have achieved a bloodless succession, and the death of the reigning monarch was usually the occasion for violent clashes between rival claimants to the throne.[2] Such infighting greatly limited the rulers' ability to guarantee the security and loyalty of southern regions such as Shawa and Amhara. When these areas both grew in economic importance because of their proximity to southern trade routes and came under the influence of dissident Tigrean-trained clergy, the Zagwe position became completely untenable. The person who benefitted most from the combination of religious, political, and economic factors described above was an Amharan warlord named Yekunno Amlak. Backed by troops from Amhara and Shawa and with the support of an important local monastic leader, he first established an independent kingdom in the southern regions and later, in 1270, deposed the last Zagwe ruler.[3]

Although the ascension of Yekunno Amlak is generally viewed as a turning point in Ethiopian history, its immediate impact on the existing political realities should not be overestimated. The problems that confronted his heirs were not markedly different from those that had troubled his Zagwe predecessors. The nobility of Tigre, for example, appear to have been little impressed by this upstart Amharan dynasty. Moreover, the early Amharan rulers suffered from succession problems similar to those that had weakened the Zagwe. Thus the first decades of Amharan rule were a period of intense internal conflict. While Yekunno Amlak is remembered as the founder of a new dynasty, Amda Ṣeyon (r. 1314–44) is recognized as the founder of the Solomonic state.[4] Having inherited a relatively stable situation from his father, Wedem Ra'ad (r. 1299–1314), Amda Ṣeyon was the first ruler of the new dynasty in a position to grapple with the threats to royal authority posed by the kingdom's military and economic vulnerability and the dynasty's lack of a clear claim to legitimacy. Although his attempts to solve these problems were only partially successful, his reign did mark the beginning of two centuries of royal ascendancy and a major shift in the balance of power in Ethiopia. Only in the reign of Amda Ṣeyon (1314–44) did the Amharan kings make their presence felt upon the whole Ethiopian plateau, including the Judaized groups around Lake Tana.

The Problem of the Ayhud: 1332–1527

The appearance in our sources from the fourteenth century onward of a number of relatively unambiguous references to Judaized groups in the Lake Tana region present the historian with a number of interesting questions. In particular, two issues of historical continuity emerge as being of major significance. First, we must consider whether such groups were in any sense the descendants of the earlier carriers of Jewish traditions discussed in the previous chapters. Second, the precise relationship between these medieval groups and those referred to in later texts as Falasha must also be defined.

The second of these questions will be examined in considerable detail below. With regard to the first, while a definitive answer appears elusive, several important points can be established. In considering the question of historical continuity over a period of many centuries, it is important to avoid too heavy a concentration on the issue of physical-biological descent. Nothing in the written sources can be interpreted as reliable evidence for the survival of a distinct well-defined Jewish community in Ethiopia for the period from the seventh to the fourteenth century. Nothing of what we know from Ethiopian history of this period makes the existence or survival of such a group seem probable. Accordingly, the search for a link between the Judaized populations of the different periods must focus not on the issues of genealogy or communal survival, but on the survival of specific ideas and various Jewish ritual elements. In this regard, there appears to be little question that the presence of Judaized groups in the Lake Tana region is the result of the diffusion of Hebraic-biblical characteristics from the Aksum region. The only alternative would be to suggest the existence of a second independent source for these elements.

There appears, however, to be no reason to assume that those who brought Jewish forms to the Lake Tana region came exclusively from groups outside the Ethiopian church. Given the previously discussed biblical-Hebraic character of Ethiopian Christianity, such elements may well have reached groups in the Lake Tana region from more than a single source. Indeed a single channel of transmission was probably the exception rather than the rule. As we shall see later in this chapter, this was not the last time in which the Church itself was to be an important vehicle for the transmission of Jewish traditions.

The earliest clear reference in any Ethiopic source to the Judaized groups in the Lake Tana region appears in the chronicle of the wars of Amda Ṣeyon. These groups are said to have offered stiff resistance to Amda Ṣeyon's attempts to consolidate his rule, and, although temporarily subdued, they rose in revolt ca. 1332. In response, Amda Ṣeyon sent troops comprised of soldiers from Damot, Seqelt, Gondar, and Hadya to fight the rebels in "Semien, Wagara, Ṣallamt, and Ṣagade. Originally these people were Christians but now they denied Christ like the Jews who crucified him. For this reason he [the king] sent an army to destroy them."[5] This expedition was apparently a success and the way was thus opened for the evangelization (or in the view of the chronicler, the re-evangelization) of these regions.[6]

Although a number of clerics active in the region around Lake Tana may have had contact with the Judaized portions of the local population, a monk named Gabra Iyasus is the first to receive special mention. As a member of the Ewostatian movement, a monastic "house" that championed a number of biblical observances, most notably the Saturday Sabbath, Gabra Iyasus might well have been particularly attracted to and attractive for such groups.[7] He established his community of Dabra San in the Enfraz region and is said to have enjoyed considerable success. "And many people came to him, and he told all of them the word of God, and all of them believed and were baptized, [even] the children of the Jews accepted his teaching."[8] The extent to which his pronouncedly biblical form of Christianity differed from the vaguely articulated Judaized faith of the residents of Enfraz must remain an open question. Certainly, if the experiences of other monastic missionaries from this period are any indication, the acceptance of Christianity involved more the addition of new beliefs and rituals than the abandonment of old ones.

Another monk who had quite a different impact on the *ayhud* was a renegade cleric named Qozmos. According to *Gadla Yafqeranna Egzi'*, Qozmos was an extreme ascetic who left the clergy of the Lake Tana region when they attempted to curtail his rigorous self-mortification.[9] Because of his miraculous powers and his ability to write, he was readily accepted by those who practiced the "religion of the Jews" in Semien and Ṣallamt. He is said to have written the *Orit* (Pentateuch) for them, and they are alleged to have viewed him as a semi-divine, even messianic figure.[10] With Qozmos at their head the *ayhud* rebelled once again, and defeated the *Kantiba* (governor) of Dambeya, who was forced to join them.[11] Perhaps because of his bitter memories, Qozmos appears to have singled out the clergy as special targets of the rebellion. "He burned numerous churches, came to the road of Enfraz, and killed Abba Qerlos, Abba Yohannes Kama, and Abba Tanse'a Madhen with thirty-six of their disciples."[12] The Emperor Dawit (1380–1412) was forced to send fresh troops from Tigre to subdue the rebel forces.[13]

Until the reign of Yeshaq, which commenced in 1413, the *ayhud* of the Lake Tana region appear to have been of only peripheral concern to the Solomonic kings. Neither Amda Ṣeyon nor Dawit intervened personally to quash their rebellions, nor was the defeated population treated with special severity. Amda Ṣeyon, for example, dealt far more harshly with the challenges to his authority in Tigre province, and appears to have been more concerned with dissident Christians than with the *ayhud*. Neither of their defeats resulted in either the confiscation of land nor a widespread dispersal of the people. Yeshaq, in contrast, moved ruthlessly against the rebel *ayhud* by personally leading the expedition against them and, following his victory, imposing Christianity upon them.[14]

What were the factors that brought about this change in policy? The rich economic resources in Wagara and Dambeya had probably been coveted by the Christian kings for some time. Only in the beginning of the fifteenth century, however, following Dawit's successes against the Muslim kingdom of Ifat, do the kings appear to have been able to give these potentially lucrative areas their full attention.[15] Similarly, Dawit's temporary settlement of the Ewostatian controversy, which had troubled the Ethiopian church for almost a century, made the *ayhud* threat to religious unity all the more prominent.[16] Finally, Yeshaq's generally harsh treatment of religious dissidents should also be considered. Maqrizi charges Yeshaq with "the object of rooting out utterly all the Muslims living in Abyssinia."[17] Yeshaq also abandoned his father's moderate policy toward the Ewostatians and sought to renew the persecution of this northern monastic movement.[18]

These external factors notwithstanding, it is doubtful if Yeshaq would have achieved such rapid success had the *ayhud* been unified in their opposition to his policies. Even in the best of times, however, the *ayhud* did not constitute a single centrally organized group. Many decades of pressure and encroachment by the Christian kingdom appear, moreover, to have produced sharp divisions as to how best to respond to this threat. Yeshaq, for example, appears to have been greatly assisted by a split that had developed between those who advocated a policy of accommodation toward the Solomonic rulers and others who favored rebellion. Most prominent among the hardliners was the Bet-Ajer, a strong leader, whom Yeshaq had appointed a governor of Semien and part of Dambeya.[19] Immediately beneath him, and far more accommodating, was his nephew Badagosh, the royal appointed liaison to the

Imperial court. When Badagosh berated his uncle for his failure to pay his tributes on time, the Bet-Ajer punished his impudent nephew. Summoned to appear before Yeshaq to explain his behavior, the Bet-Ajer refused—a clear act of rebellion. Yeshaq responded with alacrity. "And the king came and struck his tent in Wagara. The Bet-Ajer did not notice his arrival. They made war from morning to evening. After that the Bet-Ajer escaped; but the soldiers of the king surrounded him, and cut off his head."[20]

Those *ayhud* who remained loyal to Yeshaq and fought on his side against the Bet-Ajer were rewarded with grants of land. His nephew, for example, received a large fief in Wagara.[21] Yeshaq's treatment of his enemies was, however, totally in keeping with his general policy of dealing harshly with dissidents. For the first time, a group of Beta Israel were deprived of the right to own land. Yeshaq is said to have decreed, "He who is baptized in the Christian religion, may inherit the land of his father; otherwise let him be a *Falasi*."[22] While the immediate impact and universality of this decree should not be exaggerated, there appears to be little question that Yeshaq's victory over the Bet-Ajer marked the beginning of the disenfranchisement of the *ayhud* and the gradual transformation of their status and identity.[23]

Despite Yeshaq's decree and his decision to build "many churches in Dambeya and Wagara,"[24] the issue of the *ayhud* remained largely unresolved. While some *ayhud* did convert and eventually may have become committed Christians, many others were either nominal Christians or continued in their old ways. Considerable information on the religious situation of the *ayhud* in the years immediately after Yeshaq is contained in some relatively neglected passages in the *gadl* of the fifteenth-century holy man Abba Takla Hawaryat.[25] This material, which is of relevance not only for their history, but also for a general understanding of the process of ethnic and religious interaction in Solomonic Ethiopia, reveals that in the middle of the fifteenth century the *ayhud* were only temporarily subdued, at best superficially converted, and minimally integrated into the Christian kingdom.

Abba Takla Hawaryat's first encounter with the *ayhud* occurred when he confronted one of their leaders, the *seyum* of Ṣallamt, leading an army of both *ayhud* and Christians to war against the Solomonic king. The saint succeeded in both preventing the battle and strengthening the Christianity of the nominal converts in the region. At the *seyum*'s invitation he was permitted to preach to the local population, "And when they heard the sweetness of his speech and the beauty of his teaching they said to him, 'We are Christians not from out hearts but [because] we feared the command of the king and governors. But [now] we believe in the word. Baptize us.' "[26]

Not surprisingly, such activities were challenged by more traditionally oriented residents of the region and, as in the time of Yeshaq, the ruling family was split. A relative of the *seyum* himself appears to have been among those unwilling to accept the authority of the Christian holy man.[27] The Christianization of the *ayhud* was hindered, moreover, not only by the actions of their Jewish brethren, but also by the attitude of more veteran Christians. Yessahalo Krestos, a Jewish "prophet" converted by Abba Takla Hawarayt, was denied entrance to a church by its deacons because he was a catechumen and a recent convert. Only the saint's intervention gained him admission.[28] This episode, if it was at all typical, would seem to indicate that recently converted *ayhud* were not always welcomed with open arms by the Christian population.[29]

After a stay of twenty months, Takla Hawaryat left Ṣallamt and continued on to Semien. In this region as well he sought to strengthen the faith of the converted and combat the opposition of those who remained Jews.

The Emperor Zar'a Ya'eqob (1434–68), the greatest of the Solomonic rulers, also had experience with the limits of the *ayhud*'s incorporation in the kingdom. During his reign he was compelled to do battle with rebels in Ṣallamt and Semien, who "became Jews, abandoning their Christianity."[30] This rebellion, which was apparently connected to political unrest that centered around the Emperor's own daughters, was not easily quashed. Zar'a Ya'eqob's son and successor, Ba'eda Maryam (1468–78) sent troops against the same rebels and, initially at least, enjoyed little success.[31] Only after a protracted struggle was Marqos, the *azmach* (commander) of Bagemeder, able to subdue them. The defeated rebels were brutally massacred, churches in the region were rebuilt, and new troops moved in to maintain order.[32]

Marqos's victory was a serious blow to the *ayhud* and could well have prepared the ground for their final demise had not other more serious problems demanded the attention of the Solomonic rulers. After Ba'eda Maryam's death in 1478, the problem of royal succession resurfaced, weakening the dynasty and opening the way for a reassertion of local autonomy. For half a century, conflicts in the court and provinces occupied the Solomonic kings and sapped the strength of their kingdom.[33] In 1484, less than a decade after their defeat by Marqos, the *ayhud* were once again capable of going to war, and they probably enjoyed considerable autonomy during the troubled reigns of the emperors Eskender (1478–94), Amda Ṣeyon II (1494) and Na'od (1494–1506).[34] By the time Lebna Dengel came to the throne in 1508, the frontier defenses of the Solomonic kingdom were in tatters. The main threat, however, came not from the *ayhud* around Lake Tana but from the Muslims in the southeast. In 1527, the Muslim warrior Ahmad Gragn led his troops into Ethiopia. This period of decline, Gragn's invasion, its consequences for the Christian kingdom, and the role played in it by the Beta Israel, will be discussed in detail in the next chapter. This, however, must be preceded by both a more detailed analysis of the sources presented thus far and the introduction of both oral and written evidence from the Beta Israel themselves.

As the careful reader will have doubtless noted, the survey of pre-1527 sources offered above has almost completely omitted any mention of the term Falasha. Our use of the lesser known term *ayhud* has not been accidental. Not only is this the term found in virtually all the texts from the period, but also its use raises a number of important historical questions.

Who were the *ayhud* and what if any connection do they have with the Falasha of later texts? Scholars remain sharply divided as to the answers to these questions. On the one hand are those who wish to associate virtually every reference to the *ayhud* with the Beta Israel (Falasha).[35] On the other are those who claim that *ayhud* should be viewed not as an ethnic or religious designation, but as a political term referring to rebels against the Solomonic kings.[36] The truth, not surprisingly, lies somewhere in the middle. While not every mention of the *ayhud* should be automatically accepted as a reference to the ancestors of the Falasha, in many cases, including all of those cited above, just such a connection seems to have existed.

Perhaps the most common usage of the term *ayhud* in medieval Ethiopia was as a description of Christian groups viewed by an author as heretical. This usage was especially popular in the time of Zar'a Ya'eqob, who sought to purge the Church of many of its dissident elements as part of his program of religious nationalism.[37] In one text, for example, he outlines the punishments meted out to those who consult magicians before setting out to battle: "If you are a priest, your priesthood shall be stripped of you; and if you are [just] a Christian, you shall be called a Jew."[38] Moreover, since political and religious rebellion were frequently synonymous in medieval Ethiopia, the term *ayhud* was often applied to the king's political enemies. At times it is difficult to ascertain whether it was the religious deviation that occasioned the charge of treason or the reverse. In the instance of the Emperor Zar'a Ya'eqob's son Galawdeyos, who participated in a failed coup against his father, the latter appears to be the case. Galawdeyos and his fellow plotters, we are told, consulted pagan magicians and sorcerers "and later betrayed the king, breaking their oath which they swore to [him] that they would never revolt against him . . . Galawdeyos became a Jew, abandoning his Christianity and denying Christ."[39] Taken literally, the claim that Galawdeyos became both a pagan and a Jew is quite problematic. Although this seeming contradiction could perhaps be explained if we accept the designation "pagan" as equivalent to non-Christian, when it is remembered that he was also closely allied to the previously mentioned Christian saint, Abuna Takla Hawaryat, there seems little alternative but to view his alleged "Jewishness" as political in character.[40]

Given this remarkably broad usage of the term *ayhud*, it might well be asked why we believe that *any* of the usages of the term are associated with the Beta Israel. Several arguments can be put forward in favor of this contention. Firstly it must be pointed out that it is a virtual certainty that none of the groups designated in our texts as *ayhud* used this term to refer to themselves. *Ayhud* was almost invariably a pejorative term applied by a Christian author to a despised or feared "other." As in the *Kebra Nagast* and the legends concerning Yodit discussed above, the "bad Jews" (*ayhud*) were frequently contrasted to their good "Israelite" opponents. The vagueness of the term, therefore, is of little if any relevance to the questions of certain groups' internal coherence or historical continuity.[41] Members of the Stephanite monastic movement were referred to as *ayhud* by their enemies; they, in turn, joined other Christians in referring to the Beta Israel as *ayhud*. Yet clearly the Stephanites did not consider themselves as either *ayhud* or as members of the same group as the Beta Israel.[42] The existence of a large number of widely divergent groups all identified by the contemptuous designation *ayhud* is essentially the creation of their opponents, rather than evidence for a lack of clear distinctions between members of the different groups.

There are, moreover, several reasons to specifically associate at least one of the groups designated as *ayhud* with the Beta Israel. Clear evidence exists, for example, of a certain geographic continuity. In all the cases cited in our survey of sources above, the *ayhud* in question are associated with the area around Lake Tana, and in particular the regions of Semien, Ṣallamt, Dambeya, and Wagara. In later years it is in precisely this area that we find the Falasha. Simple logic would appear to indicate that some historical link may have existed between the two groups that occupied the same region a few generations apart, particularly since both appear to have been characterized by their rejection of both royal rule and Christian doctrine. Indeed, the recognition of just such a connection is implied by the manner in which several of the later sources treat these earlier episodes. The chronicler of Sarṣa Dengel (1563–97), to cite one example, refers to the *ayhud* in Semien and Ṣallamt who confronted Ba'eda Maryam (and before him Zar'a Ya'eqob) as "Falasha," thus positing a historical link between these *ayhud* and the Falasha of his day.[43] While such anachronisms should not be given too much weight, they do appear to indicate that barely a century after the events, Ethiopian historiography had equated the two groups.

Finally, it should also be noted that at least in the hagiographic sources, the *ayhud* of the Lake Tana region are credited with distinctive ethnic or religious characteristics. According to *Gadla Gabra Iyasus* the "children of the Jews," whom the saint confronted in Enfraz, had migrated to Ethiopia from Jerusalem after the destruction of the Second Temple.[44] The people of Semien and Sallamt who welcomed the renegade monk Qozmos are said to have observed "the religion of the Jews" and to have welcomed the receipt of the *Orit*.[45] When Abuna Takla Hawaryat baptized those in Ṣallamt who had previously only been superficially converted, he had them promise that they would not return to their old religion. "And he made them swear by the *Orit* of Moses because they feared the *Orit* as in Judaism."[46] Thus there appears to be little reason to question the conclusion that the fourteenth- and fifteenth-century *ayhud* of the Lake Tana region, like the Falasha of later periods, were practitioners of a particularly Hebraic form of religion.[47] Of course, the cult they maintained should in no way be seen as identical to either "normative" Judaism or later Falasha religion. Rather, they should be regarded as being among the more Judaized groups in the spectrum of medieval Ethiopian belief. However, geography, historiography, and religion all seem to link the two groups.

This connection should not, however, be exaggerated. The *ayhud* of the earlier sources are not identical to the Falasha of later texts. Important cultural, social, and religious differences exist between the two. Indeed, as indicated by its title, a major portion of this chapter will be devoted to the attempt to prove that the shift in terminology from *ayhud* to *falasha* reflects not only the passage of time, but substantial political, religious, and economic changes. At least a portion of the *ayhud* from the Lake Tana region appear to have formed the nucleus for what later became known as the Falasha. In a moment we shall turn our attention to the forces that set this process in motion. Before this, however, we must further clarify a number of points about the *ayhud* as they appear prior to the sixteenth century.

In the sources from the fourteenth and fifteenth century, the *ayhud* are not depicted as having a unified political system. Nor is religion portrayed as the crucial organizing principle upon which their society was based. The various rulers of the *ayhud* mentioned in these texts are viewed not as powerful kings ruling over a distinctly defined religious group, but as regional governors whose subjects included both *ayhud* and Christians.[48] Only in the second half of the sixteenth century do the Beta Israel appear to have achieved a relatively high degree of political centralization and religious articulation. Only in this period do the rulers of the Falasha, at least in Semien, appear to have governed a well organized community with a clearly articulated religious system.

In light of the highly diffused character of *ayhud* society, great care must be taken when generalizing concerning their experience during this period. Almost without exception, scholars have tended to interpret the scattered references found in chronicles and hagiographies as testimonies to events that affected all the Falasha. In particular, the first half of the fifteenth century has recently been depicted as a time of rapid and overwhelming change.[49] In fact, a more cautious and gradual approach is almost certainly preferable. The defeat of one group of *ayhud* by the Emperor Yeshaq was, no doubt, a major turning point in their history. During his reign a process of disenfranchisement began that eventually deprived most of the Beta Israel of their land and radically altered the economic basis of their society.[50] It must be remembered, however, that not all the *ayhud* suffered under Yeshaq. While those who opposed him lost their land rights if they did not convert, his allies added to their holdings. In fact, the Beta Israel's loss of land took place gradually and its consequences spread unevenly. Similarly, the process of Christianization among the *ayhud* was also not uniform. As *Gadla Takla Hawaryat* clearly indicates, not only did its pace vary from region to region (Ṣallamt versus Semien), it also differed within each region. In light of this diversity it is difficult to accept reconstructions of Beta Israel history that depict its transformation as both rapid and uniform.

A recognition of the decentralized character of Beta Israel society during the period is also of crucial importance to the proper analysis of the dynamics of Beta Israel political history. If one takes as a starting point the existence of an ancient Jewish kingdom with its origins shrouded in the undocumented past, the rest of Beta Israel history appears almost automatically to be little more than an account of their decline from this mythical peak. In fact, the story is much more complex. According to the extant sources the *ayhud* did not possess a centralized politically unified society. The effective military-political structure society described in Ethiopian royal chronicles from the sixteenth and early seventeenth century was not an aboriginal characteristic of the Beta Israel. It developed relatively late, probably in response to the external threat posed by the Christian empire. Their history is not, accordingly, a story of continuous and unremitting decline, but rather a gradual process of consolidation and unification followed by a series of catastrophic defeats.

No less important than the acknowledgment of the decentralized character of Beta Israel society in the fourteenth and fifteenth century is a recognition of its political openness. Whatever the nature of *ayhud* religion at the outset of this period (and our sources, unfortunately, offer virtually no information on this subject), it does not appear to have precluded them from making contacts and alliances with other groups. Indeed, while it is common, particularly among popular authors, to depict the Beta Israel's conflicts with the Ethiopian Emperors as religious wars, there appears to be little basis for this interpretation.[51] Although the clerical authors of the royal chronicles often attempted to portray their heroes' exploits in religious terms, the composition of the forces aligned in battle raises serious doubts about this view. Even when the soldiers who faced each other on opposite sides of the battlefield were from different religious communities, economic and political considerations appear to have predominated. Certainly, the Ethiopian kings of this period valued political loyalty far more than religious conformity.[52] For their part, the Beta Israel seem to have always been eager to join forces with other dissident elements in their battles against the Christian empire. The *ayhud,* who fought the soldiers sent by Dawit, were led by the rebel monk Qozmos, and the ruler of Ṣallamt confronted by Abuna Takla Hawaryat had both Jews and Christians among his soldiers.[53] In the early sixteenth century the Stephanite monk Gabra Masih was rescued by one of the *ayhud.*[54] On the other side of the political fence, it must also be recalled that the Emperor Yeshaq was assisted by some of the *ayhud.* In medieval Ethiopia, therefore, there appears to be little question that the division for the Emperor/against the Emperor held far more weight than the division *ayhud*/Christian.

Despite their limitations, the pre-sixteenth-century sources on the *ayhud* are vital to our understanding of the later history of the Falasha. Through a remarkable stroke of luck, they provide us with a crucial glimpse into the region around Lake Tana on the eve of a major transformation. Were these sources not available, we would have little choice but to describe Falasha culture and society in an essentially ahistorical manner, dating many of their characteristic features to either an indiscernible pre-historic past or, as has been common, to the time of their alleged migration from Israel. Instead, by examining our sources as a series of before-and-after pictures, we are able to trace the manner in which a distinctive Falasha culture came into being.

Falasha: A Landless Person

Perhaps the most telling indication of the major changes that occurred among the *ayhud* of the Lake Tana region in the fourteenth and fifteenth century is their acquisition of a new name: Falasha. Until recently, scholars were virtually unanimous in translating this term as "exiles," and many cited it as evidence that the Falasha were not indigenous to Ethiopia.[55] In the past two decades, however, new evidence and a more careful reading of existing sources has prompted a major reevaluation of this term, which places it more clearly in its proper historical context. Despite attempts to depict the name "falasha" as an ancient designation for the Beta Israel, there is no evidence for its existence prior to the fifteenth century. Indeed, several points would appear to indicate that only from the sixteenth century onward was this term widely used to designate Jewish elements in the Ethiopian population.

As we have already noted, the reign of the Emperor Yeshaq was a particularly significant period in the history of the *ayhud* and appears to have marked the beginning of their dislocation and loss of landrights. Following his victory over the governor of Dambeya and Semien, Yeshaq is said to have decreed, "He who is baptized in the Christian religion may inherit the land of his father, otherwise let him be a *Falasi*" [= a landless person, a wanderer]. To this decree a later scribe added the comment, "Since then, the House of Israel [Beta Israel] have been called *Falashoch* [= exiles]."[56] Although it is tempting to join this anonymous scribe in attributing the designation Falasha for the Beta Israel to the time of Yeshaq, the evidence of the texts, however, points to a somewhat later date.

None of the sources for the remainder of the fifteenth century use the term Falasha. In the early sixteenth century, however, it appears almost simultaneously in Ge'ez, Hebrew, Arabic, and Portuguese sources. *Gadla Gabra Masih*, which was written in the second quarter of the sixteenth century, and recounts its hero's encounter with a *falasa* whom it also calls an *ayhudawi*, is apparently the first Ge'ez source to explicitly make this connection.[57] A letter written in Jerusalem in 1528 by the Kabbalist Abraham Ben Eliezer Halevi is the first Hebrew text to use the term:

And from there [Suakin] some say it is three days and some say it is five days to Falasa and the journey is very difficult. And Falasa is a strong kingdom of Jews who are valiant. . . . and it is situated on high mountains and peaks and no one can ascend there to make war."[58]

Only slightly later the Arab chronicler of Ahmad Gragn's conquest of Ethiopia noted, "The Semien Province was ruled by the Jews of Abyssinia who are called Falashas in their own language; they recognize one God only and nothing else in the way of faith: neither prophet or saint."[59]

While there can, therefore, be no doubt that the term Falasha was used to refer to some of the *ayhud* in the early sixteenth century, indications are that it was not yet universally recognized. The author of *Gadla Gabra Iyasus*, who wrote after the sixteenth-century Muslim conquest of Ethiopia, reports that the "children of the Jews" encountered by his hero had emigrated (*falasa*) from Jerusalem, but does not connect this to the ethnic designation Falasha.[60] He was, therefore, almost certainly ignorant of this sense of the term.

Nor does it appear to have been applied exclusively to the *ayhud* of the Lake Tana region during this period. This is clearly indicated by an episode in the *gadl* of Ezra of Gunda Gunde, another member of the Stephanite movement. Travelling on pilgrimage to Jerusalem a group of Stephanite monks were accused as follows: "There are Falasha here hidden by the disciples of Abba Yonas; they do not bow to Mary and the Cross of the Unique [Son]."[61]

In light of all of the above references, it is difficult to accept the view that the equation *ayhud* equals *falasha* was firmly established in the time of Yeshaq. More than a hundred years later the connection between the two terms existed but does not seem to have been completely established. The chief significance of Yeshaq's decree appears, therefore, not to lie in its creation of a new ethnic identification, but rather in the reminder it provides as to one of the primary meanings of the term Falasi. Far from being an allusion to a foreign "Israelite" origin, the designation seems to be strongly associated with the Beta Israel's status as a landless people.

As noted above, one of the major sources of the Ethiopian ruler's power was his right to distribute fiefs (*gult*) to loyal subjects. The owner of a *gult* (*bala-gult*) acquired the right to tax the peasants who lived on the land in order to provide for his own maintenance and that of his dependents. Throughout the fourteenth and fifteenth centuries vast parcels of land were conquered and placed under imperial rule, providing incomes for a growing number of royal retainers from the army, the court, and the church. Yeshaq's victory was, for example, followed by the distribution of *gult* to a number of his allies. In one crucial respect, however, his treatment of his enemies appears to have departed from the usual norms. In the Ethiopian land tenure system the *bala-gult* had no actual rights to the land itself. These remained the hereditary property (*rist*) of the peasants from whom he collected his taxes. In contrast, to the rights of a *bala-gult,* which were by definition dependent on the quality of his relationship with the emperor or some other powerful figure, rights to *rist* were generally far more stable. *Rist*-holders only rarely saw their land alienated and redistributed.[62] This appears to have been precisely the fate that befell a portion of the *ayhud*. While those who were willing to convert to Christianity were able to retain their *rist,* the others became *falasi*. Colonists were moved in to take over the land they vacated.[63]

Although we possess no detailed information on the subject, the Beta Israel may have adopted a number of strategies in response to the decline in their access to land. A significant number were, at least superficially, converted to Christianity in an attempt to retain their economic position.[64] Others probably continued to work their traditional lands, no longer as independent agriculturalists, but as tenant farmers for the recently arrived colonists.[65] Yet a third group appear to have migrated to regions, which had not been affected by Yeshaq's decree or where the quality of the farmland was low enough to discourage the immediate arrival of covetous settlers. While the inhospitably cold mountains of Semien immediately come to mind, lowland regions, traditionally despised by highland Ethiopians, may also have been included. Although probably not the first *ayhud* to settle in these regions, these migrants would have significantly increased the local population, creating new economic and political demands on its leadership.

Whether as a result of tenancy, the low productivity of their lands, or the demands of migration-induced population pressures, the Beta Israel probably began to seek ways to supplement their income from agriculture. On the basis of the existing sources, both written and oral, it is impossible to determine with any certainty precisely when they began to engage commercially in handicrafts such as pottery, weaving, building, and, most important, smithing. As with so many of the changes in this period, the process was probably gradual and uneven, taking place over generations or even centuries. Nevertheless, there would seem to be little question that the major catalyst for this economic transformation was their loss of *rist*-rights, which began in the time of Yeshaq.[66]

The fifteenth century appears, therefore, to have marked the beginning of a series of changes that transformed the *ayhud* on many levels. Singled out and deprived of their *rist*, they responded by both concentrating themselves in peripheral areas and assuming a special economic identity either as landless tenants or craftsmen. Whichever strategy they pursued, they added new depth to their previously vague group identity, and began to distinguish themselves from the various other groups designated as *ayhud*. How far this process of redefinition would have gone simply as a consequence of geographical and economic forces is difficult to determine. The question is, in any event, completely hypothetical for almost immediately a major religious-ideological component came to the fore.

Falasyan: A Monk

Until recently the existence of monasticism among the Beta Israel was just one of the many enigmatic elements in their history and culture. In recent years, however, research by a number of scholars working with oral traditions gathered from Beta Israel informants has enabled us to better understand this phenomenon and place it firmly in its correct historical context.[67] Their research has enabled us to see that in the religious sphere no less than in the political-economic realm the first half of the fifteenth century marked the beginning of a series of major transformations of the Beta Israel.

According to Beta Israel tradition, the major catalyst for these changes was the arrival in their midst of a charismatic holy man known as Abba Sabra. Although generally believed to have been a Christian, Abba Sabra is said to have clashed with the reigning monarch and to have sought refuge in the isolated regions inhabited by the Beta Israel.[68] Rather than converting the Beta Israel to Christianity, he eventually joined them, bringing with him the Christian institution of monasticism. Aided by his students and disciples, most notably Ṣagga Amlak (who supposedly was a son of the Emperor Zar'a Ya'eqob), he irreversibly altered the basis of Beta Israel religious life. In fact, almost every major feature of Beta Israel religion as known today is attributed to the monastic heroes of this period.[69]

While there is obviously a strong hagiographic element in these traditions, the essential story of a renegade monk joining forces with the Beta Israel in the fifteenth century and influencing their religious practice is eminently plausible. Indeed, in light of what we know of this period from other sources, the Beta Israel traditions offer a remarkably accurate picture of the religious milieu and, in particular, the crucial role played by monasticism.

Ethiopian monasticism traces its origins to the end of the fifth century and the arrival of two groups of monks from Syria. The impact of their activities on the understaffed and underresourced church of the period can scarcely be overestimated.[70] Yet despite the crucial role played by these foreign missionaries, teachers, and translators, it was not until the end of the thirteenth century that the monastic ideals and institutions they represented became the dominant force in Ethiopian Christianity.

During the early Solomonic period (1270–1527), four major monastic movements arose. Each represented an attempt by regional groups to oppose the encroachment of the Solomonic kings on traditional rights and privileges. As the kings expanded their domain and reduced local autonomy, members of local noble families abandoned the political arena and took up the monastic life. Although Ethiopia's monasteries had probably served as refuges or prisons for political failures and malcontents prior to this period, the changing political conditions of the time dramatically increased the numbers of those assuming the monastic garb. Although the different monastic movements differed significantly in the time and locale of their development, and each had its own distinctive ritual practice and theological tenants, all four were characterized by an initial period of anti-monarchical activity during which their members defied and denied the authority of the Solomonic kings.

It was Shawa province that first came under Solomonic domination and it was here too that we witness the earliest development of a new militant monastic movement. The rebel clerics of Shawa, and to a lesser extent Amhara, refused royal gifts, denounced royal polygamy, and denied royal jurisdiction over their monasteries. The second of the monastic movements, that named for the fourteenth-century holy man Ewostatewos, flourished in the northern province of Tigre. The Ewostatian movement championed traditional Ethiopian religious practices such as the Saturday Sabbath in opposition to the dictates of the Solomonic kings and the Egyptian bishops. At the height of their conflict with the official leaders of the Church, the Ewostatians did not even recognize the right of the *Abuna* to consecrate clergy. In the middle of the fifteenth century, just as the Ewostatians were being reconciled to the central Church, there arose once again, in northern Ethiopia, the Stephanite movement. Members of this third movement, founded by Abba Estifanos, were distinguished by their refusal to bow before Mary or the cross. Since both these cults were strongly supported by the court, the Stephanites' heteropraxy was to a considerable extent symptomatic of their opposition to royal domination of the church, especially during the reign of the powerful emperor Zar'a Ya'eqob.[71]

The rise of monasticism among the Beta Israel was in many ways a similar phenomenon to its flowering in Shawa and Tigre. While it is true that the Beta Israel differed from the Christian groups insofar as they probably lacked any monastic tradition prior to the fifteenth century, this difference does not appear to be crucial.[72] Although Tigre province had a long tradition of monasticism prior to the fourteenth century, in Shawa the institution was unknown before the middle of the thirteenth century. More important, among the Beta Israel as in the other three cases, the development of monasticism seems to be intimately connected to the encroachment of the Solomonic kingdom. As Quirin has noted, "the institution of monasticism was developed as a means of revitalizing the moral and ideological basis of their society after their defeat by Yeshaq."[73] By adopting and adapting the Christian practice of monasticism, the Beta Israel were able, in a manner similar to their Christian counterparts, to articulate elements of a distinctive regionally based religious identity and express their opposition to the central institutions of the Christian empire.

In addition to the obvious structural resemblances between Christian and Beta Israel monasticism, there is ample evidence in support of a historical link similar to that suggested by Beta Israel oral traditions. As we have already seen, rebel clerics such as Gabra Iyasus (Ewostatian), Gabra Masih (Stephanite), and Qozmos all had contact with and/or cooperated with the *ayhud*. In a text from the *Miracles of Mary*, a Christian monk is said to have joined a community of Jews living in the mountains during the reign of Zar'a Ya'eqob.[74] The claim that Abba Sabra joined the Beta Israel in the aftermath of his difficulties with this Emperor is, therefore, eminently plausible. He, like others, may have sought a purer, more traditional form of religion than that offered by the zealous reforming emperor. Even the assertion that one of Zar'a Ya'eqob's sons was among his disciples cannot be rejected totally out of hand in light of that ruler's political difficulties with some of his children.[75]

In one major respect, however, the rise of monasticism among the Beta Israel would appear to have differed from the development of similar movements elsewhere in Ethiopia. Crucial to the development of each of the Christian movements was the displacement of local nobles and their subsequent recruitment into the ranks of the monastic leadership. In both Shawa and Tigre the emergence of the monastic movements coincided with the end of serious political opposition to imperial rule and a sharp curtailment of local autonomy.[76] It has in the past been common to offer a similar interpretation of the factors behind the rise of Beta Israel monasticism. Quirin, for example, has stated that Beta Israel monasticism "provided a new practical leadership after the demise of the secular leaders."[77] However, a careful reading of the sources raises serious questions concerning this interpretation. There is, as we have seen, little evidence that the *ayhud* possessed a centralized political structure prior to the sixteenth century. Already by the time of Yeshaq, moreover, the ruler of Dambeya and Semien is said to have been a royal appointee. Indeed, the Falasha rulers of the sixteenth and seventeenth century appear to have been far stronger and to have enjoyed a greater deal of autonomy than their predecessors. Accordingly, far from being the substitute for a failed and waning political elite, the Beta Israel monks appear to have preceded the emergence of a clearly defined and well-organized secular leadership. In a society faced with military, political, and economic challenges on an unprecedented scale, they provided the religious ideological basis around which to organize.

According to Beta Israel tradition, virtually every major element of their religious system originated as part of the "monastic revolution" of the fifteenth century. Of course, allowances must be made here, as with most oral traditions, for a certain degree of telescoping. The religious changes in question almost certainly took shape over an extended period, rather than in a single brief episode.[78] This caution should not, however, lead us to minimize the significance of this period for the cultural development of the Beta Israel. Although it is tempting to view the contribution of the monks as an essentially conservative one, preserving or reviving an ancient tradition, this would appear to drastically underestimate their role in the emergence of the Falasha. Although the Beta Israel have frequently been depicted as heirs to a particularly archaic form of Judaism, their religious system developed in Ethiopia independent of direct contact with earlier Jewish groups. Far from acting primarily as guardians of the status quo, the monks were major innovators, gradually defining and articulating a religious system with much greater depth than that of the earlier *ayhud*.[79] Moreover, this religious system provided the ideological foundation for the organization of a society that differed significantly from its predecessors. To a considerable extent the Beta Israel monks can be said to have created a society in their own image—one in which religious identity, physical isolation, and concepts of purity played a central role. Accordingly, the monks must be credited with being the crucial catalysts in the "invention" of the Falasha, and it may well be more than a coincidence that one meaning of the term *falasyan* is monk.[80]

Falasha Literature

Thus far in our consideration of the changes that took place among the Judaized population of Ethiopia in the fourteenth and fifteenth century, we have considered primarily the evidence of the Christian Ethiopic sources and the Beta Israel's oral traditions. Further support for the thesis argued above is found in a third, somewhat surprising source, the literature of the Beta Israel. Although religious rather than historical in character, these texts when properly analyzed offer a number of important hints as to the cultural history of the Beta Israel, and, as we shall demonstrate, offer rather striking confirmation for the testimonies provided by the two previously examined types of sources.

No aspect of Beta Israel culture has been the subject of as continuous a record of first-rate scholarship as the community's religious literature. As the result of the efforts of scholars such as Joseph Halévy, Carlo Conti Rossini, A. Z. Aešcoly, Wolf Leslau, Stefan Strelcyn, Mordechai (Max) Wurmbrand, and Edward Ullendorff it is possible to provide surprisingly detailed descriptions of many Beta Israel compositions.[81] To be sure, much work still remains to be accomplished in this field. It is possible, nevertheless, to suggest a number of characteristics generally typical of Beta Israel literature and of considerable relevance for the reconstruction of their history.

Almost without exception the literature of the Beta Israel neither originated within their community nor reached them directly through Jewish channels. Rather, the majority of Ethiopian "Jewish" texts reached the Beta Israel through the mediation of Ethiopian Christian sources. Perhaps the most striking example of this phenomenon is the best known of all Beta Israel texts, *Te'ezaza Sanbat* (The commandments of the Sabbath), long considered the most original of Beta Israel compositions. *Te'ezaza Sanbat* is in fact a composite work that draws from a variety of sources. The first section of the published editions of this work (which does not appear in all manuscripts) is dependent on an Arabic (Christian?) source.[82] The next section is a skillfully edited and censored version of a Christian homily on the Sabbath (*Dersana Sanbat*).[83] After a short interlude this is followed by a list of laws and commandments for the Sabbath that draws heavily on the book of Jubilees, particularly Chapter 50. A similar interweaving of sources continues throughout the book.[84] According to Beta Israel tradition, *Te'ezaza Sanbat* is one of a number of texts and other innovations that can be attributed to the fifteenth-century monastic leader, Abba Sabra. Even if we withhold judgment on his personal role in the work's composition, there seems little question that *Te'ezaza Sanbat* was created from a variety of sources by someone familiar with Ethiopian Christian literature. In this, it is not substantially different from most other Beta Israel compositions.

With one or two exceptions, the Beta Israel appear to have chosen works whose Christian versions already displayed a clear biblical Jewish tone.[85] The deaths of major biblical figures, the celebration of the Sabbath, and the fate of the soul after death are all themes devoid of any exclusively Christian content. Thus the Christian versions could be adapted for Beta Israel use without the necessity of major rewriting. Indeed in most cases only the most minimal and obvious changes were introduced: the "Sabbath" became the "Jewish or First Sabbath," *Egzi'abher* (God) was substituted for Jesus, the sign of the cross became simply a sign. Only in rare instances were more substantial attempts made to rewrite or edit the sources. In this context it is worth remembering that the previously discussed Hebraic-biblical character of Ethiopian Christianity must have greatly assisted the Beta Israel in their search for appropriate works to adapt. It should, moreover, be noted that the reign of the Emperor Zar'a Ya'eqob, which is remembered by the Beta Israel as the period of Abba Sabra and Ṣagga Amlak, was a time of both remarkable literary production and of strong Jewish influences within the Ethiopian Orthodox Church.[86] In short, it was a period extremely well suited to the kind of adoption and adaptation of literary works undertaken by the Beta Israel.

The powerful impact of Ethiopian Christian literature on that of the Beta Israel need not have been accompanied by a major influx of Christians or even a considerable number of texts. The presence of several "units" in the Beta Israel corpus suggests that the total number of manuscripts that reached the Beta Israel was probably not large. Four works, the *gadlat* (Testaments) of Abraham, Isaac, and Jacob, and the Homily of Abraham and Sarah in Egypt, appear to have come to the Beta Israel as a single group. Not only do they appear together in almost all the Beta Israel versions discovered to date, but a fourteenth- or fifteenth-century Christian manuscript preserves the same arrangement.[87] The Beta Israel texts may well have been copied from just such a manuscript. Three Beta Israel texts, (*Te'ezaza Sanbat, Maṣḥafa Mala'ekt*, and *Mota Aron*) incorporate material from homilies by Jacob of Sarug, and here again a single manuscript may well have been the source.[88]

Perhaps even more significant, at least seven of the approximately twenty Beta Israel texts were translated from Arabic sources.[89] Since translation from Arabic to Ge'ez did not begin in earnest until the early fourteenth century, none of these works can predate this period.[90] Indeed, several authors have suggested that most of these texts came to the Beta Israel in the fourteenth or fifteenth century, a view that accords well with much of the other material presented above.[91] In fact, this period is probably best viewed as the *terminus post quem* for these texts. One of them, *Nagara Muse*, dates to the eighteenth century![92]

On the basis of our present state of knowledge, it appears that Beta Israel literature offers strong support for the view that the early fifteenth century was a crucial period in the emergence of a distinctive Falasha culture. Despite its overwhelmingly biblical/Jewish character, this literature offers no evidence in favor of the view that their religion is an ancient form of Judaism. Archaic elements and ancient forms in Beta Israel texts can almost always be shown to have reached them through the Ethiopian Orthodox Church. Many of these, moreover, could not have entered Beta Israel culture prior to the fourteenth century. That some of these texts entered considerably later serves as an important caution against viewing the processes of adoption and adaptation as having taken place with tremendous rapidity in a few short years or even decades. Given the ritual-cultic importance of books such as the *Arde'et, Mota Muse*, and *Gadla Abraham*, which are read respectively at purification ceremonies, funerals, and on New Year's, these findings have a significance beyond the realm of literature per se. Funerals, purification rituals after childbirth, and holiday observances that incorporate such texts could only have assumed their present form after the composition, translation, and transmission of these works to the Beta Israel. What (if any) form such rituals had prior to the introduction of these texts remains ultimately unknowable; the relatively late date of their current structure appears certain. The association, moreover, of crucial *rites des passage* and annual observances with the heroes of Biblical Israel must have contributed significantly to the Beta Israel's sense of legitimacy and peoplehood.

One final point connected to the subject of Beta Israel literature must be considered before we summarize the findings of this lengthy and wide-ranging chapter. The possibility cannot be excluded that in the course of their transformation from an ill-defined group of *ayhud* to the far more clearly delineated Falasha, the Beta Israel acquired not only literature, but literacy. Our sources offer only the briefest of hints in this respect, but they are nevertheless worth some attention.

For a variety of reasons it is difficult to credit the idea that the Beta Israel were from antiquity a literate culture. Scholars are virtually unanimous in the view that the Beta Israel were never familiar with Hebrew.[93] The various Agaw languages they spoke and used in some of their prayers did not exist in a written form independent of their use of Ethiopic script.[94] Moreover, given the limits of literacy in traditional Ethiopia (even many Christian priests were illiterate), it is hard to believe that the isolated *ayhud* of the Lake Tana region were literate from an early date. Indeed, the failure of scholars to raise the issue of when they became literate would appear to be yet another example of the manner in which Beta Israel culture has been treated in a static and ahistorical fashion with many of the elements that can be documented only from the fifteenth century onward treated as if they must have existed from antiquity. As noted above, the fourteenth-century rebel monk Qozmos is said to have written the *Orit* for them. Perhaps only through his intervention did the *ayhud* gain possession of written scripture. Given what we have learned about their religious, economic, and social development from the fourteenth century onward, it certainly appears plausible that only in this period did they become a literate culture.

As a number of recent studies have shown, the acquisition of literacy, even on a limited scale, may have far-reaching consequences for a traditional society.[95] Religious beliefs become more clearly articulated and more open to reflection and critique. Group social identity can be better defined and borders between groups more explicitly delineated. A class of religious specialists often emerge who function as custodians and interpreters of the written sacred texts. Indeed, many of the processes that transformed the *ayhud* into the Falasha are precisely those that are commonly associated with the impact of literacy. Thus, while no definitive proof can be offered in favor of the claim that the Beta Israel acquired not only literature but literacy from the fourteenth century onward, the suggestion is an attractive one and is in general agreement with the available data.

Summary and Conclusions

As is abundantly clear from the preceding discussion, the fourteenth through sixteenth centuries were a crucial period in the history of the Beta Israel. Prior to this time we are able to offer only the most speculative reconstructions concerning the history of Judaized groups in Ethiopia. From the fourteenth century onward, however, Ge'ez chronicles and hagiographies begin to present scattered reports concerning groups of *ayhud* in the regions around Lake Tana. Even these seemingly straightforward reports present the historian with a number of interesting problems. While it is tempting, for example, to view the *ayhud* of this period as the descendants of earlier Judaized groups from the Aksumite period and later, the historical reality is probably more complex. The presence of Judaized elements around Lake Tana in the period of the so-called Solomonic dynasty was probably the result of influences on the region from groups both within and outside the Ethiopian Orthodox Church. A further difficulty found in the interpretation of these references to the *ayhud* results because this term, far from referring to a single clearly defined group, was primarily a pejorative terms used by authors to denigrate their enemies. Only a small portion of those identified in the sources *ayhud* appear to have a direct historical connection to the people later identified as the *Falasha*. Even those *ayhud* who on the basis of beliefs and geography can be identified as constituting "proto-Falasha" population were not politically united or socially isolated from their non-Jewish neighbors.

A variety of factors appear to have combined to bring about the transformation of these vaguely defined *ayhud* of the fourteenth and fifteenth century into the *falasha* of later periods. First, the gradual disenfranchisement of groups of *ayhud,* who lost the right to own *(rist)* land, had several important consequences. Those who did not convert to Christianity were forced to either become tenant farmers or concentrate themselves in peripheral areas where the agricultural quality of the land was low. In both cases, a need developed to supplement their diminished income from farming with crafts such as pottery, weaving, and smithing. Their previous inchoate group identity began to take on new social and economic overtones. At about the same time we witness the emergence of a new form of religious leadership as monks (*falasyan*) become the primary carriers and interpreters of a far richer and more clearly articulated religious identity than had previously existed. These monks, several of whom were originally Christian, are credited with introducing almost every major element of the Beta Israel religious system. Under their leadership biblical-Hebraic elements found in Ethiopian Christianity were adopted and adapted to develop a distinctive Jewish group identity. This process, which is clearly attested to in the Beta Israel's own traditons, can also be amply documented through the study of their religious literature. Thus, a combination of social, political, economic, and religious factors from the fourteenth to sixteenth century helped transform a number of vaguely defined and politically disparate groups of *ayhud* into a far more centralized and distinctive group known as the *Falasha*. In the next chapter, we shall analyze the consequences of this new cohesiveness and examine the period of their most important conflicts with the Christian Ethiopian emperors.

4

Resistance and Defeat: 1468–1632

During the period from 1468 to 1632 the Beta Israel displayed their most sophisticated political-military organization, were involved in some of their most dramatic conflicts with the Ethiopian emperors, and suffered some of their most serious defeats. Although most aspects of their cultural, economic, and social development remain obscure, their role in the wars and succession struggles that characterized this era are unusually well documented. Once again we are able to clearly demonstrate that the events shaping the Beta Israel can only be properly evaluated in the general context of their times.

The Falasha described in the royal chronicles of the sixteenth and seventeenth century differ significantly from the *ayhud* described in the previous chapter. The area under their control had shrunk significantly. If in the past Semien, Ṣallamt, Dambeya, Ṣagade, Waldebba, Walqayit, and Wagara all had sizeable Beta Israel populations, by the middle of the sixteenth century only Semien and to a lesser extent Dambeya and Wagara still harbored an organized Jewish presence.[1] Scattered Beta Israel lived elsewhere, but they probably did not have any formal organization beyond the village level. One feature associated with the constriction of the area densely settled by the Beta Israel was a rise in the degree of political organization. From the middle of the sixteenth century until the loss of political autonomy ca. 1625, the Beta Israel of

Semien were ruled by members of a single family, one of whom served as paramount ruler and military leader. Despite the appearance of a relatively high degree of political centralization, some caution should be exercised before we refer to even this form of government as a "kingdom." First, as our sources make abundantly clear, during all of the period in question the residents of Semien were in a tributary relationship to the Christian Ethiopian emperor. While on occasion their rulers tried to withhold this tribute, these acts of defiance represent typical examples of the manner in which regionally based vassals sought to exploit the weakness of individual emperors and not serious assertions of absolute independence.[2] So too the prominent role of Gedewon, governor of Semien, in support of a series of challengers to the rule of the Emperor Susenyos (1607–32) appears to be not an indication of the Beta Israel's continued independence but rather a sign that they had been reduced to attempting to achieve the most favorable terms possible within the framework of the Christian empire. By the sixteenth century the issue of Beta Israel independence had largely been decided in the negative. The Beta Israel of Dambeya seem to have been almost completely subdued, and although occasional victories were achieved in Semien, only the cowardly and incompetent Minas (1559–63) was truly stymied in his attempt to defeat the Beta Israel. Finally, it should be noted that the Beta Israel's relatively long period of resistance in the Semien was much more the product of the region's harsh physical conditions than of either sophisticated military techniques or large numbers of troops.[3]

Symptons of Imperial Decline: 1468–1527

Even the difficult conditions of the Semien region would probably not have delayed the incorporation of the Beta Israel had all Ethiopian emperors pursued the aggressive policies of government centralization and religious nationalism displayed by Zar'a Ya'eqob.[4] In fact, his rule emerges as something of an exception, and in most of this period the Ethiopian emperors made little effort to penetrate the periphery of their empire and radically reorganize the principles that guided its societies. Thus, immediately upon assuming the throne, his son, Ba'eda Maryam, reversed his father's administrative reforms.[5] Although he attempted to continue Zar'a Ya'eqob's policies in the religious sphere and achieved a victory over the Beta Israel that had eluded his father, in general he was not as successful a ruler. The next fifty years, moreover, witnessed a far more serious deterioration of imperial control. When Ba'eda Maryam died in 1478, his son and successor Eskender was only six years old. The first eight years of his reign were most notable for the struggles that took place between the various regents who sought to exercise power in the name of the infant king.[6] Although the next eight years saw somewhat more stability, Eskender's sudden death in 1494 at the age of twenty-two once again plunged the kingdom into turmoil. Eskender's son, Amda Ṣeyon II, was at most seven when he came to power and died within half a year. The next claiment to the throne, Eskender's brother Na'od, was crowned at age twenty in 1494, but only began to rule effectively about a year later, after he had subdued a number of rivals and rebels. Na'od's reign, which lasted until his death in 1508 was one of the longest of the period.

Not surprisingly, the succession struggles and internal battles that characterized the last quarter of the fifteenth century produced a marked weakening of imperial control over frontier areas. Thus, Ba'eda Maryam's previously mentioned victory over the Beta Israel was no more successful at resolving the issue of their status in the empire than those of his predecessor. By 1484 the Beta Israel were once again in conflict with the Christian Emperor (Eskender), who took at least four years to subdue them.[7] A recently published passage from the *Life* of Abuna Habta Maryam, indicates that Na'od's troops may have also clashed with the Beta Israel. In it we read that God "made Na'od king when the Jews who deny [Christ's] birth [became powerful in Ethiopia], these who, since ancient times, lived leading men and women astray."[8] This episode may perhaps be the same as that referred to by the sixteenth-century Jerusalem kabbalist Abraham Halevi. According to a letter he wrote in 1517, one of several reports he authored on the Jews of Ethiopia, a succession struggle erupted in 1504 between the sons of a recently deceased Beta Israel ruler. Eventually one son asked the Ethiopian emperor to come to his assistance.

And in the year which the men of the sinful kingdom, the kingdom of Portugal rose against the Marranos in that very year and that time there arose a war between the Habeshites and the Israelites. And because the star of Jacob sank, and fell and was dark and blacked out at that time, the hand of Samael [an evil angel] triumphed over the Jews and the Habeshites defeated them. And the hand of the Habeshites was severe, severe and hard on the Jews who were in this kingdom until they eliminated their name from the kingdom. And those who remained fled to the mountains and there they strengthened themselves and defended themselves.[9]

Indeed, perhaps the clearest testimony to the continued struggles between the Beta Israel and the Christian emperors of this period is the regular mention in Hebrew sources of Ethiopian Jews brought as slaves to the markets of the Middle East. The appearance of these "Jews from the land of Prester John" marks their first serious encounter with World Jewry and is noteworthy in a number of respects. These sources established the basis for later rabbinical opinions affirming the Beta Israel's status as Jews.[10] Moreover, their interest in describing the heroism, military prowess, and political autonomy of the Beta Israel makes them (their tendency to exaggerate notwithstanding) a useful supplement to existing Ethiopian sources of the wars of this period.[11]

Despite the emphasis of these Jewish sources, for most of the period from the mid-1400s until they achieved victory with the help of the Portuguese in 1543, the Christian emperors of Ethiopia were preoccupied not with the Beta Israel but with a major Muslim threat to their control of the Ethiopian highlands. Both Ba'eda Maryam and Eskender suffered serious military reverses in their campaigns against the Muslims of the southeastern region of Adal and probably had only limited resources to devote to the Beta Israel.[12] In fact, Eskender and Na'od lost their lives in battles against the Muslims of Adal and Ifat respectively, and in the early sixteenth century an even more serious challenge faced their successors.

Na'od's death in 1508 led to yet another minor assuming the throne as his son, Lebna Dengel, age twelve, came to power. Rather predictably, the succession of a series of young and inexperienced princes had resulted not only in a weakening of the country's frontier defences, but also in a general decline of royal power at court. In many respects royal courtiers appear to have welcomed the ascension of minor candidates as an opportunity to retain power in their own hands for as long as possible.[13] By far the most formidable court figure of the late fifteenth and early sixteenth century was Queen Helena, a widow of Ba'eda Maryam. With minor interruptions she exercised her influence over political struggles and foreign affairs for almost half a century.[14] With the ascension of Lebna Dengel, she once again served as regent, and with characteristic perspicacity sought to take advantage of the Portuguese offer of an anti-Muslim alliance.[15] Unfortunately, by the time the Portuguese were finally able to respond to this request the political situation was dramatically altered. Not only had Lebna Dengel ended the regency and assumed power, but his devastating victory in 1516 over the Muslims of Adal as well as other successes had left him brimming with confidence. For the first time in half a century the emperor appeared to be on the verge of asserting his authority over his rivals both at court and in the provinces.[16] By the time the Portuguese embassy arrived in 1520, Queen Helena's offer was only a vague memory. When they departed six years later no agreement had been reached.

The Muslim Conquest and Its Aftermath: 1527–63

Lebna Dengel's victory over the Muslims of Adal in 1516 damaged the prestige of the sultanate's ruling Walasma dynasty as much as it enhanced his own. Following a period of internal struggle, Ahmad ibn Ibrahim, a resourceful military commander popularly known as Gragn, "the left-handed," emerged as the ruler of Adal.[17] Having assumed the title of Imam, he led his army in a series of raids along the periphery of the Christian kingdom, which culminated in 1527 with a two-pronged attack against the frontier provinces of Dawaro and Ifat. In 1529 Gragn's seasoned and well-armed troops met and defeated Lebna Dengel's numerically superior forces in a battle at Shembra Koure. The *futuh* (conquest) of Ethiopia had begun.[18] During the next twelve years highland Ethiopia witnessed devastation on an unprecedented scale, as churches were burnt, monasteries destroyed, and numerous Christians forcibly converted to Islam. Only in those areas "where a very long history of ethnic and religious fusion had been effected, namely, in Tigre, Lasta, Amhara, Bagemder, eastern Gojjam, and in small isolated pockets in Shawa" did Christian culture survive and retain enough resilience to begin the slow process of rejuvenation.[19] In many respects the Church never completely regained the vitality of its earlier golden period.

Initially the Beta Israel appear to have welcomed the Muslim disruption of imperial rule and viewed it as an opportunity to reassert their independence. According to Gragn's chronicler, they served as guides to the Muslim troops who invaded Semien and fought against the troops of Lebna Dengel.[20] By 1542, however, they had discovered that Muslim rule also presented clear disadvantages. Thus, when the Portuguese, led by Dom Cristovao (Christopher) da Gama, began to move inland in order join up with the troops of Lebna Dengel's successor, Galawdewos (Claudius), the Beta Israel allied themselves with the European Christian forces. A Beta Israel who had been in command of a strategic highpoint in Semien known as *Amba Ayhud* helped Dom Cristovao to conquer it from the Muslims.[21] In return for his assistance, he was restored to his command. Indeed, following the initial defeat of the Portuguese by Gragn and da Gama's death, the Emperor Galawdewos, his mother Sabla Dengel, and the remaining Portuguese took refuge at *Amba Ayhud*.[22] In February 1543 they set out from there for their final victorious campaign against Gragn. In return for their support the Beta Israel had many of their traditional rights in Semien restored.[23] Indeed, Galawdewos's entire reign (1540–59), a period most notable for his valient attempts to reconstruct the institutions of imperial government, appears to have offered the Beta Israel a welcome respite from the earlier years of war and conflict.[24]

Following Galawdewos' death in 1559, he was succeeded by his youngest brother Minas.[25] From the outset, Minas showed himself an ineffectual, even cowardly leader. Rather than personally rallying his troops to defend the country's frontiers and confront the Muslim troops led by Nur, he delegated this crucial task to his cousin Hamalmal. Minas himself chose to spend the rainy season of 1559 in Emfraz, a mountainous area overlooking the northeastern shore of Lake Tana. Minas's personal motives aside, his selection of this area as a site for the imperial camp is representative of an important trend in the geopolitical development of sixteenth-century Ethiopia. As a result of the campaigns of Ahmad Gragn and the subsequent migration of the Oromo, the political center of the Ethiopian empire gradually moved northward. The growing imperial presence in the Lake Tana region was probably the most important factor behind the Ethiopian emperors' frequent clashes with the Beta Israel during this period.[26] The incessant demands for demonstrations of loyalty and financial support placed an intolerable burden on the governors and people of Dambeya, Wagara, Semien, and other surrounding regions.[27] The shift of the country's political center to the region around Lake Tana also made it imperative that this area be militarily subdued. Not surprisingly, the period from the beginning of the reign of Minas's successor, Sarsa Dengel (1563–97) to the end of

Susenyo's rule in 1632 also saw a series of campaigns against the Agaw populations to the south (Agawmeder) and the southwest (Metekkel) of the lake.[28] Only after the subjugation of the Beta Israel ca. 1625 did these other campaigns become more determined and bring lasting results.[29] In retrospect, the wars against the Beta Israel from 1560 to 1632 can be seen to have been the first stage in a more extended struggle, which lasted until 1683, by the Christian emperors of Ethiopia to subdue the peoples of the Lake Tana region.

When Minas set out to war in October 1560, however, it was in a futile and unnecessary campaign against the Beta Israel of Semien. Although the Beta Israel had agreed to submit to imperial rule and were willing to continue to pay regular tribute, Minas demanded that they convert to Christianity.[30] When they refused to comply, Minas gathered his troops, including regiments from Tigre, and set out to conquer them. Unfortunately for Minas, he greatly underestimated the forces and resources necessary to wage a successful campaign against the Beta Israel's mountain strongholds, and suffered an ignominious defeat. Despite the attempts of his clerical supporters to gloss over this episode by claiming that it merely showed that the time for the final defeat of the Jews had not yet arrived, taken together with his previous failures to demonstrate leadership, it was a major embarrassment and significantly undermined his legitimacy.[31] Although Minas managed to hold on to power, the remainder of his brief reign saw few noteworthy achievements, and he died of fever in 1563.

Sarṣa Dengel 1563–97

Following Minas's death, his mother, Sabla Wangel, moved quickly to place her grandson the thirteen-year-old Sarṣa Dengel on the throne. Although regional leaders from both Amhara and Tigre, including several who had earlier rebelled against Minas, opposed his accession, Sarṣa Dengel retained power. In fact, his reign (which lasted until 1597) was one of the longest in Ethiopian history. Rather surprisingly, his extended period on the throne contributed little to the consolidation of imperial power and the repression of regional forces. Indeed, as several scholars have recently pointed out, his reign was characterized by weakness and vacillation, compromise and appeasement. He dismantled important frontier defenses and pursued policies that disrupted peaceful provinces and reduced the morale of his soldiers.[32]

No aspect of Sarṣa Dengel's reign was more characteristic of his shortcomings then his three campaigns against the Beta Israel, which began in 1579 and lasted for almost a decade.[33] By far the best documented of any of their clashes with the Christian emperors, these battles have probably received far more attention than they intrinsically merit. As Quirin has astutely noted, "they were rather less significant in their causes or their consequences for the Beta Israel than either those of Yeshaq in the fifteenth century or Susinyos in the early seventeenth."[34] Ironically, the most meaningful feature of these campaigns was probably the very fact that they were undertaken at all. By setting out to war against the Beta Israel at a time when the Oromo posed a major challenge to his empire's southern frontiers, Sarṣa Dengel was guilty of a major miscalculation that weakened not only his rule, but that of his successors.[35]

Like his father before him, Sarṣa Dengel chose the region of northwest Ethiopia around Lake Tana as the site for several of his camps and spent considerable time, particularly in the rainy season, in the area.[36] Guba'e in Emfraz, was a special favorite of his, and some time before 1586 he built the first Gondar-style castle there.[37] As always, the royal presence in a region placed a major burden on the surrounding population, who were largely responsible for provisioning the imperial entourage.[38] Thus, the royal court, rather than serving as an integrating factor, was perceived by much of the populace as a predatory force that left them stripped of their resources.

According to his chronicler, Sarṣa Dengel's initial campaign against the Beta Israel in 1579 was provoked by the refusal of Radai, chief of Semien, to deliver his tributes.[39] While there appears to be no reason to doubt this testimony, the timing of Radai's act was, to say the least, peculiar. Had he waited a few months more, Sarṣa Dengel would have been occupied with his wars against the Oromo and unable to respond in force. Radai almost certainly must have assumed that the Emperor would personally ignore his challenge and delegate responsibility for the region to one of his generals. Instead, the Emperor abandoned his plans to fight the Oromo and committed himself to a difficult and costly campaign in Semien. Even if we remember that Radai's refusal to pay taxes was coupled with other provocative acts, including the renaming of mountains in Semien after those of biblical Israel, it is difficult to accept Sarṣa Dengel's decision uncritically.[40] The economic resources of this region, renowned for its impassable roads, cold weather, and devastating hails, could scarcely have been crucial to the short-term financial well-being of the state.[41] Nor does the political threat posed by the Beta Israel appear to have warranted the neglect of the far more serious challenge from the Oromo. Nevertheless, Sarṣa Dengel devoted almost a decade to subduing the people of Semien, and even then the task remained largely incomplete.

Perhaps the greatest obstacle to the speedy subjugation of the Beta Israel was their strategy of retreating into well-defended mountain strongholds. From the heights of these lofty plateaus, the Beta Israel could easily roll large stones down upon the royal troops who sought to ascend along the treacherous and narrow paths.[42] The resistance of the Beta Israel to capture, enslavement, and conversion was, moreover, remarkably fierce. While Radai and his family eventually surrendered and were sent into exile in Waj,[43] other Beta Israel martyred themselves. One woman in particular is remembered for leaping off the edge of a great precipice shouting, "Adonai help me," and dragging her captor with her to his death.[44] As in the past, the defeat of the Beta Israel resulted in deaths, conversions, enslavement, and the loss of more land. Several of the regiments drafted to fight in Semien appear to have been settled in the region, rather than being allowed to return to their home provinces. This policy was not only costly to the Beta Israel, but also lowered troop morale and removed much-needed soldiers from regions being overrun by the Oromo.[45] In the final analysis, moreover, none of these policies restored peace in Semien. Three years later, some time after the rainy season of 1582, Radai's brother Kalef, who had escaped capture in the previous war, led yet another insurrection against the king.[46] Although little is known about this campaign, Sarṣa Dengel was ultimately no more successful than in his earlier campaign, for the Beta Israel rebelled yet again in December 1587.

Sarṣa Dengel's third campaign against the Beta Israel came in response to a raid led by their leader Gushen on the people of Wagara. In response, the emperor rose from his camp at Guba'e and marched through Wagara to Semien and the Beta Israel stronghold of *Warq Amba*. Initially, the Beta Israel enjoyed a certain degree of success, scoring a major victory against the imperial troops camped at the foot of the nearby *Sakana Amba*. The emperor, however, quickly recouped by stationing new troops at the site, who laid siege to the *amba* and starved its occupants into submission. The captured Beta Israel were settled alongside the camp of their conquerors, but when they attempted to escape a massacre ensued. Losses among the Beta Israel were heavy and the emperor alone is said to have received almost two hundred widows and numerous orphans as part of his share of the captives.[47] According to a tradition preserved by the Ethiopian church, so much blood was split when Sarṣa Dengel had the Beta Israel killed that his tent had to be moved three times to avoid being soiled by it.[48] *Warq Amba* was speedily subdued and by the end of January 1588 Gushen and many of his supporters had died, flinging themselves to their deaths from the heights of their fortresses.[49] Rather mysteriously, Gedewon, an important member of the Beta Israel ruling family, escaped unharmed.[50]

Despite the ferocity that characterized Sarṣa Dengel's three campaign's against the Beta Israel, his victories do not appear to have produced any dramatic long-term changes in the status of the Beta Israel. The loss of life, enslavement, and forced conversions must all have been severe blows for the surviving population. Moreover, the settlement of some of the victorious troops in the region probably increased the Beta Israel's financial burden and fostered resentment. They did not, however, lose their autonomy in the Semien region for long and even received official confirmation of their position in the province following the death of Sarṣa Dengel in 1597.

Dynastic Struggles 1597–1607

Maryam Sena, the wife of Sarṣa Dengel, bore the emperor three daughters, but no sons. As a result, he designated Zadengel, the son of his brother, Lessana Chrestos, as his heir. Sometime later, however, he changed his mind and came to favor Zamaryam, his son by his Beta Israel mistress Harago. When Zamaryam died shortly after his introduction to the court, Sarṣa Dengel reinstated his nephew as his presumptive heir. The birth of another son, Ya'eqob, to Harago in 1590 produced yet another change of mind with the advantage falling once again to the half Beta Israel son.[51]

Ya'eqob was only seven years old when his father died and he was crowned as emperor. The selection of this small boy rather than the older and abler Zadengel was less a reflection of a desire to comply with the late emperor's choice of an heir than a shrewd political move on the part of the nobles, the warlords, and the Empress, Maryam Sena. By placing Ya'eqob on the throne as regent, they were able to retain their hold on the reins of power. Zadengel was sent into exile on an island in Lake Tana.[52] Although Ya'eqob's mother, Harago, received no official position at court, her brother Gedewon was confirmed as governor of Semien.

Not surprisingly, no serious attempt was made to challenge Ya'eqob's rule during the seven years of his regency. However, when he decided in 1603 at age fourteen to actively assume power the coalition of groups who had placed him on the throne had little interest in seeing him discard his role as figurehead. Because of his youth, moreover, he had neither led nor won the loyalty of the various royal military units, who were chaffing at their relatively long period of inactivity. This combined lack of experience, allies, and trustworthy advisors made it easy for Maryam Sena and the nobles to overthrow Ya'eqob and replace him on the throne with Zadengel. Although Ya'eqob tried to escape to his uncle Gedewon in the Semien, he was captured and placed on trial for usurpation.[53] Ya'eqob was charged with being a pagan, a practitioner of Oromo divination techniques, a sexual deviant, and not the son of Sarṣa Dengel. How much his half-Beta Israel antecedents influenced the proceedings is difficult to reckon. Certainly the fact that in his moment of need he turned to his uncle, the ruler of the Beta Israel of Semien, would appear to indicate that his link to his maternal kin remained strong. The charge of paganism, moreover, while a common accusation in Ethiopian court intrigues, may also have been based on his "non-Christian" background. Before the proceedings against Ya'eqob had reached their obviously preordained conclusion, Zadengel intervened. Rather then being maimed or disfigured, which would have permanently ended his political ambitions, Ya'eqob was sent into exile in Enarya.[54]

Zadengel became Emperor at age twenty-six and assumed the throne name of Galawdewos. He was an honest, courageous, and educated ruler who made a serious attempt to rectify some of the damage caused by the neglect and errors of his predecessors. He tried, for example, to stop the advance of the Galla by leading his troops into Gojjam. He also made a serious attempt to curtail the power of the nobility and reassert imperial authority. This latter program, which included the creation of a powerful "king's army" (*malak hara*) and the arming of the peasantry, ultimately led to his downfall. As noted above, already in 1597 the nobles and the empress Maryam Sena had placed Ya'eqob on the throne because they feared that Zadengel would limit their freedom of action. When their worst fears were confirmed, they wasted little time in acting. Some sought to restore Ya'eqob to the throne. Others favored the aspirations of the warrior chief, Susenyos, who as a great-grandson of the Emperor Lebna Dengel could legitimately stake a claim to the throne. Not surprisingly, Zadengel received little support from either the nobility or the military elites. His assiduous courting of the Portuguese, including a ban on the observance of the Saturday Sabbath and an offer to convert to Catholicism, lost him much popular support. Eventually, the Abuna absolved the population of their oath of allegiance to the monarch and excommunicated him. In October 1604, a little more than a year after assuming power, Zadengel was killed in Dambeya by rebel forces.[55]

Although Susenyos appeared assured of the throne and was backed by much of the nobility and the army, his support largely evaporated when Ya'eqob reappeared. Once again, the nobility and warlords sought to place on the throne the younger and weaker candidate. Susenyos was forced to flee and become a *shifta* (bandit). Ya'eqob sought to appease him by offering him the governorship of Shawa, Amhara, and Walaqa. Susenyos, however, viewed himself as the legitimate heir and saw little reason to settle for a secondary role. He was, moreover, an excellent general and a skilled tactician. In March 1607, following two years of turmoil, he defeated and killed Ya'eqob and claimed the throne.[56]

Defeat and Adaptation 1607–26

More than a decade of succession struggles provided the Beta Israel with an extended respite from their wars against the Ethiopian emperors. From 1597 to 1607 all the contenders for the throne had more important matters to deal with than the fate of the residents of Semien and Dambeya. Ya'eqob's death and the rise of Susenyos, moreover, did not immediately result in a universally accepted monarch assuming the throne. Rival claimants and disgruntled nobles continued to plague Susenyos throughout the early years of his reign. One of the most serious was a Tigrean monk, who, hiding his face in a veil, claimed to be the half Beta

Israel Emperor Ya'eqob. Large parts of the population, including the prestigious monastery of Dabra Bizan, supported him and Susenyos was forced to lead his troops to Tigre and personally subdue the rebel.[57] While there he took the opportunity to have himself crowned yet again, this time in the ancient Ethiopian capital of Aksum. While Susenyos was occupied with the Tigrean challenge to his reign, large parts of Bagemder, Wagara, and Dambeya rose up in support of Arzo, a grandson of Minas. The Emperor's brother, Yemane Chrestos, put down this threat.[58]

The revival of imperial interest in the Beta Israel of Semien was directly related to the numerous challenges to Susenyos' rule. In 1614 the dispossessed nobility of Ṣallamt, Wagara, and Semien rose up in support of yet another pretender to the throne claiming to be the late Emperor Ya'eqob. Among the supporters of "Ya'eqob," who is identified in the Ge'ez sources as Takluy and by Bruce as Amdo, was Gedewon, leader of the Beta Israel of Semien.[59] When Takluy was captured by Walda Hawaryat, the governor of Ṣallamt, Gedewon freed him and offered him refuge in the mountains of Semien. From there Takluy was able to raise a large army and challenge royal control of much of the surrounding territory by raiding the plains of Shewada and Ṣallamt. In response, Susenyos appointed Yolyos, the husband of his favorite daughter, one of his most loyal followers and until then the governor of Tigre, as governor of Wagara, Semien, Ṣallamt, Wag, as well as the southern parts of Tigre. Yolyos promised to subdue the rebels saying, "I shall vanquish and kill this pretender and Gedewon the Falasha and plant onions on Segenet."[60] Despite Yolyos's boasting, his troops were not immediately successful and he was forced to ask the Emperor to personally intervene after Takluy killed Abraham, the governor of Ṣallamt. Marching from Wagara to Semien, Susenyos joined Yolyos and laid seige to the Beta Israel fortress of Amba Misraba. Their soldiers conquered the *amba* and killed all its inhabitants. A similar fate awaited those Beta Israel who sought refuge on an *amba* called Hotch. Finally, Gedewon and Takluy were surrounded at Segenet. For two months Susenyos's troops laid seige to the *amba,* inflicting heavy losses on its defenders. Gedewon himself was only saved by the bravery of one of his chiefs, Wod Qematra, who was killed by a musketeer. Finally, Gedewon handed Takluy over to the Emperor in exchange for a pardon and peace. The false Ya'eqob was crucified as punishment for his rebellion.[61]

Gedewon's surrender to Susenyos may well have guaranteed his own safety, but it offered no such promises to the bulk of the Beta Israel population. In punishment for the support they offered his rival, Susenyos ordered his governors to massacre the Beta Israel men wherever they found them. Their wives and children were sold into slavery. Only a few escaped.[62] The Beta Israel of Dambeya and perhaps others who had not participated in the rebellion were spared on condition that they convert to Christianity. Indeed, Susenyos is said to have spent the whole of the rainy season at Gorgora on the north-west shore of Lake Tana in order to insure compliance with his decree.[63] Virtually all of them complied, and as a test of their sincerity the Emperor demanded that they plow their fields on the Sabbath.[64]

Susenyos' pronouncements are of interest in several respects. First, they clearly indicate that even prior to their final defeat the Beta Israel were geographically dispersed and politically divided. In addition to the two large concentrations of Beta Israel in Dambeya and Semien, smaller groups, perhaps not even organized communities, existed in a number of other regions.[65] Only a small portion of these appear to have followed Gedewon in supporting the pretender Takluy/Ya'eqob's aspirations to the throne. Second, Susenyos' policies appear to indicate a clear departure from previous attempts to deal with the Beta Israel. While earlier rulers including Yeshaq and Minas had sought to impose Christianity on the Beta Israel, wholesale extermination outside the heat of battle had not previously been attempted. Moreover, with the exception of Minas' ill-advised attempt to force the Beta Israel to convert, the emperors had usually been satisfied with professions of *political* loyalty and prompt payment of tributes. Susenyos' decrees mark a dramatic attempt to settle once and for all the problem of the Beta Israel.

Despite the severity of his proposals, their impact on the Beta Israel was almost certainly less than one might initially expect. Susenyos' control of his realm was never very strong and it is probable that in many regions local rulers simply chose to ignore his edicts. The continued survival of the Beta Israel of Semien is the most obvious evidence that Susenyos' call for their extermination was not completely carried out. In other regions, the demand that the Beta Israel labor on the Sabbath must have been especially problematic. The issue of the Saturday Sabbath had long been a bone of contention within the Ethiopian Church and between the Ethiopian Christians and the Portuguese Jesuits.[66] The Tigrean "Ya'eqob" who challenged Susenyos early in his reign drew much of his support from the traditionally pro-Sabbath monastery of Dabra Bizan. Moreover, Susenyos, like Zadengel before him, had sought to remedy the weakness of his internal position by relying increasingly on the Portuguese for support. Gradually he also moved toward his own personal conversion.[67] By the time Susenyos sought to quash the rebellion of 1614, relations with the Orthodox clergy had deteriorated to such an extent that they withheld their support for his campaign.[68] In this context Susenyos' prohibition of Sabbath rest for the Beta Israel can scarcely be viewed as simply a demand for a visible sign of their conversion. To many Orthodox Christians Sabbath labor was an anathema, and Susenyos' demands must have increased their concern regarding his attitude toward their own observance. The singling out of so problematic an issue for the Beta Israel may, moreover, raise legitimate questions as to which church the Emperor sought to incorporate them.

It is also against the background of the internal religious divisions that plagued Ethiopia during his reign that we must understand Susenyos' continued difficulties with Gedewon and the Beta Israel. In 1617 Yolyos, the king's son-in-law and hitherto loyal supporter, joined a group of nobles, courtiers, and the Abuna in an attempt to overthrow Susenyos and his Catholic younger brother Sela Krestos. Both Yolyos and the Abuna died in battle.[69] Far from serving as a warning to Susenyos, his victory in 1617 merely made him even more determined to establish Catholicism as the state religion. In June 1620 he issued a proclamation condemning the Ethiopian church's alleged monophysite theology and prohibiting the observance of the Sabbath. Although the initial response to these decrees came from the clergy of Tigre, by the fall a far more widespread opposition had surfaced. In October 1620 Yona'el, the governor of Bagemder who had himself played a crucial role in quelling the rebellion of 1617, declared himself a defender of the Orthodox church. In the same month a popular uprising of the peasants in Damot further demonstrated the depth of feeling surrounding these issues. Not to be deterred, Susenyos publicly converted to Catholicism in March 1622 and began a wholesale transformation of the ties between church and state. By 1624 vast areas of Ethiopian custom were under attack including the right to divorce, the tradition of weekly fasts, and the observance of biblical dietary laws. The hours of Mass and other services followed the practice of the Catholic Church and the Gregorian calender had been introduced.[70] Not surprisingly, opposition to Susenyos and the Portuguese was widespread with peasants, clergy, and nobility joining forces against the imposition of Catholicism.[71] Their efforts reached a climax in June 1632 when the primacy of Ethiopian Christianity was restored and Susenyos was forced to abdicate in favor of his son Fasiladas.

It is in the context of this general dissatisfaction with the Emperor that we can begin to understand Gedewon's decision in 1624 to participate in yet another rebellion against imperial rule. Although the Emperor responded speedily and sent one of his most able and experienced generals, Gedewon initially enjoyed considerable success. The imperial troops were defeated and their pack animals and provisions seized as booty. Susenyos had little choice but to engage in a holding action and order his governors to prevent the spread of the insurrection.[72] Gedewon's rebellion soon gained momentum, however, as he succeeded in developing his movement into a more general challenge to Susenyos' rule. While the population of Shawa and Amhara united behind the claims of one Walda Gabriel to the throne, Gedewon led large parts of Bagemder in supporting the aspirations of a great-grandson of Minas, whose father, Arzo, had also challenged Susenyos' rule.[73] For more than two years Gedewon and his candidate succeeded in thwarting imperial attempts to subdue them. Aided by disaffected clergy angry at Susenyos' attempts to impose Catholicism, Gedewon had the son of Arzo named as king and together they set out to conquer the Semien region. Only around 1626 did the imperial governor of Semien, Malke'a Krestos, succeed in defeating them. The son of Arzo was hung from a cedar tree. Gedewon was decapitated and his head sent to Susenyos.

Following Gedewon's death, Susenyos sought to exterminate the rest of the Beta Israel in Semien. Leading a large body of troops to the province, he divided up his army and commanded his generals to seal off the province so that no one could escape. While he was only partially successful in this genocidal policy, he did succeed in putting an end to close to three hundred years of conflict between Judaized groups and the Christian emperors of Ethiopia. Although the Beta Israel continued to form a recognizable group, after this final defeat never again did they represent a political-military threat to imperial rule. Thus, their resistance to assimilation and their strategies for preserving their identity took other forms than that of armed conflict.

Epilogue

Given the abundance of documentation concerning the Beta Israel's wars with Sarṣa Dengel and Susenyos, it is tempting to focus exclusively on these dramatic episodes in describing their history during this period. Other more subtle trends and events remain almost totally hidden from our gaze. Nevertheless, a number of processes are clearly worthy of comment both in their own right and because they foreshadow larger tendencies in later years.

Once again it must be remembered that although the Semien region held the most visible and best organized grouping of Beta Israel, it was by no means the only region in which they resided. Dambeya, for example, held a considerable concentration of Beta Israel. Wagara, Tigre, Jenfekera, and several other regions contained smaller populations.[74] Although no clear evidence exists on this point, these disparate groups were probably linked through a common religious system and kinship ties. They were almost certainly not politically united, for there is little indication that Beta Israel in other regions actively supported the rebellions based in Semien. In all likeliehood, moreover, they differed significantly with regard to their economic base and the extent of their incorporation into and accommodation with the dominant society.

Thus while in the sixteenth and early seventeenth century the Beta Israel of Semien still exercised a degree of political autonomy and presumably possessed a diversified economy, in other regions occupational specialization was far more developed. The association of the Beta Israel with weaving and smithing, which may date to as early as the fifteenth century, was certainly well established by the time of the Portuguese.[75] So too their activities as masons and carpenters, which were to become so important with the development of the city of Gondar, also seem to have their roots in this period. Indeed, one of the most striking testimonies to the complexity that characterized imperial relations with the Beta Israel is the oral tradition stating that Susenyos was the first king to use them as builders and rewarded them with land at Azezo and Abba Samuel.[76]

At the least, such traditions raise serious questions concerning any attempt to explain imperial attitudes to the Beta Israel on the basis of an overriding racial animus or other monolithic motives. They appear to indicate, rather, that those Beta Israel whose occupational skills were cherished by the Christian rulers received better treatment then their co-religionists in other regions. This consideration, for example, would explain Susenyos' decision to spare the Falasha of Dambeya (albeit at the price of their conversion), while the rest of their brethren were to be executed.[77] In these illustrations of the true complexity that character-ized Susenyos' policy toward the Beta Israel, we find, moreover, our first hints of a pattern that came to predominate in later periods. During periods of strong central rule, those Beta Israel who through economic specialization made themselves valuable to royal patrons survived and even improved their standing. In contrast, a lack of marketable skills or a reduction in central control paved the way for decline and exclusion.

In the next chapter we shall examine these processes in greater detail as they appear in the Gondar period (1632–1769) and the Era of the Princes (1769–1855). For the moment, it is sufficient to note that the roots of these trends significantly precede either of these periods. During the period discussed in this chapter and particularly in the late sixteenth and early seventeenth century, different Beta Israel groups pursued dif-fering strategies for survival. While those in Semien protected by the harsh geographic conditions of their homeland continued to exercise a military-political option, other groups pursued less dramatic (and less well-documented) social and economic accommodations. With the final defeat of the Beta Israel of Semien in the 1620s, the latter course of action was to serve as a precedent for the next generations of Beta Israel life. The successes and failures of this era will be the subject of our next chapter.

5

Glory and Decline: 1632–1855

Susenyos' final victory over the Beta Israel of Semien was unquestionably one of the major landmarks in the history of their people. In retrospect, however, it appears to have been less a radical turning-point than the culmination of more than two centuries of conflict. From the time of Yeshaq in the fifteenth century onward, those Christian emperors who possessed sufficient military power had sought to limit the political autonomy of the *ayhud* and later the Falasha. Over the course of time, more and more of the Beta Israel were dispossessed and remained economically viable only through supplementing their agricultural work as tenant farmers with income earned as craftsmen. This economic specialization coupled with the emergence of a distinctive Beta Israel religious tradition under the leadership of monastic clergy enabled those Beta Israel who no longer enjoyed independence to preserve their identity. By the end of the sixteenth century, only those in Semien retained a significant degree of autonomy and continued to offer military resistance to the Christian king. Other groups had previously reached an accommodation with the dominant society in which they retained limited rights due to their economic skills. Following their final defeat, the Jews of Semien regrouped and followed a similar course. Thus, contrary to what we might expect, Susenyos' victory did not mark the beginning of an inexorable downward spiral for the Beta Israel.

To be sure, the period immediately after their defeat was one of the most trying in their history. Not only did they have to contend with his punitive treatment of even those who had not taken an active role in the wars, but also they faced harsh natural conditions. In 1634 locusts, famine, and epidemics struck the regions of Semien, Dambeya, and Wagara. So difficult were conditions that the Emperor Fasiladas (1632–67) was forced to wander from region to region in search of sufficient provisions to support his court.

> The pestilence entered through Dambeya and soon assailed the camp and court at Danqaz with such fierceness that it was necessary to move the site to Libo. There the attacks continued in such a manner that they did not spare the imperial tents: within them the pestilence killed some pages of the emperor, forcing him to go running away and changing to various places, wandering like another Cain. From Danqaz the disease passed to Wagara, to the mountains of Samen and to the famous Lamalmo. . . . The great armies and swarms of locusts . . . mowed down with the teeth all the crops, brought with them hunger as they usually do, followed by such scarcity and shortage of crops that many people died from sheer hunger.[1]

Many of the already devastated Beta Israel doubtless died of starvation. In time, however, conditions improved, and the next century and a half, known as the Gondar period because of the establishment of a new imperial capital in the city given that name, is remembered in Beta Israel tradition as an era when they lived "in peace and welfare."[2]

The Establishment of Gondar

Throughout all of the early medieval period, from the rise of Yekunno Amlak in ca. 1270 to the conquest of Ethiopia by Ahmad Gragn in the second quarter of the sixteenth century, the emperors of Ethiopia built no cities, but lived in mobile tent cities which served them as "wandering capitals."[3] From the middle of the sixteenth century onward a tendency developed to establish imperial camps of greater permanency in northwest Ethiopia in the region around Lake Tana. Sarṣa Dengal, for example, returned repeatedly to Emfraz (Guba'e) and eventually built a stone castle (the first such building in the country) on the site.[4] As we noted in the previous chapter, the growing royal presence in this region was probably the primary contributory factor to the increasingly frequent clashes with the nearby Beta Israel. The tendency toward a more permanent type of settlement and the erection of palaces and churches of stone accelerated during the reign of Susenyos. It culminated in the reign of his son and successor Fasiladas with the establishment of the city of Gondar, the country's first permanent capital since the Zagwe had reigned in Lalibala in the thirteenth century.

Unfortunately, the dearth of sources from the period immediately following the Portuguese expulsion from Ethiopia makes it difficult to reconstruct the reality behind the numerous legends that surround the founding of Gondar.[5] Certainly, the mention in the short chronicle that in the fourth year of his reign (1635/36) Fasiladas established a *madina* (town or residence) at Gondar appears significant.[6] By the time the Yemenite ambassador Hasan ibn Ahmad al-Haymi visited Ethiopia in 1648, Gondar was well established with Fasiladas' castle its most imposing feature.[7] Over the next two decades, a number of castles and no fewer than seven churches were also constructed in the city.[8]

Over the course of time Gondar grew from a small village to a city whose population has been estimated as between forty to eighty thousand.[9] It served as the political, economic, religious, and cultural capital of the kingdom. During the Gondar period Ethiopian art, architecture, and technology reached previously unattained heights.[10] New traditions of biblical interpretation and liturgical chant were developed and consolidated.[11] Yet in retrospect it almost appears as if this vast explosion of creative energy in and around Gondar left little to spare for the surrounding provinces. During the Gondar period the power of the king atrophied and the area of effective royal authority grew smaller and smaller. Eventually, provincial nobles in the north and south were able to assert their control over crucial economic resources and military prerogatives and reduce the rulers of Gondar to mere figureheads.[12]

Economic Specialization and Social Mobility

The most striking feature of Beta Israel life in the Gondar period is their identification with a number of specialized crafts and occupations, including smithing, weaving, pottery, building, and soldiering. By their very nature such pursuits, particularly the latter two, were largely dependent upon patronage from royal or noble figures interested in exploiting these skills. Accordingly, the type and extent of specialization among those Beta Israel (quite probably a majority) residing in isolated rural areas were probably far different than in and around Gondar itself. Once again our sources only permit us to speculate on this matter. What is clear, however, is that it was on the basis of these skills that some Beta Israel were able to gain favor with the Gondari kings and enhance their economic and political standing.

As we have already noted, the economic specialization of the Beta Israel during the Gondar period was not a completely new phenomenon. Rather, it grew in two distinct ways from the base of earlier attempts to supplement their agricultural income through crafts. On the one hand, the Gondar period saw the continuation of the Beta Israel's association with such relatively low status occupations as smithing and pottery.[13] On the other hand, their proximity to the court owing to their previous service as craftsmen facilitated their introduction to such jobs as masons, carpenters, and, in the case of women, paintmakers.[14] Their role as soldiers was apparently a natural outgrowth of the reputation for bravery they had acquired during their long years of conflict with the Ethiopian kings.[15] To the extent that the Beta Israel were able to substitute highly valued occupations for less prestigious ones, their social status improved.

The Gondar period, for example, saw a significant decline in their employment as weavers. While in the early seventeenth century they were "almost the only weavers of cotton," a century later they had been replaced, at least in Gondar, by Muslims.[16] In contrast, they continued to play a major role as blacksmiths and potters and may have even expanded their involvement in these occupations.

Already in the time of the Portuguese the Beta Israel had enjoyed a reputation as "excellent smiths," valued for their ability to make and repair agricultural implements and weapons.[17] It was probably their connection to toolmaking that led most directly to them being among the first Ethiopians to be trained as masons and carpenters. Thus when the Jesuit Pero Paes directed the building of Susenyos' palace at Gorgora ca. 1614, he

gave Directions for making Hammers, Mallets Chizzels, and all other Necessary Tools, handling them himself, and teaching the new workmen to dig, hew, and square stones for the Fabrick; and the same he did to all the Joyners and Carpenters.[18]

However they first came to these professions, the Beta Israel rapidly acquired a reputation as skilled masons and carpenters. Tradition credits them with an important role in almost all the major building projects of the Gondar period.[19] Thus, they are said to have contributed to the construction of castles, churches, bridges, and walls during the reigns of both Fasiladas and Yohannes I (1667–82). Half a century later, in the reign of Iyasu II (1730–55), they participated in the redecoration of Fasiladas' palace. On their work Bruce noted,

The roof, in gaiety and taste, corresponded perfectly with the magnificent finishing of the room; it was the work of the Falasha, and consisted of painted cane, split and disposed in Mosaic figures, which produces a gaier effect than it is possible to conceive.[20]

Beside their position as artisans and craftsmen, the Beta Israel also enhanced their prestige and social mobility by serving as soldiers in the imperial army. The emperors of Ethiopia had for centuries strengthened the core of troops who owed them personal loyalty by incorporating soldiers from previously hostile regional armies into the imperial service.[21] For the kings this policy assisted them in maintaining a large professional army, whose troops did not owe allegiance to any local noble ruler. For the conquered people, particularly non-Christians, military service represented their most important avenue of social advancement. Following their defeat by Susenyos, several units of Beta Israel soldiers were added to the existing imperial troops.[22] In the reign of Yohannes I, Beta Israel troops known as *Kayla* fought alongside him in his wars against the Oromo.[23] According to one tradition, one of the Gondar kings had five hundred Beta Israel soldiers in his army.[24] Given the Beta Israel's long history of warfare and the accompanying marshall ethos, it is hardly surprising that many would have chosen to pursue the opportunities available in a military career.

In return for the services they rendered the Gondari kings as both artisans and soldiers the Beta Israel were rewarded in the standard manner with titles and land. Although not accorded title of sufficient importance to gain mention in the various royal chronicles of the Gondar period, the individuals and circumstances under which they were awarded their positions are vividly remembered in Beta Israel oral traditions.[25] According to these, prominent Beta Israel were designated as either *azmach* (general) or *azaj* (commander), a title that carried with it administrative and miliary connotations, as well as *bajerond* (treasurer), which referred to a chief of the workers.[26] During the early Gondar period, the former of these (*azmach*), which was also more prestigious since it involved authority over both non-Beta Israel and Beta Israel, is said to have predominated. In later year and particularly in the late eighteenth and early nineteenth century, the conditions of the Beta Israel declined and only the more limited ethnic-occupational title of *bajerond* appears to have been awarded.

The significance of these titles for an understanding of Beta Israel history in this period is at least twofold. First, insofar as the Beta Israel were appointed to the title of *azmach* with relatively broad responsibilities, we can claim that a genuine trend to incorporate them into the kingdom was at work. In contrast, the emergence of the *bajerond* as their primary form of appointment bespeaks a trend toward economic and ethnic differentiation.[27] Second, the appearance of Beta Israel officeholders in both positions, but particularly the *azmach,* is indicative of the formation of a new externally created form of leadership that gained its authority not through internal criteria of religious or political authority, but via recognition by the dominant society.[28] What, if any, tensions surrounded the emergence of this new elite cannot be documented. Certainly, it should be remembered that in rural society on the village level the traditional leadership of elders and the monastic clergy must have continued to function. Indeed, with the demise of the traditional secular rulers and their replacement by "foreign" governors and imperially appointed titleholders, the prestige of the Beta Israel monks as internally legitimated groups and the primary carriers of the communities' distinctive traditions may well have increased substantially.

The second noteworthy benefit that derived to the Beta Israel from the military and particularly the artisanal services rendered the kings was a limited reversal of the policy of disenfranchisement that had affected their existence for over two centuries. The effects of this shift in policy should not be exaggerated. Landlessness and tenancy remained a major fact of Beta Israel life in most regions throughout this period. Nonetheless, as their traditions amply attest, in the area around Gondar some Beta Israel were able to acquire good agricultural land either through grants or official recognition of their rights to live and work in the region.[29] To the extent that this occurred it marked a significant departure from earlier trends and represented a decided normalization of Beta Israel life. In some cases, most notably Kayla Meda (Kayla field) and Abvorra, their residence at the site appears to predate the Gondar period, and the kings simply recognized their claims to the area.[30] In many others, their connection to a specific locale seems to date from their participation in the erection of a church or castle at the site. In either case, this recognition of land rights coupled with the acquisition of prestigious titles offers a clear indication of the manner in which their skills as artisans and soldiers created the possibility of substantial political and economic mobility for some Beta Israel in the Gondar period.

Social and Religious Trends

Beta Israel craftsmen were just one of a large number of people drawn to the city of Gondar. Economic specialization, density of population, and ethnic diversity were all important characteristics of the new Ethiopian capital.[31] Foreigners, Muslims, Beta Israel, and representatives of numerous regional groups were all found in the city. For those Beta Israel residing in and around Gondar, their proximity to and daily interaction with the predominantly Christian population must have posed a challenge. Clearly it was impossible to observe ideal standards of social purity under conditions that dictated repeated contact with outsiders.[32] While the geographic separation of the Gondarine population on the basis of social status, religion, and economic function into separate quarters put some limits on contact between the separate groups, these quarters were not ghettos. The population flowed freely in and out of the sections of the city and representatives of different faiths often lived side by side. It was in response to this situation that a religious council convened by the Emperor Yohannes I in 1668 decreed that

the *Afreng* [i.e., Franks] must return to their country and leave ours; but those who have joined our faith and have received our baptism and eucharist can remain here with us or leave if they wish. As for the Muslims, they must remain separate and live apart, forming a separate village of their own; no Christians may enter their service, neither as a slave nor servant, neither husband nor wife may live with them. **The Falasa, called Kayla, who are of the Jewish religion, must not live with the Christians, but must separate themselves from them and live apart, forming a village.**[33]

Despite this pronouncement, the separation between the groups was only partially implemented, so that a decade later in 1678 Yohannes found it necessary to repeat the decree.[34] Less formal, but probably at least as important as a practical barrier to contact, were the popular beliefs that identified Beta Israel smiths and potters as dangerous beings to be feared and avoided.[35]

While these common prejudices and superstitions may have given the Beta Israel leaders some concern, they probably viewed the legislated segregation with more than a little approval. Although present-day informants are at pains to stress that conversion to Christianity was minimal and separation from outsiders voluntary, at the least the threat of assimilation must have been ever present.[36] Giacomo Baratti, an Italian traveller who visited Ethiopia in the seventeenth century reported that among the Beta Israel in Tigre,

> great numbers have embraced that profession that did teach love and kindness to strangers [i.e., Christianity], hoping to meet with greater advantages when they should become brothers, for there is no invitation more powerful upon the spirits of a man to oblige him to imitate himself in Religion than a sincere affection expressed by the expressors of it. . . . The Jews have here their Synagogues, but they are at present so little frequented, that I think the name will be one day lost by reason of their great numbers that daily turn Christians.[37]

It must be remembered that with their complete loss of political autonomy, the Beta Israel forfeited whatever coercive power they may have used in the past to maintain group solidarity. Thus, Abba Yeshaq reports that in the days of Beta Israel self-rule a person who violated the Passover could be stoned to death. In later days, only a sacrifice was demanded.[38] In reality, even this sanction could only be enforced through group pressure and the threat of ostracism, which in the relatively fluid state of Gondarine society probably carried little weight.

Whatever the extent of assimilation, the processes of religious acculturation begun in earlier periods clearly continued. This is best illustrated by the example of the text known as *Nagara Muse* (The conversation of Moses). *Nagara Muse* purports to be a record of a conversation between God and Moses on Mt. Sinai. In response to a series of inquiries God outlines the rewards that result from certain types of good deeds and the punishments meted out for specific sins. This is then followed by a second more philosophical set of questions concerning the nature of God.[39] The text is of Syriac origin and the Ge'ez versions, both that of the Ethiopian church and the Beta Israel, are derived from an Arabic source.[40] As is usual, the Beta Israel text is an adapted and censored version of the Christian. What is particularly noteworthy for the present discussion is that the translation is explicitly stated to have taken place in the 1750s, toward the end of the Gondar period.[41] Thus, even though we are unable to say precisely when this text reached the Beta Israel, it stands as clear evidence that their religious system continued to develop and absorb new material well into the eighteenth century and beyond.[42]

Of course, none of the changes that took place during this period were comparable in magnitude to those of the fifteenth and sixteenth century. The Beta Israel clergy, prayerhouses, and schools in the Gondar region existed to preserve their religious values and institutions, not radically transform them. Thus, the monastic clergy retained their leadership role and their liturgy survived in its traditional form.[43] Ge'ez, probably understood only by the clergy, continued to be the language of prayer and scripture. The strength of all these aspects of traditional life were, however, to be sorely tested when the "peace and welfare" of the Gondar period gave way to the chaos and insecurity of the Era of the Princes.

Zemane Masafent

Although Iyasu II (1730–55) and the dowager empress Mentewwab continued the Gondari tradition of large-scale construction, during his reign the centrifugal forces loosening the provinces from imperial rule accelerated at an alarming pace.[44] For most of the period, his effective control was limited to the provinces immediately around the capital. Shawa, Lasta, and Tigre, for example, were for many years only nominally parts of the kingdom. Even in Gondar itself, Iyasu was only grudgingly accepted by the traditional nobility. Thus his power rested on the fragile coalition of his mother's kinsmen from Qwara and an increasingly important coterie of Oromo (Galla) officials, guards, and soldiers. It was apparently in an attempt to gain support from the latter group that Mentewwab arranged her son's marriage to the daughter of an important Oromo chief from Wollo province. In fact, she succeeded in doing little but stiffening the opposition to Iyasu from the Amhara ruling classes and increasing his dependence on others, most notably Ras Mika'el of Tigre. Nonetheless, when Iyasu died in 1755 he was widely mourned. "From Gondar to the ends of the earth, Muslims and Christians, Qemant and Falasha soldiers armed with shields . . . all cried and wailed."[45]

Mentewwab and her brother Walda Le'ul placed Iyasu's minor half-

Oromo son Iyo'as on the throne.[46] By this time, however, the balance of power between the provinces and the court had swung so much in favor of the former that Iyo'as' rise to the throne could only be secured with the consent of and at the price of major concessions to a number of local governors. So long as his uncle Walda Le'ul directed the state, Iyo'as (and in his name Mentewwab) clung to power. Following his death at the end of 1766, repeated attempts were made to dethrone Iyo'as. In January 1769 he was assassinated on the order of Ras Mika'el of Tigre. An elderly brother of the Emperor Bakaffa (1721–30) was taken from the royal prison of Amba Wahni and enthroned as Emperor Yohannes II. The Zemane Masafent (lit. The Era of the Judges) had begun.[47]

After a few months Yohannes II was poisoned and his son Takla Haymanot II succeeded him. In reality, the identity of the reigning incumbent and heir to the imperial title was of little consequence. The ruling "King of Kings" was little more than a figurehead to be "enthroned and dethroned at the whims of governors, who fought among themselves for the position of *ras* of the kingdom or *ras bitweded*, lit. 'the favorite duke.' "[48] Although the prestige of the Solomonic dynasty lingered on and no attempt was made to usurp the throne itself, effective power rested in the hands of local governors and military leaders. As they vied with each other for supremacy and to increase their domains the country was plunged into a state of almost constant small-scale warfare.

For the population in general and the peasants in particular the *Zamane Masafent* was a period of severe hardship. In the best of times the lot of the peasants and in particular those who labored as tenant farmers was not a happy one. For them the endless military conflicts of the *Zamane Masafent* aggravated an already difficult situation. The soldiers of the different regional armies lived off the land, ravaging both enemy territories and those of their masters.[49] Insecurity, poverty, and depopulation were characteristic of the period, especially in the area around Gondar that was repeatedly conquered and pillaged. Small wonder that, as we shall discuss below, the condition and status of the Beta Israel, who had depended on royal patronage and protection, declined.

The *Zamane Masafent* also marks the end of a comparatively long period of isolation following the expulsion of the Jesuits during which few outside observers visited the country. In 1769, the same year that

Iyo'as was assassinated. The Scottish traveller James Bruce arrived at the coastal city of Massawa and began his justifiably famous travels through Ethiopia. Much of the credit for reawakening European interest in Ethiopia in general and in the Beta Israel in particular must rest with Bruce. Although more than thirty years were to pass before further exploration was attempted in Ethiopia, his arrival can be said to have begun a new era.[50] In the first half of the nineteenth century, a number of foreign visitors journeyed through Ethiopia and it is largely on the basis of their accounts that we are able to reconstruct some aspects of Beta Israel life in this period.[51]

Economic Decline and Religious Challenges

While the political instability and incessant warfare of the Era of the Princes brought hardship to most of the Ethiopian society, few groups were as vulnerable to its depredations as the Beta Israel, who had depended on royal patronage for employment, political recognition, and political security. Not surprisingly, therefore, the period was one of the bleakest in their history and its effects lingered on long after centralized government had been restored.

Iyasu II was the last of the Gondarine kings to engage in monumental construction. Of his successors, only Takla Haymanot II (1769–77) was able to undertake a substantial building program. The seven churches he founded in or around Gondar were, however, minor projects compared to those of earlier kings, and he erected no castles or palaces.[52] Only two other emperors of the period were able to build even a single church.[53] The impoverished emperors of this period lived not in fine stone palaces and castles, but in small thatch-roofed wooden houses "erected like a pigeon-house."[54] The decline of new construction was, moreover, accompanied by a general neglect of many existing buildings. Already by the time Bruce visited Gondar in 1771, Fasiladas' palace was in disrepair.[55] Half a century later it was in an advanced stage of disintegration and all but uninhabitable.[56] Of the city's churches, only a handful were in good condition.[57] Thus despite a steady need for repairs as a result of both fires and warfare, much of the city was allowed to fall into a state of ruin.

For the Beta Israel, who had played a major role in the construction and maintenance of the Gondarine castles, fortresses, and churches, the abandonment of this tradition was a considerable setback. To be sure, for many years numerous Beta Israel continued to work as masons and carpenters, and retained their reputation for excellence.[58] However, the decline in both the number of large-scale projects and the quality of skills demanded gradually led to a corresponding decrease in the number of Beta Israel engaged as builders and the level of experience required. Neither the limited construction of private residence nor the increasingly infrequent minor repairs made on larger edifices utilized tremendously sophisticated building techniques.[59] As the need for skilled masons and carpenters diminished, fewer and fewer Beta Israel were able to support themselves in this manner.

At the same time as their economic base in construction was reduced, the Beta Israel witnessed a similar decline in their potential as agriculturalists. As we have already noted, the internecine warfare and insecurity of the *Zemane Masafent* made the already difficult lot of the peasants ever harder to bear. In the case of the Beta Israel, several factors appear to have combined to shift a disproportionate burden onto their shoulders. First, the area in and around Gondar was one of the hardest hit by the frequent depredations of roving armies.[60] Despite its clear deterioration, control of the capital was still invested with important symbolic significance, and the various *rases* (princes) and warlords regularly clashed over rights to the city. Residents of both the city itself and the surrounding countryside suffered. Second, it must be remembered that despite their limited successes of the Gondar period, the vast majority of Beta Israel did not possess *rist,* but rather worked the land of others as tenant farmers. As such they were particularly vulnerable to economic exploitation and dislocation.[61] Third, there are indications that from the middle of the eighteenth century onward, the Beta Israel not only found it difficult to acquire land, but also saw their existing holdings encroached upon.[62] Thus, services rendered as builders and soldiers were rewarded not by grants of land, but by monetary compensation or payment in the form of slaves. At the same time, deprived of the protection of a strong central government interested in preserving the security of valuable artisans, the Beta Israel were placed in a defenseless position in which their lands and goods were liable to be seized and redistributed. Bruce's account of "Heaps of platters and pots, that had been used by Mahometans or Jews," being brought for purification, would appear to indicate that the Beta Israel often fell prey to marauding armies.[63] As Gobat reported, "Their cattle are often taken from them. They carry no arms, either for attack or defence."[64]

In the wake of the reduction of their income from both construction and agriculture, the Beta Israel had little choice but to increase their involvement in what to the dominant society were less prestigious pursuits such a weaving, pottery, and, in particular, smithing. Virtually all the reports concerning their occupational status from the first part of the nineteenth century give prominent attention to their association with despised professions and the stigma attached to them.[65] Although in some cases the designation of the Beta Israel as *buda* (possessors of the "evil eye") was applied primarily to those who worked as smiths or potters and was more closely associated with certain occupations than with any one ethnic group, in many instances the label appears to have come to refer to all Falasha. Certainly, whatever the wider referents of the term, the Beta Israel were by far the ethnic group most closely identified with the phenomenon of *buda*.[66] Indeed, as we shall discuss in greater detail below, this association with supernatural powers largely shaped the attitude of Christian society to the Beta Israel and offered them a limited amount of privacy and protection.[67]

The economic decline and social isolation experienced by the Beta Israel in the Era of the Princes was accompanied by grave threats to their religious system. At times, their very survival appeared in danger, but toward the end of the period they experienced a revival. In some cases, the changes engendered in their religious practice can be directly related to the general deterioration in their condition. Thus, when increased poverty created a shortage of animals for sacrifice, changes were introduced into some rituals. In the case of the purification ceremonies performed forty days after the birth of a boy and eighty days after that of a girl, the reading of the *Mashafa Arde'et* (Book of the disciples) was substituted for the sacrifice.[68] These adjustments, however, appear as only minor difficulties when considered in the light of a major crises that struck the Beta Israel in the late eighteenth and early nineteenth century. Under pressure from Oromo princes, themselves only recently converted to Christianity, large numbers of Beta Israel abandoned their faith. As a unique document reports: "At the time of the princes called *ras* Mariyya, *ras* Gugsa, and *ras* Ali, the religion of Israel disappeared again, and this decline lasted twenty years.[69] In fact, given the dates of the rulers concerned and in light of some oral traditions, the period of crises may well have been closer to forty years.[70] In the 1830s, for example, the French travellers Combes and Tamisier commented that the Ethiopian Christians, "detest the Jews out of habit, and the latter exposed to continual harassment, are rather inclined to abandon their faith."[71]

The survival of Beta Israel religious life was due in large measure to the energetic response of their monastic leaders and the surprising resilience of some of their religious institutions. When Antoine d'Abbadie and his brother Arnauld visited Ethiopia in the 1830s, the outstanding Beta Israel leader of the Hohuara (Janfekera) region was Abba Yeshaq, a venerated monk and priest. So widespread was his reputation for learning, that Christian clergy would visit him with inquiries on matters of biblical interpretation.[72] In the 1840s, Abba Wedaje, the chief monk of Qwara, led a religious revival that "brought his people back to their religion."[73]

Danger and Purity

Of all the material we possess concerning the religious situation of the Beta Israel in the early nineteenth century, none would appear to be as representative of the manner in which their social status was evolving than a decree by an important Ethiopian official concerning the observance of the monthly celebration in honor of the Archangel Michael. Troubled that the Beta Israel were observing the holiday at the same time (and together with?) their Christian neighbors, he required them to move their celebration from the eighteenth day of the solar month to the same day of the lunar month.[74]

While this decree itself is of comparatively minor significance, it serves to neatly define one of the central dilemmas of the relationship between the Beta Israel and Christian Ethiopians: over the course of the centuries the combination of a common biblical ethos and a long history of contact and mutual acculturation between the two societies had resulted in their possessing religious systems and cultural identities that were remarkably similar. As we have already discussed in some detail, the two groups shared biblical elements in their religions, a clear correspondence between their religious hierarchies of monks and priest, a *corpus* of literature, a common Israelite self-image. In some cases, moreover, even blatantly Christian elements appear to have linked the two groups. Samuel Gobat asked a Beta Israel "Rabbi" to show him his books: his copy of Psalms was found to include *Weddasse Maryam* (The Praises of Mary), "which the Christians have added to them, with all the repetitions of 'In the name of the Father, and of the Son, and of the Holy Ghost.' "[75] At the least this would seem to point to a certain laxity in the checking and censoring of works received from Christian scribes. It can, however, not be ascribed to mere ignorance of one priest. Abba Yeshaq, the most learned of Beta Israel monks, included in his list of Beta Israel works, *Fekkare Iyasus* (The teachings of Jesus), a work whose Christian provenance and contents are undeniable.[76] Thus, in practice the two religious systems overlapped not only with regard to shared biblical elements, but also to a much lesser extent with some shared Christian themes. Nor did the two groups differ significantly in language, dress, or physical appearance.[77]

Yet, at the same time and with the overt encouragement of their religious and political leadership, both groups remained socially distinct and economically identifiable. While day-to-day contacts existed between members of each group—indeed for many Beta Israel such interactions were probably an economic necessity—neither viewed these as desirable. Moreover, the stereotyped images that members of each community held of each other created a picture of opposing attributes that could easily make one question if the two groups belonged to a single society, much less the same nation and cultural heritage. Popular belief among many Ethiopians closely associated the Beta Israel with the notion of *buda* ("evil eye") and accused them of harming their victims by transforming themselves into hyenas at night and drawing out their blood or life force.[78] For their part, the Beta Israel viewed Ethiopian Christians as polluting apostates bordering on superstition and polytheism. Although this seemingly paradoxical situation in which the two communities shared an impressive array of cultural traits and yet viewed each other as foreign and "wholly other" almost certainly did not originate in the Era of the Princes. It is only in this period that we are able to fully document it and explore its implications.

While almost all commentators on the Beta Israel have given attention to both their status as a despised caste-like group and their abhorrence of contact with non-Beta Israel, in many cases these two phenomena have been treated in isolation from each other, as separate systems. On the one hand, it is claimed, we have the Beta Israel desire to limit contact and contamination by outsiders in order to prevent assimilation; on the other, the Ethiopian Christian fear of the dangerous magical powers of smiths in general and by association the Beta Israel in particular.[79] In fact, as we shall demonstrate below, there is ample justification for viewing the two sets of beliefs and prohibitions as closely interrelated. Both, it would appear, are attempts to create symbolic boundaries between the two culturally similar groups.[80]

The interrelationship between the two sets of beliefs and practices can best be demonstrated by examining the manner in which Beta Israel and Ethiopian Christian stereotypes of each other revolve around a small number of interconnected key symbols. One set of these ideas, for example, revolve around the concept of magical transformation. As we have already noted, Christian prejudice and superstition about the Beta Israel is intimately connected to the latter's identification with a number of a despised professions most notably as smiths and potters. Common to both these occupations is the "magical" transformation of matter (earth/ore) through the use of fire. This same theme of magical transformation is one of the dominant metaphors in the Ethiopian image of the *buda* so often applied by Christians to the Beta Israel. The *buda*, it was claimed, could change him/herself into a hyena.[81] He could, moreover, alter the form of his victim to that of a hyena, ass, cow, cat, or other animal.[82]

To be sure, not all Christians accepted these beliefs. One of those encountered by Plowden, for example, objected to the concept, noting

I find it impossible to believe that God has given such superior powers to some men, that they should be able to convert themselves from a human being, as He formed them, into a quadruped, or to render themselves invisible, as this would entirely pervert and endanger the order of creation.[83]

Gobat notes a similar objection from the mouth of a Falasha who argued that, "If boudas exist, you are obliged to believe that they can do nothing contrary to the will of God."[84] In fact, while some Beta Israel appear to have accepted the possibility of the *buda*, other viewed it as yet another example of the superstitious Christian belief in magical transformations. While some of these such as the Eucharist and baptism were related to universal Christian beliefs, others were associated with the particular circumstances of Ethiopia. Thus, the fact that Beta Israel smiths and carpenters were called upon to make both crosses and the *tabot* (ark) for the Church led them to mock the Christian "worship" of these objects as virtually idolatrous in character.[85] Thus the Christian Ethiopian feared the Beta Israel smith because of his "magical" ability to create metal objects from ore and fire; the same smith mocked the Christian for his superstitious belief in the cross's transformation into an object of veneration.[86]

Yet another even more developed system of beliefs existed around the key symbol of blood. As we have already noted, one aspect of the *buda*'s power was his ability to drain the blood of his victim.[87] This could be accomplished, moreover, not only by vampire-like means, but also by creating the need for the victim to be treated by the recognized medical technique of bleeding. "The drawing of blood by the cupping-machine is peculiarly favourable to his [the *buda's*] operations, and enables him more firmly to keep possession of his victim."[88] In part at least, the association of the *buda* with blood may be connected to the smith's involvement in a wide variety of impure activities that may result in the drawing of blood. These include the creation of weapons, punishment of prisoners and criminals, and treatment of diseases.[89] This linkage appears to be made explicit in the claim that the Beta Israel were the descendants of the smiths who made the nails for Christ's crucifixion and were thus referred to by a name meaning "may his blood be upon us."[90] Mention is also made of the Beta Israel practice of performing blood (animal) sacrifices.[91]

Significantly, the treatment of blood also played a major role in the Beta Israel's depiction of how they differed from the impure Christians. Thus, while the Christians accused the *buda* of vampire-like behavior, the Beta Israel viewed the Christians as consumers of blood not merely because of the theology of the Eucharist,[92] but particularly with regard to the Ethiopian practice of eating raw meat (Brundo), which they viewed with special abhorrence.[93] The missionary Flad, for example reports that, "In cooking meat they are extremely particular, each little bit is cut off separately, and washed again and again in water, *until every trace of blood disappears*."[94] In a similar fashion, the Beta Israel custom of isolating a woman in a special hut when she menstruated may have had as much to do with distinguishing themselves from the Christians, as with issues of internal order.[95]

Finally, it should be noted that mutual avoidance is a central *leitmotif* that governed Beta Israel-Christian perceptions of each other. For their part, the dominant Christians sought to avoid contact with the Beta

Israel *buda,* whom they viewed as essentially nonhuman and dangerous. Similarly, the Beta Israel sought as much as possible to limit contact with outsiders whom they viewed as polluting. To this end they had developed a wide ranging series of purity behaviors that included taboos on the acceptance of objects particularly food from outsiders, rigorous laws of exogamy, extremely strict Sabbath observances, and rigid sanctions against those who violated these rules.[96]

On the one hand, one group's total rejection of the other meant that it was extremely difficult to render the other group's cultural ideas acceptable; and on the other hand, sanctions were employed . . . to deter anyone from attempting to bridge the gap or mitigate the cultural cleavage. Such sanctions were justified on physical as well as moral grounds designed to protect the survival of the people and their culture.[97]

In the final analysis, of course, the functional and symbolic similarities between Beta Israel and Christian images of each other should not cause us to overlook the basic inequality that governed the relationships between the two groups. For all their cultural and religious affinities, the Beta Israel and Ethiopian Christians did not compete for recognition as true Israelites on a level playing field. Political power and economic prestige, particularly in the form of landrights, were almost exclusively in the hands of the Christians. As the Era of the Princes drew to a close, the Beta Israel were politically powerless, economically impoverished, and socially marginalized.

The period from 1632–1855 is one of the most complex in the history of the Beta Israel. Indeed, as we have noted above, it has, in fact, two distinct phases. From 1632 to 1769, under the patronage of Emperors and courtiers based in the newly built capital at Gondar, the Beta Israel enjoyed a considerable degree of economic success and social mobility. By serving the needs of their imperial and noble benefactors the Beta Israel were able to reverse earlier processes of decline. In some cases, they were rewarded with land and titles. Although their constant interaction with the surrounding population doubtless led to instances of conversion and assimilation, most appear to have preferred to remain within the boundaries of their own community. As in the past, however, acculturation continued and may have even accelerated in the areas around Gondar. In general, they can be said to have lived in "peace and welfare."

The assassination of the Emperor Iyo'as in 1769 marked the culmination of a long process of imperial decline and ushered in the Era of the Princes. As different governors and local rulers vied for supremacy, the situation of the peasants in general and the Beta Israel in particular declined dramatically. As the demand for skilled builders decreased, the Beta Israel were forced in growing numbers into such despised professions as smithing and pottery. Moreover, the lack of a strong central government made them increasingly liable to the depredations of the various armies that sought to control the Gondar region. No less significantly, their religious system came under serious attack and went into a downspin, which only the intervention of some outstanding monastic leaders halted. The revival of Beta Israel religion these monks sparked could not have come at a more opportune time, for from the mid-nineteenth century onward the Beta Israel came to face yet another threat to their existence in the form of European Protestant missionaries.

6

A Mission to the Jews

Throughout the *Zamane Masafent* individual local rulers sought to rise above their peers and assert dominant control over the Ethiopian highlands. Only in the middle of the nineteenth century, however, was one of them successful. During the period from November 1852 to February 1855, Dejjazmach Kasa of Qwara fought four major battles that effectively removed his major rivals in central and northern Ethiopia from the political scene. His coronation in February 1855 as King of Kings Tewodros II marked the end of the Era of the Princes and ushered in a new period in Ethiopian history.[1] Supreme authority and political-military power were united in a single person for the first time in more than a century. Although many provinces remained only partially subdued, and Shawa was effectively independent, centralization had, to a significant degree, been restored.

Even before the rise of Tewodros reintroduced a measure of centralization to Ethiopian politics, Protestant missionaries began to take an interest in the country. Relying heavily on the writings of Bruce, the Church Missionary Society began to make plans for an Ethiopian mission.[2] The arrival of Samuel Gobat and Christian Kugler in Ethiopia in early 1830 heralded in the era of the modern missions. While Kugler confined himself largely to Tigre, Gobat continued on to Gondar. During the next seven years, three of which he spent in Ethiopia, Gobat revealed himself to be a sensitive and skillful representative of the Protestant cause.[3] In later years, after illness forced him to leave Ethiopia, the Protestant missions often suffered due to their lack of someone with comparable tact and understanding. Gobat met on several occasions with Beta Israel, and strongly supported the establishment of a mission to them.

Gobat's immediate successors took comparatively little interest in the Beta Israel, and it was only in 1855 with the arrival of J. Martin Flad that the possiblity of a mission to the Beta Israel appears to have been seriously considered.[4] Even Flad did not arrive intending to work among the Jews. However, an extended period of inactivity in the Gondar region, while the missionaries attempted to reach an accommodation with Tewodros, placed him in contact with the local Beta Israel and began a lifelong involvement with their evangelization. By May 1858 a school for the Beta Israel had been established in Gondar and in 1860 the London Society for Promoting Christianity amongst the Jews established a mission to the Falasha, headed by a converted German Jew, Henry Aaron Stern. Within in a short time, Flad's differences with his fellow missionaries over their method of operation in Ethiopia had led him to break company with them and devote himself completely to the Falasha mission.[5]

The Ethiopian Context

Although it is tempting to consider the activities of the London Society in Ethiopia within the context of the countless other missions established in Africa in the nineteenth century, such an approach is of only limited value. To be sure, the missionaries active among the Beta Israel were motivated by much the same spirit as their contemporaries elsewhere on the continent.[6] Their arrival was, moreover, symptomatic of the growing European involvement in Africa during this period. Indeed much of the early history of the London mission must be viewed against the background of growing Ethiopian concern with foreign encroachment on its soil.

The setting in which the London Society operated, however, was in a number of ways unique.[7] The presence in Ethiopia of an ancient and well-established national church was an issue of continual concern to the missionaries. Owing to the political-ecclesiastical situation in Ethiopia, it was unthinkable to attempt to pursue missionary activities without the approval of both the Emperor and the Abuna. Accordingly, when the leader of the London mission, Stern, arrived in Ethiopia in March 1860, he immediately set out to obtain an audience with the Emperor Tewodros II.[8] Although the king's reaction was generally favorable, he insisted that Stern obtain the consent of Abuna Salama, the Egyptian bishop who headed the Ethiopian Church.[9] While scarcely an admirer of the Abuna, Tewodros was too shrewd a politician to risk a disagreement or misunderstanding with him over what appeared, at the time, to be a minor issue. Despite some initial reservations (he thought "the mission to the Jews a pretext for interfering with the belief of the Christians"), Salama eventually gave his "permission to preach [to the Jews] and hold assemblies in every village and town of his vast diocese."[10]

Two important limitations, however, were placed upon mission activity. First, the missionaries were to proselytize only among the non-Christian inhabitants of Ethiopia. No attempt was to be made to "convert" local Christians to Protestantism. Second, while given limited freedom to practice their religion as they chose, all converts were considered members of the Ethiopian Orthodox church. In short no separate Protestant church was to be established.[11]

In accepting these conditions, Stern was consciously attempting to make the best of a highly unsatisfactory situation. Neither he nor any of his fellow missionaries believed the Ethiopian church to be a proper vehicle for spreading their message. They were horrified at what they viewed as ignorant clerics exploiting a superstitious population.

The whole of the village, together with their priests, a stupid, ignorant, vicious-looking lump of humanity, crowded around us. We asked them many questions about their religious belief and their hopes of salvation. The ignorant and poor people naturally turned to their priest for a reply, but they might as well have expected an answer from the fragments of rock which lay strewn over the turf, as from this self-conceited, proud, and bigoted minister of the Church.[12]

In practice, the missionaries appear to have exploited any lapse in royal vigilance in order to meet with and preach to local Christians. In addition, they genuinely questioned the willingness of any Beta Israel to join a church that had treated them so poorly in the past.

One *great* stumbling-block to the Jews is the entering into the Abyssinian Church, and I believe it must be so to every right-minded Israelite. If in this country there were a free toleration for every creed, so that everyone could openly confess the pure Gospel, I have no doubt that some would have joined us; but as now there is nothing for it, but to be incorporated with the so much abhorred Amharas, they take no step.[13]

Under such circumstances, it is hardly surprising that relatively few of their converts were truly prepared for integration with the national church. Rather, it was hoped that such "English Protestants" (or as they became known in later years "Yato Flad-Lessotch" [Mr. Flad's Children]) would form the basis for a Reformed Church in Ethiopia.[14]

Another aspect of the London mission's development directly related to the influence of the Ethiopian situation was the emergence of a native ministry. Although conventional histories of the London Society have frequently tended to give the lion's share of attention to such European missionaries as Stern and J. Martin Flad, during most of its history the mission was actually run by the so-called native agents, Debtera Beroo, Michael Aragawi, Hiob Negoosie, and so forth.[15] Indeed throughout the period from 1864 to 1922, no European representative of the London Society was active in Ethiopia for more than a few months at a time.

The overwhelming responsibility given to the native agents was less a consequence of any commitment to them on the part of the London Society than a simple product of Ethiopian political realities. In October 1863, responding to a variety of slights, both real and imagined, the gifted but erratic Tewodros II imprisoned the missionaries Stern and H. Rosenthal.[16] Several months later the remaining missionaries to the Beta Israel were also incarcerated. Only in April 1868 did a British expeditionary force led by Sir Robert Napier succeed in freeing the captives. (Faced with ignominious defeat, Tewodros committed suicide.) The missionaries returned home to Europe. Neither of Tewodros's successors, Yohannes IV or Menelik II, encouraged the return of the European agents. In fact, of the captives only Flad returned to Ethiopia and for only short periods.[17] Thus, while he remained the titular head of the mission until his death in 1915 and proudly suggested in his autobiography that his work there was over sixty years, most of this period was served in abstensia.[18] The London Society's Ethiopian mission was Ethiopian therefore not only in its locale and target population, but also with respect to its staff.

The Missionary Appeal

Without doubt the central questions for any analysis of the mission-Beta Israel encounter concern the manner in which the missionaries sought to attract the Beta Israel and the elements to which the Beta Israel themselves responded. Before we proceed to our own examination of these issues, it is necessary to consider previous attempts to answer these questions and in particular the oft-repeated claim that the missionaries primarily used physical coercion and financial inducements to procure converts.[19] While it is, of course, impossible to totally disprove such accusations, and instances of coercion and bribery may actually have taken place, it is difficult to accept that either practice represented a characteristic feature of missionary activity during the period we are concerned with. Certainly neither technique formed part of approved missionary policy. Also in light of the evidence available and the conditions under which the London Society operated, it does not appear likely that either practice could have been a major weapon in the missionary arsenal.

Of the two charges levelled against the missionaries, that of using physical coercion seems to rest upon the weakest foundation. The missionaries themselves, whether the early Europeans or the Falasha converts, had no direct means of forcing the Beta Israel to accept Christianity. Indeed, if their testimonies are to be believed, converts and "inquirers" were far more likely to be abused by irate relatives than vice-versa.[20] Certainly, the missionaries do not appear to have been able to prevent a number of their converts from "backsliding" and returning to their previous faith.[21] In a similar fashion, while it is tempting to assume that the missionaries had access to the resources of the Christian Ethiopian state in their struggle to convert the Beta Israel, this assumption receives little support from the evidence at hand for the period in question. Tewodros II, his successors, and the local governors of his time appear to have been fairly scrupulous in ascertaining that all conversions were made freely, or at least not under conditions of obvious duress.[22] It must be remembered that neither the political nor ecclesiastical leadership of Ethiopia was overflowing with sympathy for the "English Protestants."[23] In general, permission to operate appears to have represented the limit of local support for their cause. At times, even this minimal concession was difficult to procure, and the missionaries complained of harassment by soldiers and other officials.[24]

A second major objection to the accusation of coercion is based upon the consideration of the theological assumptions that motivated the mission. Contrary to the common stereotype of the missionary, the representatives of the London Society appear to have been deeply committed to achieving genuine conversions.[25] Baptism and acceptance into the Church represented, in their view, the culmination of a process of inner transformation: of turning to Christ. They spoke scornfully of Orthodox converts who had not been properly taught and hence lacked any real understanding of Christianity.[26] According to their own testimony, they lobbied (successfully) against the Emperor Yohannes IV's attempts to convert the Beta Israel by decree.[27] At least in some cases the missionaries' cautious attitude toward baptism resulted in a considerable degree of tension between them and potential converts. At any given time the mission had, in addition to those already baptized, a substantial number of "inquirers" learning the principles of Christianity.[28] The circumstances of such trainees were especially difficult. Even though they had made a significant break with their Beta Israel kin, they were not yet Christians. Not surprisingly, the missionaries occasionally found themselves under pressure to normalize the situation of such inquirers through a speeded up baptism and conversion ceremony.[29] Here, as elsewhere in Africa, they resisted such pressures with only limited success.

Although we see that there was an underlying pressure to convert that flavored the atmosphere in Christian Ethiopia, this cannot be considered evidence that the missionaries of the London Society depended primarily upon overt coercion to win new adherents. Their theology of conversion and the means at their disposal did not incline them to employ such a procedure.

The situation with regard to the procuring of converts through financial inducements is, however, somewhat more complex. Once again, it can be stated with confidence that the mission was theologically opposed to any attempt to "buy" converts. Tewodros' attempt to win over Beta Israel masons employed in Gondar by offering them money was, for example, the subject of much critical comment on the part of the missionaries.[30] The mission in Ethiopia also did not possess substantial resources for the subvention of the Beta Israel had this been its goal. Nevertheless, it would be a mistake to totally discount the economic factor in evaluating the mission's impact upon the Beta Israel.

Almost from its inception, the London Society sought to provide some financial assistance to those inclined to consider its message. Stern, for example, reports buying corn and clothing for the inquirers with fifty Maria Theresa dollars.[31] During crises, most notably the great famine of 1888–92, such sums could mean the difference between life and death.[32] Salaries were also paid during most of the mission's history to the local agents and native teachers. In 1871, Debtera Beroo, the mission leader, received an annual salary of twenty-one pounds. His assistant, Kindy Fanta, was paid fifteen pounds per annum, and two teachers received four pounds ten shillings each.[33] Prior to this period, however, all the missions' native agents appear to have primarily supported themselves through crafts and handiwork.[34]

Mention should also be made of the fact that a number of the earliest converts, including several who became native agents, came from backgrounds of extreme poverty and vulnerability. The brothers, Samani and Sanbatu Daniel, were fatherless and entered the mission through Theophilus Waldmeier's orphanage.[35] Agashy Scheloo had lost his mother and was placed under the protection of Beta Israel monks.[36] Beroo, long the effective head of the mission, had seen his family reduced to ruin by persecution and disaster.[37] A blind youth is also mentioned among the mission's earliest converts.[38] For these "Falasha Christians" and perhaps for others the mission offered if not wealth, at least security. The record thus appears on the whole inconclusive. While no clear evidence exists that the missionaries emphasized the material benefits of conversion, their relative wealth and command of outside resources must certainly have been sources of attraction. Nonetheless, it seems difficult to believe that this alone was the factor that led most Beta Israel to convert.

More generally, it should be noted that conversion to Christianity may at first have seemed to offer Beta Israel converts the possibility of removing the stigma of their caste-like despised status.[39] In practice, this scarcely appears to be the case. Beta Israel converts whether to the mission or the Orthodox Church largely retained their ethnic identity as Falasha and the former carried the added burden of being identified with the foreign Protestants. Many, moreover, continued to work as smiths and potters.[40]

The first step in the missionaries' program to convert the Beta Israel was a concerted effort to undermine their faith in both their religious practice and leadership. Once again from an African perspective, the Jews of Ethiopia offered their opponents a unique challenge. While countless other African groups confronted Christian missionaries with "superstitions" they sought to uproot, no other group was as consistent in claiming biblical legitimacy for its religious system. Even within the framework of the missions to the Jews, the monks and priests of the Beta Israel represented an unparalleled phenomenon. On the one hand, they lacked the Talmud, which members of the London Society viewed as the chief source of Jewish unbelief. On the other hand, they possessed a number of decidedly un-Jewish (and nonbiblical institutions) such as monasticism. Not surprisingly, the missionary attack was also in its own way unique.

According to the missionaries, the problem with the Beta Israel religion was not merely its failure to acknowledge Christ, but also its distorted and degenerate form of Judaism. Over and over again in their disputes with the Beta Israel clergy the missionaries returned to the same theme: your claims of biblical authority are false because much of your religion is nonbiblical in character. Sacrifices, monasticism, and the laws of purity were the elements most frequently singled out for condemnation.

The following conversation has been recorded:

When he [a young Beta Israel] had asserted that the Lord had given the law in Egypt, and I had corrected his errors, he exclaimed impatiently, "Yes, and this law we keep, and no other will we hear."
I.—What was the law that the Lord gave to the children of Israel on Mount Sinai?
"The ten words," he replied quickly, looking round victoriously on the assembly.
I.—Do you know them?
Again he blundered.
When he had repeated them aloud, in order that all should hear it, I asked, "Now tell me, is there anything in these ten words about washing, about the separation rules, about abstaining from defiled things, which you just before affirmed was the religion of the children of Israel?"[41]

The Pentateuch in the Ethiopic language was then brought forward and they began to read some part of a passage that was interpolated after the book of Deuteronomy was finished. Upon this I called his attention to a few words immediately preceding the interpolated passage, namely, "Here endeth the law of Moses"; upon this they were silent, and I said, "You who pretend to keep the law, are great transgressors of the same since you add to it, in direct contradiction to Moses's command."
They—We keep the law.
We—How is that possible? Where is the blue fringe on the borders of your

garments? Where is your tabernacle? Where is your altar? Where are your priests of the sons of Aaron?[42]

In addition to critiquing Beta Israel religious practice, the missionaries also complained frequently about their religious leadership, the priests and monks.[43] These clerics attracted the ire of the missionaries for a variety of reasons. First, as evangelical Protestants the missionaries had a deeply ingrained aversion to a religious hierarchy staffed by monks and priests. They were, for example, no less bitter in their denunciations of the clergy of the Ethiopian Orthodox Church.[44] The Beta Israel religious leaders were in their opinion doubly blameworthy because they claimed biblical sanction for their office.

To be sure, not even the missionaries were totally immune to the attraction of the greatest of the Beta Israel religious leaders. In one truly extraordinary passage, Stern, reporting on his meeting with the famous monk and prophet, Abba Mahari, wrote, "There was something imposing and majestic in the appearance of the man, which one could scarcely behold without admiration and reverence."[45] Far more typical, at least in his opinion, was his encounter with a "wild fanatical looking monk, with a grin of contempt which imparted to his black face and capacious mouth a most repulsive expression, with an air of pride and self-complacency."[46]

Stern and his colleagues not only attacked the priesthood and monasticism as institutions, but also exploited every opportunity to engage individual clerics in disputations in order to demonstrate their opponents' ignorance.[47] Their task was not a difficult one. The Beta Israel monks were honored in their community because of their piety and the communal and ritual roles they filled, not for their skill as debaters. They conceived of their religion more as a tradition of communal and personal obligations passed on by word of mouth and through ritual practices than as a clearly articulated, logically developed, scripture-based system. Few, if any, Beta Israel clergy possessed a complete Bible. The art of citation and argumentation, at which the missionaries were so skilled, was totally foreign to them. Inevitably, they came out second best in the confrontations engineered by the missionaries. Increasingly, they came to cite "tradition" rather than biblical precedents in their discussions with the missionaries.[48]

The missionary strategy of provoking clashes with the Beta Israel clergy was ideally suited to their work among these people. To this day most Beta Israel possess only a rudimentary understanding of the symbols and rituals that make up their religious traditions. Their clergy, especially the monks and priests, were not only the paramount ritual experts, but also the chief guardians of the community's historical traditions and beliefs. Most Beta Israel had no pretensions to such knowledge and, when they encountered the missionaries, simply referred them to the priests.

With our fellow-traveller, the Falasha, we had on the way a religious conversation, which we continued till it was late. We tried to convince him that Jesus Christ is the promised seed of Abraham, in whom all nations are blessed. . . . Next day we travelled together until we reached Ferka, where our ways separated. Before we parted, he said: "You have told me a great many things I did not know before; and, being an unlearned man, I invite you to visit me at Fentsha. If you convince our Kahen (priest), that Jesus is the son of God, and the promised Messiah, I will believe in him."[49]

Under such circumstances, the missionary assault on clerical prestige and status can be seen to have held the promise of totally undermining the Beta Israel religious system. In fact, the missionaries seem to have been confident that this was happening.

Respecting the Jews, or Falashas, one remarkable feature is at present observable, namely, that they have been greatly divided in their religious opinions, as also in respect of their adherence to the monks. . . . They feel our superiority over their teachers, they perceive our acquaintance with the work of God; and comparing it with the ignorance of those teachers, they are astonished. . . . Hence a great division has arisen, and although we must not as yet be too sanguine, yet we may freely say that the balance is in our favour.[50]

The Beta Israel, they believed, were ripe for a mini-reformation and the abandonment of the monastic system.[51] In fact, as we shall discuss in the next chapter, demography appears to have played at least as large a role as theology in encouraging the decline of Beta Israel monasticism.

The missionary appeal to the Beta Israel was not, of course, confined to attacks on their clergy and their religious practices. Nor was it limited to preaching the Gospel and spreading the Christian message. For many Beta Israel their first contact with the missions resulted neither from their desire to acquire a new faith nor from their attempt to defend their tradition, but from their interest in obtaining a copy of the Bible in Amharic. From the perspective of the missions to the Jews, the Ethiopian experience was once again rather unusual. The production of Bibles and even the mass circulation of inexpensive copies of the Hebrew Scriptures were common undertakings of the London Society. In Ethiopia, however, the missions were both the first and, for many years, the only source of such literature. Printed books of any kind remained a rarity in Ethiopia well into the twentieth century. Certainly the Beta Israel had no means of mass producing religious literature, nor was the production of scriptures in the vernacular a task they were capable of pursuing. Thus, when the London Society began to distribute Amharic Bibles, no rival Jewish source for such books existed.

It is difficult to overestimate the impact of the mission's "generosity" on the Beta Israel. In a single step printed books *and* the Scriptures in the vernacular reached them. A limited number of hand-copied parchment manuscripts of the *Orit* in Ge'ez were suddenly supplemented by hundreds of Amharic Bibles (including New Testaments, Christian parables, and missionary tracts).[52] Initially, the number of Beta Israel capable of reading the books they received was very limited.[53] Much of the attraction of the texts must accordingly have lain in their novelty and the simple prestige of ownership. The missionaries quickly followed the distribution of books with the second stage in their plan to attract the Beta Israel: the establishment of schools.[54] The London Society was, of course, in no way unique in establishing schools or using education as a lure for potential converts. Throughout the African continent, the educational endeavors of the missions were among the most positive side effects of their religious activities.[55] Moreover, schools were a regular feature of the mission to the Jews wherever it existed. Yet, here again, the mission to the Beta Israel was somewhat remarkable at least in the African context. In other parts of Africa, the tasks facing the missionaries included reducing the local languages to a written form, translating the Bible into that language, familiarizing potential converts with the Bible, and teaching them to read and write.[56] Among the Beta Israel, written languages (Amharic and Ge'ez), biblical texts (Ge'ez), a basic familiarity with much of the Old Testament, and limited degree of literacy already existed. The missions thus found a much firmer base upon which to work and faced a much simpler task. True, the Bible had to be translated into Amharic, but this had already been accomplished by 1840.[57] More significant, the teaching contained therein represented not a strange novelty introduced to the Beta Israel by the missionaries, but a more accessible version of their most revered text. In a similar fashion, the educational opportunities created by the mission appeared not as an unheard of and hence unappreciated innovation, but rather as the offer of an already prestigious skill on an unprecedented scale. Small wonder that throughout the history of the mission, education proved to be one of "Christianity's" most attractive features.[58]

Beta Israel Converts

Of course, any discussion of the Beta Israel-mission encounter would be incomplete without a discussion of those Beta Israel who converted to Christianity. Before presenting our conclusions on this subject, however, it is necessary to add a few prefatory remarks by way of a caution.

As we have noted in previous chapters, only in the last quarter of the twentieth century do we begin to have reliable demographic data concerning the Beta Israel. It is, therefore, impossible to give anything but a general figure as to their total population during the first decades of the mission's presence. Contemporary estimates of between fifty and one hundred thousand Beta Israel appear fairly reasonable, although, as we shall discuss in the next chapter, even the lower figure may be a bit high for the period immediately after the great famine of 1888–92. Obviously, any figures given for the number of converts can only be properly evaluated in the context of the total target population and thus our general ignorance on this subject severely limits the usefulness of the missionary data. A second factor that must be considered concerns the nature of the missionary reports themselves. As noted above, the Ethiopian mission of the London Society was unusual if not unique in that converts entered an existing national church rather than the mission's own denomination. While those baptized under the auspices of the mission could be easily counted and registered, this was not the case for those Beta Israel who sought to enter directly into the Ethiopian Orthodox Church. The figures presented in the various missionary publications concern the number of individuals baptized *by the mission,* not the total number of converts to Christianity. Beta Israel who were led to Christ through the mission's influence but did not accept its organizational framework did not figure in mission reports.[59] The figures they offer are, therefore, the minimum number of those converted during a given period.

The number of Beta Israel baptized by the mission was never large.

More than two years passed before the Society achieved its first conversions.[60] Neither the 65 claimed until 1868, nor the 1470 until 1894 represent overwhelming success. Rarely did the number converted in a single year exceed forty and this figure was achieved only when minor dependents of adult converts were counted.[61] Thus, in most years, the rate of conversion achieved by the mission did not exceed 0.1 percent of the total population. Even so, this relatively small figure represented a constant source of concern to the Beta Israel. Once it was firmly established, the community of "Falasha Christians" was self-sustaining and not dependent on the traditional Beta Israel for either new members or spouses. Here again the limitations of the missionary reports are apparent. No attempt was made, for example, to record the number of children born to converts. Only rarely were attempts made to estimate the total number of living Falasha Christians. In 1885 a figure of eight hundred to nine hundred was cited.[62] As time passed, however, and converts scattered over wider and wider areas of Ethiopia, such estimates became even more difficult to make. At the turn of the century, missionaries report "finding" groups of previously unrecorded converts on several occasions.[63]

Mission converts were not drawn equally from all sectors of the Beta Israel population. As we have noted above, there are some indications that the mission's relative wealth and security made it especially attractive to the poor and disadvantaged. The young appear to be another group particularly open to the missionaries' appeals. For its part the mission was especially interested in attracting youths, who might serve as teachers or missionaries.[64] Moreover, its educational activities gave it a natural base from which to proselytize. Many of the Beta Israel who accepted baptism were minors or young adults.[65] In contrast, older adults proved extremely resistant to the mission's entreaties. Few converted, and many of those who did were following in the footsteps of their children or other younger relatives.[66]

Another group that deserves special mention as particularly susceptible to conversion are the *debterotch* (sing. *debtera*). Among the Beta Israel, as with their Christian neighbors, the *debtera* represented a secondary unconsecrated clerical group responsible for performing the liturgy. In general, a *debtera* was a person who was prevented from continuing in or seeking elevation to a higher religious position by some personal, physical, or familial flaw.[67] As a group they were generally well educated and often served as scribes.[68] Among the Ethiopian Christians the combination of the valued skill of literacy with limited recognition and opportunities for advancement was a frequent source of tension between the *debtera* and the higher clergy. The tendency of many *debtera* to engage in officially forbidden magical practices was one of several sources of tension between them and the church establishment.[69] A similar situation may well have existed among the Beta Israel.[70] Moreover, Flad notes that many Beta Israel *debterotch* studied in Christian schools.[71] It is therefore hardly surprising that the *debterotch* proved to be among those most eager to acquire Amharic Bibles and to support the missionary criticism of the monastic clergy. They also appear prominently among those who eventually accepted Christianity.[72]

Finally, we must recognize the importance played by family ties in the spread of Christianity. To a considerable degree, the achievements of the London Society among the Beta Israel rested on its ability to convert entire family groups rather than single individuals. Repeated mention is made of the baptism of several members of a single family.[73] In other cases, relatives who initially opposed Christianity were later baptized themselves.[74] Debtera Beroo eventually converted not only his mother and brother but also two of his mother's brothers.[75] Goshu Mersha was joined in the mission by his wife, two brothers, and a sister.[76] Many converts were thus able to transfer their religious allegiance without a notable disruption of their social, particularly kinship, ties.[77]

Beta Israel Responses

Given the relatively small number of Beta Israel who converted to Christianity during the period from 1860 to 1888 and the limits of the missionaries' success among many groups in the population, it is perhaps tempting to minimize the overall impact of the mission. This would be a serious error. Although the Falasha Christians were the group by far the most influenced by the mission, it is a mistake to consider them the only group affected by the encounter. Many of those who responded most tellingly to the missionary initiative did so from within the framework of traditional Beta Israel society and religion. As will be demonstrated below, some who rejected Christianity underwent transformations no less dramatic than those who converted.

During the first two years of the London Society's activities in Ethiopia, relations between the missionaries and the Beta Israel were tense but cordial. Despite the warnings of the clergy, the Society's agents encountered little organized opposition to their presence. The turning point in Beta Israel relations with the mission came not, as might be expected, with the first conversions, but rather a month earlier in 1862. Significantly, the immediate cause of the crises was not the actions of the any of the European missionaries, but rather the eruption of tensions within Beta Israel society itself. Kindy Fanta, one of the mission's inquirers, was accused by the clergy of his village of having become a Christian. Together with the young man's parents they cursed and excommunicated him. In response, he abjured them in the name of the Emperor (May the Emperor die, if you do so and so) not to sacrifice. As a result of his action a central feature of Beta Israel traditional religion was suddenly in mortal danger.[78] For the Beta Israel, as for many peoples challenged by Christian missionaries, the attempts of the missionaries to regulate or abolish aspects of their traditional religion and culture had a decisive impact on their attitude toward the mission and its representatives.[79] Their hitherto passive hostility toward the London Society was radically transformed. Almost immediately they began to initiate a series of steps in an attempt to resist the missionary challenge. The Beta Israel employed a variety of techniques and policies to minimize Christian inroads into their communities. Although none of their efforts totally succeeded in removing the Christian threat, limited gains were made.

Initially, the Beta Israel sought to fight the ban of sacrifices (and a month later the first baptisms) through the Ethiopian legal system. As numerous studies have documented, imperial Ethiopia had a well-developed legal system with a variety of levels of courts concluding, at least in theory, with final appeal to the Emperor.[80] The Ethiopians were, moreover, a particular litigious people much enamored with the verbal give and take of the legal process. Within this context, the Beta Israel search for a legal remedy to their problems was, even considering their relatively low social, political, and economic position, natural and predictable.

The Beta Israel began their campaign against the ban on sacrifices at the court of the governor of Dambeya. Although generally sympathetic to their claims (he *requested* that the missionaries rescind the ban and himself suspended it prior to the hearing), the governor reached no verdict and referred the disputants on to the king.[81] The appearance of a number of important Beta Israel religious leaders before the Emperor

Tewodros II in October 1862 remains one of the most famous and best documented events in their history. Not only do traditions concerning this event still survive in the memory of community members, it is also the subject of the earliest surviving historical text written by the Beta Israel themselves.[82]

Although officially on the subject of sacrifice, the case before the Emperor appears to have encompassed other issues. Beta Israel traditions depict this incident as primarily an argument concerning the Unity or Trinity of God; a view that finds some support in the missionary literature.[83] The arguments presented at Tewodros' court did not produce a clear-cut verdict. The Beta Israel were not, as they had feared, forced to convert. Nevertheless, it appears likely that their right to sacrifice was suspended or at least limited.[84] Even this disruption was, however, short-lived and ceased with the death of Tewodros in 1868.[85]

In most cases, the Beta Israel resorted to the Ethiopian courts not with regard to society-wide concerns such as the ban on sacrifices, but rather in an attempt to prevent or at least hinder individual conversions.

I'aasoo, one of the first inquirers, [has] had great trouble with his father-in-law, who wished to persuade his daughter to leave her husband. He [the father-in-law] had challenged him to appear with him before the governor. The latter [the governor] was not able to decide in a matter of divorce, as this is generally done by the priests. But still, he said, he was of the opinion that if his daughter wished to remain with her husband, the king would not permit him to take away his daughter by force.[86]

Such legal harassment of the earliest converts was apparently quite common, and the missionary Rosenthal complained in November 1863 that converts had to contend with their converted brethren who "bring them before governors and princes to injure their lives."[87]

Rather surprisingly, despite their general lack of success the Beta Israel continued to resort to legal attempts to prevent conversions. According to the mission's *Annual Report* of 1883, Beta Israel priests were temporarily successful in convincing the governor of Qwara to ban the missionaries from his province. He ceased to interfere only when the missionaries could prove they had the king's permission.[88] In fact, having received the permission of Ethiopia's political and ecclesiastical leadership, the missionaries were in an excellent political-legal situation. As long as they used neither violence or coercion, their Beta Israel opponents had little hope for a legal remedy to their problems.

Of course the major weapon available to the Beta Israel in their struggle against the missionaries was not the Ethiopian legal system, but their own ability to enforce communal sanctions. To this end they employed two techniques: (1) the isolation of foreign missionaries; (2) the expulsion and excommunication of Beta Israel converts. Neither practice represented a totally new phenomenon among the Beta Israel. As we have seen, from the fifteenth century onward the custom known as *attenkugn* had dictated that any member of the community who came in contact with an outsider had to undergo ritual purification before rejoining society. It remains unclear to what extent the laws of *attenkugn* were applied prior to the nineteenth century. In all probability the degree of observance among the general population varied in different periods and under different conditions, while the clergy, especially the monks, were stricter in their behavior. Beta Israel laboring as builders and living in Gondar were, for example, probably rather casual in their attitude toward this custom. Certainly, most Beta Israel do not appear to have avoided contact with the foreign missionaries during the first years of missionary activity. In contrast, from 1870 onward representatives of the London Society found an increasing number of villages closed to them.[89] It is difficult to avoid the conclusion that while *attenkugn* existed long prior to the missionary "invasion," it was mobilized and intensified in an attempt at resistance.

In this context, it must be remembered that the Beta Israel, unlike the Ethiopian national authorities, had neither the power nor authority to physically exclude missionaries from preaching in the country. They could, however, deny them entry into their villages and refuse all contact with them. They could also attempt to exclude local converts from contact with other Beta Israel.

The pattern that emerges here is worthy of comment, for it marks an area of significant contrast between the Beta Israel and most African targets of missionary action. In general African peoples appear to have adopted a decidedly inclusive attitude toward converts to Christianity. Faced with defections, they were usually quite ready to abandon their customary tolerance and openness in favor of coercion and persecution.[90] Christian converts were frequently forced to participate in traditional rituals, and even Christian corpses were, on occasion, hijacked to ensure them a traditional burial.[91] The Beta Israel, in contrast, devoted most of their energy to the *exclusion* of local converts.[92] To be sure, "Falasha Christians" were encouraged to recant and return to the fold.

No evidence exists, however, that they were either expected or urged to participate in traditional rituals so long as they remained Christians. While the Beta Israel do not appear to have been as extreme as some Jewish communities who excommunicated any member who made use of missionary services, neither did they attempt to hold on to lapsed members by force.[93]

Of course, in practice, neither of the methods described above was completely successful. Although the missionaries were repeatedly confronted by individuals, villages, and even entire regions in which they were not welcomed because the Beta Israel clergy had threatened to excommunicate those who met with them, such sanctions were rarely 100 percent effective. A number of factors would appear to lie behind the Beta Israel's relative lack of success.

First, it must be stressed yet again that however convenient it may be to talk about the Beta Israel "community," the Jews of Ethiopia possessed neither centralized communal institutions capable of making decisions for the group as a whole nor efficient mechanisms for enforcing decisions made at anything other than the village level. The exercise of sanctions was therefore totally dependent on the ability of the clergy to mobilize popular opinion in support of such a step. Consensus, not compulsion, was the name of the game.[94]

At this point, a second important factor came into operation. Those members of the community whose cooperation was most crucial for the successful application of sanctions, namely the relatives of converts, were also those most tempted to violate such measures. Moreover, as previously noted, they were the individuals most vulnerable to conversion. To excommunicate a Jewish Beta Israel because he or she insisted on maintaining contact with his converted son or daughter, brother or sister, was to do nothing less than push him into the arms of the Christians. It is therefore scarcely surprising that the only truly effective sanctions were those supported (and even initiated) by the convert's own kin. Kindy Fanta, one of the first Beta Israel converts, was excommunicated not by the priests but by his parents.[95] Several of the first group of Falasha Christians had to take refuge from their angry relatives in the houses of the missionaries.[96] Many of those who refused to convert cited their hesitation to break off their relationship with a parent or spouse as the excuse for deferring their decision.[97]

A third reason for the relative inefficiency of the communal sanctions related directly to the composition of the London Society's staff. The Falasha Christian agents enjoyed much easier access to their unconverted brethren than their European counterparts: neither race, language, dress, or culture separated them from their Beta Israel. In addition, they had a vast network of kinship ties and an intimate knowledge of community life upon which to base their activities. Most important, because of their continued *ethnic* identification as Beta Israel, the laws of *attenkugn* do not appear to have been used to exclude them from participation in rituals and celebrations. They were therefore able to continue their involvement in communal life, and also to exploit ritual occasions to preach their message.

In 1882 missionaries Debtera Alamy and Debtera Lena met with the priests of the village of Abea in Qwara on the day of "a great annual sacrifice."[98] One year later Michael Aragawi and Goshu Mersha went on an extensive missionary tour during which they stayed with the latter's *Jewish* relatives and attended several weddings. The same year Gebra Heiwot attended and participated in the *Seged,* a pilgrimage festival.

Hundreds of Falashas, men and women were gathered together. All arrived carrying a big stone on their neck, crying "O God, have mercy on us: Elohe, Elohe, gracious God, forgive us." The priest asked Gebre Heiwot to read to the people certain parts of the Pentateuch in Ethiopic, which one of them translated into Amharic. After this, your Agent read in Amharic all the Messianic prophecies, and preached Christ. Whereupon the priests became the opponents, and ordered him to leave the place, forbidding him to come again. A number of Falashas followed him, to whom he spoke freely: all accepted tracts, promising to read them, to see who was in the right way.[99]

Other native missionaries are reported to have entered Beta Israel monasteries, talked with monks, attended harvest *(Ma'rar)* celebrations, and preached on the Sabbath in the *masgid.*[100]

The experience of the native missionaries would therefore appear to indicate that the Beta Israel laws of purity were not always applied as strictly or as comprehensively as some contemporary authors would seem to have believed.[101] In fact, the most probable explanation for the continued access of converts to their brethren is probably that such laws were applied far more strictly against non-Beta Israel than against "Falasha Christians." Indeed, in contrast to what has commonly been assumed, it may well be that at least in the nineteenth century the laws of *attenkugn* were as much an ethnic barrier as a religious one.[102] Whatever the reasons, the laws of *attenkugn* represented only a minimal barrier to the "contamination" of traditional believers by their converted brethren.

Migration as Resistance

Not surprisingly, some Beta Israel religious leaders believed more drastic remedies were in order. During the first two decades of the missionaries' activity in Ethiopia, at least three attempts were made by large numbers of Beta Israel to leave Ethiopia. The first ended in disaster, the results of the others remain unclear.[103]

In 1862 a large group of Beta Israel drawn from almost all the regions in which they resided attempted to reach the Holy Land by marching through northern Ethiopia to the Red Sea. At their head stood several prophets, the best remembered of whom is the holy monk, Abba Mahari. They failed to reach their goal and by the time they reached Tigre province many had died of hunger and disease. Some of those who survived remained in Tigre, while a remnant straggled back to the south, suffering further loses along the way. The missionary Flad offers a vivid account of their journey and the tragedy that befell the participants. His report is largely echoed by Joseph Halévy, who appears to base himself on oral traditions still graphically recalled by the Beta Israel.[104]

Despite this wealth of documentation, the precise relationship of this episode to the mission's presence is the subject of some controversy. According to Halévy, the decision to set out for the Land of Israel was made in the wake of the disputation before Tewodros. He claims that after the debate, during which the king was greatly impressed by the courage of the Beta Israel, they were granted a reprieve for four years. As a result,

Some of the priests who had been ordered to appear at Gondar to assist at the controversy, and who had feared a fatal termination, fell subsequently into a singular state of religious exaltation ... they believed ... that the time had arrived for a return to Jerusalem.[105]

This sequence of events also appears in many oral traditions and has been echoed by some recent scholars.[106] This evidence notwithstanding, a number of reasons exist for questioning this chronology and the attempt to draw a direct connection between the migration and the appearance before Tewodros. First, Flad, who was a contemporary witness to both events and is generally more reliable than Halévy on such matters, draws no connection between the two events. Second, oral traditions claim that the attempted journey was over by the end of the rainy season, that is, no later than September 1862, while the debate before Tewodros was in October of that year. Third, the absence from the disputation of Abba Mahari, one of the Beta Israel's outstanding leaders, is probably best explained as a consequence of his participation in the journey during the same period. Indeed, at least one contemporary source appears to confirm the suggestion that at the same time as some members of the community remained in place and sought to fight the missionaries through the Ethiopian legal system, others sought to leave the country. Writing to the rabbis of Jerusalem in the fateful year of 1862, Abba Ṣagga, one of the parties to the disputation at Tewodros' court, noted

There is come among us a great stir in our hearts. For some say that the time is come for our people and we shall be separated from the Christians and go up to your country, Jerusalem, and be united with your brethren and offer sacrifices to the Lord, the God of Israel, in the Holy Land.[107]

On the whole, it appears far more plausible to suggest that the attempted journey preceded the disputation at the court by several months. It may well have been set off by the conversion of the first Beta Israel in June 1862 or the almost simultaneous ban of sacrifices imposed on the community. However, at the root of this dramatic episode lay not only these "push" factors, but also such "pull" factors as the Beta Israel's attachment to the Holy Land, their growing realization that other Jewish communities existed outside Ethiopia, and the general messianic fervor in Ethiopia associated with the figure of Tewodros II.[108]

In contrast to the attempted exodus of 1862, the reported migrations of 1874 and 1879 remain among the least known episodes in Beta Israel. None of the standard histories of the Beta Israel make any mention of them not do they appear to have made a major impression on the communities' oral traditions. In both cases, however, the connection between the calls to emigrate and the missionary threat is even more explicit than in 1862.

In the November 1874 issue of *Jewish Intelligence,* Flad wrote:

I was told early in the morning, that the chief priest of the Falashas, Aba Maharee, was making preparations to go with many Falashas into the low country of Wogerra. Some evil disposed individuals had spread the story that I had come with a letter from the Queen of England to King John, entreating him to have all the Falashas baptized. Beroo and our people told me that when the intelligence of my arrival reached him, Aba Maharee ordered special prayers to be offered up in all their synagogues for our destruction. . . . Seeing that they were disappointed in their hopes, when they learned that we were in good health . . . the Falasha priests took it as a bad omen, and resolved to emigrate to the low countries. The following is the proclamation which was read in the synagogue: "Aba Maharee invites all those who wish to die as Falashas to leave West Abyssinia, and to follow him to a place of refuge. Those who do not care for their fathers' religion may remain; but let them remember that there is only one true religion—that of Moses." This proclamation caused a great excitement in the Falasha villages.[109]

Although it appears that Flad was successful in persuading Abba Mahari that no mass baptism was, in fact, intended, it is not completely clear if the call to find a "place of refuge" was cancelled. This appears likely, since no further mention is made of the attempt to lead a second exodus, and Abba Mahari is mentioned again in 1877.[110] In 1879 yet a third call was made to migrate away from the missionaries.

There arose a prophet among the Falashas, proclaiming that the God of Israel had revealed it to him in a dream "that Europeans from distant lands would come and force all the Falashas here abouts to receive baptism." Whereupon many Falashas, as soon as they heard this, became unsettled, and went to the Kola (low country).[111]

Several factors must be considered if we are to accurately understand these radical attempts to escape the missionaries. As we have already noted, the Beta Israel lacked both the legal and political means to exclude representatives of the London Society from their midst. Under such circumstances, migration offered them their only chance to achieve total separation from the missionaries. In addition, it should also be remembered that the Beta Israel generally had no hereditary land rights and worked primarily as tenant farmers for Christian landlords. Accordingly, their ties to land as an economic resource were limited, and migration may have even offered them the opportunity of acquiring land in underpopulated, less desirable locales. Significantly, two of the migrations are said to have been toward the low-lying hot regions usually avoided by highland Ethiopians. Finally, it must also be remembered that the Beta Israel possessed a strong tradition of Exodus as a means of redemption and a powerful attachment to the Holy Land and the city of Jerusalem.[112]

The prophetic activities of Abba Mahari and his anonymous successor are among the clearest indicators that even the most steadfast Beta Israel traditionalists were touched by the challenge posed by the mission. Their experience serves as a vivid reminder that the impact of the mission can by no means be measured solely in terms of the relatively small number of Beta Israel who converted.

The arrival in Ethiopia of the missionaries of the London Society for Promoting Christianity amongst the Jews inaugurated the Beta Israel encounter with Western modernity and thus forms a necessary starting point for any understanding of their history in the second half of the nineteenth century and beyond. The London Society's missionaries' criticism of animal sacrifice, purity laws, and monasticism offered a serious challenge to the Beta Israel's image of themselves as heirs to a biblical tradition and undermined the standing of their most important leaders. Through their activities the missionaries exacerbated existing tensions in Beta Israel society, such as those between the *debterotch* and the clergy and between young and old. They also created new pressures by offering alternatives to the traditional means of acheiving prestige and success. As we shall discuss in greater detail in the next chapter, the true depth of the mission's impact in many of these areas was only fully revealed in the last years of the century, when a great famine placed an additional strain on the already troubled fabric of Beta Israel life. Before we proceed to this topic, however, we must briefly depart from the main thread of our story to consider what was in the long run perhaps the most significant feature of the missionaries' encounter with the Beta Israel. The agents of the London Society were the first group to consistently treat the Jews of Ethiopia as "Jews" in the universal sense of that term. In doing so, they brought the Beta Israel to the attention of World Jewry and set in motion processes both in Europe and Ethiopia that irreversibly transformed the course of their history.

The Jewish "Discovery" of the Beta Israel and the Halévy Mission

Despite the publication of Bruce's *Travels* in 1790, Jewish perceptions of the Beta Israel in the first decades of the nineteenth century differed only slightly from those common in the medieval period. In particular, almost two centuries after their defeat by Susenyos, rumors continued to circulate concerning an independent Jewish kingdom in Ethiopia.[113] By the middle of the century, however, more reliable information began to arrive via travellers and missionaries. Filosseno Luzzatto, working through an exhaustive reading of available sources as well as information newly gathered using Antoine d'Abbadie as an intermediary, compiled a remarkably complete picture of Beta Israel history and culture.[114] Missionary reports, moreover, were extensively quoted in many Jewish newspapers, increasing their readers' familiarity with events in Ethiopia and creating a deep sense of the need for urgent action on behalf of their brethren in Ethiopia.[115]

In addition to these numerous reports from foreigners in Ethiopia, this period in also noteworthy for the first direct contacts with World Jewry initiated by the Beta Israel. In 1855 an Ethiopian Jew named Daniel ben Hanina arrived in Jerusalem with his thirteen-year-old son Moshe. Having learned of the existence of Jews in the Israel, Daniel had come with the blessings of the Beta Israel priests, so that his son might study Torah with the rabbis in the Holy City. After a short stay Daniel returned to Ethiopia, bearing a letter to the leaders of the Beta Israel community signed by some of Jerusalem's leading rabbis.[116] His son remained behind, but after a short time disappeared, only to resurface in the company of the Anglican Bishop and former missionary in Ethiopia, Samuel Gobat. It was probably no accident that one of the same Jerusalemite rabbis "betrayed" by Daniel, Joseph Schwarz, later became one of the first Jewish authorities to cast doubt on the Jewishness of the Beta Israel.[117]

In the letter sent to Ethiopia with Daniel ben Hanina, the rabbis of Jerusalem invited the Beta Israel, if they were interested, to send three or four representatives to study with them in Jerusalem. They had, they reported, considered sending two embassaries to Ethiopia with Daniel, but decided to refrain until they had determined the community's openness to such an initiative. The Beta Israel appear to have sent at least two responses in reply to the letter from Jerusalem. One, which has survived only in a fragmentary quotation, referred to the obvious differences between Ethiopian practice and that of rabbinic Judaism. "Send us educated men from among you that we might teach them the principles of the religion of Israel which are accepted by us."[118] The second, which we have cited above, was apparently more widely circulated, was written by Abba Ṣagga against the background of the missionary ban on sacrifices and Abba Mahari's abortive attempt to journey to the Holy Land, and was brought to Jerusalem by the missionary Bronkhurst.[119]

As reports about the Beta Israel multiplied and concern regarding their situation grew, calls began to be heard that practical steps be taken to come to their assistance. A number of early attempts by Jewish travellers to reach Ethiopia ended in failure, and interest in the idea began to lag.[120] Indeed, the plight of the Beta Israel might have been forgotten were it not for the enthusiastic intervention of Rabbi Azriel Hildesheimer, spiritual leader of the Jewish community of Eisenstadt, Hungary. In March 1864 he circulated a letter to Jewish leaders in England, Germany, and parts of the Austro-Hungarian Empire, in which he described in great detail the plight of the Beta Israel.[121] These letters received only a limited response, which prompted Hildesheimer to shift his tactics. On October 11, 1864, he issued a public appeal for aid to the Jews of Ethiopia, which was published in virtually all the leading Jewish newspapers of the time.[122] In this proclamation Hildesheimer sought to deal with three issues: Were the Falasha really Jews, could a Jewish mission save them, and how could such a project be organized? Basing himself on the Radbaz, Luzzato, as well as missionary sources, Hildesheimer affirmed the Jewishness of the Beta Israel ("We are brothers, the sons of one Father"), and suggested three practical steps: (1) Holy books and religious objects should be collected; (2) Three Amharic-speaking European Jews be chosen to go to Ethiopia as representatives of World Jewry; (3) Political action be initiated to ensure the intervention of consuls and other international figures on behalf of these representatives.

Hildesheimer's proclamation produced a large and overwhelmingly positive response.[123] None was more significant in the long run than that of Joseph Halévy, a thirty-eight-year-old teacher from Adrianople, Turkey. In a passionate letter written only a few weeks after Hildesheimer's appeal, Halévy offered to travel to Ethiopia and detailed his qualifications for this difficult mission.[124] Despite the growing concern about the Beta Israel and widespread support for Halévy's mission, two years passed before the *Alliance Israélite Universelle*, the most important Jewish philanthropic organization of the period, agreed to fund Halévy's journey to Ethiopia.

It is difficult to believe that a more suitable candidate for such a mission than Halévy existed anywhere. He had already established himself as a brilliant scholar with a firm basis in Judaica, Ethiopian languages, and Oriental studies. Halévy set out in the spring of 1867 and travelled through the Middle East before reaching Ethiopia.[125]

The period of Halévy's sojourn in Ethiopia is one of the most eventful and best documented in Ethiopian history.[126] In June 1863 Tewodros II, responding to a variety of snubs and insults (both real and imagined), seized and imprisoned the missionary Stern. In the months that followed other foreigners were similarly incarcerated. After an extended period of drawnout negotiations, the British government decided in mid-August 1867 to mount a military expedition to free the captives. The undertaking was delegated to the Bombay government and the command was entrusted to the commander-in-chief of the Bombay army, Sir Robert Napier. The army that Napier finally assembled (at a cost of almost nine million pounds) was by far the greatest military force in Ethiopia. Small wonder that Halévy found accommodation scarce and prices exorbitant. Although he initially planned to accompany the British expedition and thus gain entry into the interior of the country, Halévy eventually abandoned this plan and set out on his own. The decision was a wise one, for it was not until early 1868 that the British began their slow march to Magdala, where they encountered and defeated Tewodros.

Halévy first encountered the Beta Israel at the end of 1867 and spent several months visiting their villages. Although initially suspected of being yet another "white Falasha" missionary, he eventually achieved a high degree of acceptance.[127] While he was critical of some aspects of Beta Israel religious practice, he does not appear to have attempted to promote major changes in the manner of either the missionaries or later Jewish representatives. Moreover, while his reports have clearly been tailored to suit the susceptibilities of his European Jewish audience, comparison with other sources reveal him to be a generally reliable witness who recorded the people he encountered and the places he visited with considerable accuracy.[128] When he left Ethiopia, he took with him a young boy named Daniel entrusted to his care by the community elders and priests and an important collection of Beta Israel manuscripts. In his report to the *Alliance*, Halévy strongly affirmed the Jewishness of the Beta Israel and called for steps to strengthen them against the mission and bring them closer to World Jewry.[129]

Despite Halévy's recommendations, no practical steps were taken on behalf of the Beta Israel for almost forty years. In large measure, this lack of action can be traced to the attitude of the *Alliance*. Never enthusiastic supporters of a mission to Ethiopia (they had decided against such a project the day before Hildesheimer composed his appeal), the *Alliance* decided to take no further action. In later years, Halévy was to claim that he had been the victim of harsh personal attacks from representatives of the *Alliance*. The original manuscript of his travelogue, which was deposited at the offices of the *Alliance*, was lost in a fire.[130] Plans for a follow-up mission in 1875 were cancelled. Thus the primary long-term acheivements of Halévy's mission remained in the scientific rather than the philanthropic realm. Life for the Beta Israel in Ethiopia continued unchanged and largely unaffected by events in the Jewish world. Meanwhile, conditions in Ethiopia took a dramatic turn for the worse.

Kifu-qen: *The Great Famine of 1888–92*

Despite the growth of Jewish interest in the Beta Israel, almost forty years were to pass between Halévy's visit to Ethiopia and the journey of his student and follower Jacques (Ya'acov) Faitlovitch. In the meantime, events in Ethiopia continued to shape the fortunes of the Beta Israel in a dramatic fashion.

Kifu-qen (lit: awful day[s]), the great famine of 1888–92, devastated vast areas and left in its wake an impoverished, starving, and mourning population. Its impact on the Beta Israel was enormous and far-reaching and they justly view it as one of the seminal events in their history. Certainly its immediate effect far exceeded that of the Protestant missionaries, although, as we shall demonstrate below, in some cases the famine can be seen to have completed processes begun by the mission. Major changes in demography, settlement patterns, and religious structure followed in its wake. Indeed, it may be argued that with the exception of the *aliyah* movement of the 1980s, no single episode in Beta Israel history had as decisive an impact on the character of their society.

Causes of the Great Famine

According to Pankhurst, the initial cause of the Great Famine in Ethiopia was the concurrence of three *natural* disasters: a major epidemic of cattle plague, drought, and an outbreak of locusts.[1] While there can be no doubt with regard to the essential accuracy of this assertion, it must be noted that already from 1885 onward clashes between the dervish soldiers of the Sudanese Mahdist state and the Christian rulers of Ethiopia had seriously disrupted the economy of Western Ethiopia and the Dambeya region in particular. "Fighting and concomitant troop movements and looting, impoverished the countryside, notably Tigray, Bagemder and Gojjam. The latter provinces were ravished by the armies of both Mahdists and Emperor Yohannes."[2] In June 1885 the Mahdists invaded and pillaged Chelga. The following year they despoiled large parts of Qwara. In 1887 victorious Christian soldiers "devastated the whole of Dembea [Dambeya]," and later the same year Dervish soldiers defeated King Takla Haymanot and "made all the province of Dembea a wilderness."[3]

The result of these invasions and fighting was that all the country where the Falashas lived was utterly devastated. There were no houses, no animals to plough with, no ploughs, no seed for sowing purposes, no instruments wherewith even to dig the ground, for those who returned from their flight; and therefore arose a terrible famine.[4]

To this day, Beta Israel informants strongly associate the onset of the famine with the Mahdist invasions. In the words of one informant,

In the time of Yohannes . . . most of the priests were trapped or more correctly were slaughtered and fled to abandoned places. Dervishes came—Sudanese— they killed them and burnt everything they found . . . there were two invasions in two years. No one engaged in farming. For four years there was a famine.[5]

They also closely connect the onset of the *Kifu-qen* with the death of the Emperor Yohannes IV in March 1889 and the chaos that ensued until the rise of Menelik II to power.[6]

Thus we see that by the time the cattle plague, which inaugurated a series of natural disasters, had reached the region around Gondar and Lake Tana where most of the Beta Israel resided, the economy of the area was already in ruins. The Mahdists' incursions into Ethiopian territory continued, moreover, throughout the period of the famine and for several years thereafter.[7] In most of the regions inhabited by the Beta Israel, therefore, chronic political and military instability preceded the famine, aggravated its impact, and delayed recovery.[8]

As for many people, the first of the *natural* disasters to strike the Beta

Israel was a devastating outbreak of rinderpest. Infected cattle imported through Massawa from India by the Italians were probably the initial carriers.[9] In a matter of months from mid-1888 onward the plague swept southward from Eritrea and Tigre into Bagemder, Lasta, Gojjam, and Shawa. By one estimate, 90 percent of the country's cattle died.[10] Gabra Sellassie, the chronicler of Emperor Menelik II, relates that in Bagemder province, which had been famous for its cattle, neither bulls nor cows remained.[11] Initially, people did not recognize the seriousness of their situation. "People refused to eat the meat of cattle which died [of plague], later they would have eaten their skins."[12] The loss of cattle not only deprived the population of their meat and milk, but also of their labor. Agriculture was crippled. "This terrible famine was caused in part by the prevailing cattle plague all over Abyssinia, and there was no possibility of agriculture of any kind being carried out."[13]

The period 1888–89 witnessed not only the rinderpest, but also a span of excessively hot and dry weather. From early January 1989 onward, moreover, locusts and caterpillars began to devour the meager remains of the already depleted harvest. Flad, for example, reported that caterpillars, "appeared in such masses that they destroyed the crops and what was left over was annihilated by swarms of locusts."[14]

One of the clearest indications of the impact of the famine in the agricultural sector was the sharp rise in prices for food and livestock. By early 1891 "two dishes of corn (barely enough to feed a family for a day) cost 1 dollar . . . , more that eight or nine times the normal cost, and as much as a weaver might earn in a week."[15] Wheat prices rose from 1 dollar to between 24 to 30 dollars. "A cow cost 80–90 dollars (formerly 3–4 dollars); an ox, 60 dollars (formerly 4–6 dollars)."[16]

As the famine spread, conditions continued to deteriorate and larger and larger groups of people became caught up in the web of suffering and misery. "For four years there was no bread. Nothing only [food] in the forests. Everyone was like animals—picking leaves from under a tree, picking and eating, picking and eating."[17] In a heartrending letter written in August 1892, the chief missionary agent Mikael Aragawi reported

Day by day the members of our household stand before me weeping and saying "Give us bread, give us clothing to cover our nakedness" but I have nothing to give them. Daily I go with them into the woods to seek fruits, herbs, and roots,[18] what we find we cook and eat, mostly without salt, because it is too dear. For two years we have not tasted meat or butter, far less eaten to satisfying. Many Abyssinians feed upon the carcasses of asses and hyenas; they eat to satiate their hunger and they die. Mothers have cooked and eaten their own offspring. Horrible things are done, about which I cannot write more.[19]

In their weakened condition, many famine victims lacked the strength to resist infections and epidemics of typhus, smallpox, cholera, dysentery, and influenza took many additional victims. Their widespread wanderings in search of food served, moreover, to spread the diseases from region to region.[20]

As the human population weakened and declined, wild beasts began to roam freely throughout and even dominate large parts of the country. In June 1891 Aragawi reported to Flad that "hyenas, leopards, and lions, are nearly the only inhabitants of the country between Ferka and Digel Ber."[21] In some regions people ceased to sleep in the open for fear of wild animals, however, even those in their huts were not always safe.[22] In some cases, people began to build their beds on raised platforms in the hope that this would protect them and their families.[23] Eventually no time nor place was safe. In August 1892 Aragawi wrote, "the wild beasts—lions, hyenas, leopards and others—have increased in such numbers that they attack in open daylight and devour them."[24]

Animal predators were not the only threat to the famine-weakened population. Others were killed by roving bands of *shifta* (bandits) who took advantage of the collapse of law and order in famine-ravaged areas.[25] For the Falasha Christians, who were dependent on their ability to travel both in their missionary work and in order to receive advice and support from their patrons abroad, the growing insecurity was an especially heavy burden. At times they were able to bribe their way past the *shifta,* but on at least one occasion their agent was murdered and his money (one hundred thirty-three pounds sterling), mules, books, and correspondence stolen.[26] Following this tragedy, Flad recommended suspending all payments to the native agents noting, "The country (at present) seems to be full of rebels and thieves."[27]

The Demographic Impact

As we have noted at several points, the lack of accurate population data is a characteristic problem for Ethiopian history in general and the history of the Beta Israel in particular. Nowhere is this clearer than in our attempts to evaluate the effects of the Great Famine. Given the dearth of reliable statistics, it is virtually impossible to offer more than rough estimates regarding the absolute number of people who perished, the percentage of the total population they represented, or how this affected population density. Most authorities tend to estimate the average rate of mortality in the different regions as between one- and two-thirds.[28] In Bagemder and the Lake Tana region, however, because of the previously mentioned political-military troubles, the figures may have been considerably higher. One observer estimated the mortality rate in these regions to be as high as 75 percent, and this does not appear unreasonable since nearby regions of the Sudan are known to have been particularly hard hit by the famine.[29] In fact, so great was the depopulation of the Bagemder region that even several decades later laborers had to be imported to make up for the shortage.[30]

The figures given by representatives of the London Society concerning the fate of their converts appear to largely confirm the more general figures above. In 1885, shortly before the onset of the Mahdists' incursions, the mission's *Annual Report* estimated the total number of "Falasha Christians" as eight hundred to nine hundred souls.[31] At least thirty families of proselytes (approximately one hundred twenty individuals) were martyred following the destruction of Gondar in 1887.[32] Even the missionary agents conceded, however, that the Mahdists' victims were greatly outnumbered by those of the famine.[33] During a four-month period from May to August 1890, one hundred seventy-seven members of the mission community perished.[34] In June 1891 Mikael Aragawi reported a further twenty-four deaths, and by the time Flad visited Ethiopia in 1894 the number of converted families known to have survived the famine stood at fifty-eight, probably less than three hundred individuals.[35]

Needless to say, no similar data exist with regard to the mortality rate among unconverted Beta Israel. On face value there seems to be no reason to assume that they were spared the enormous loses suffered by their Christian kinsmen and neighbors. Indeed, since they did not have access to either foreign money or assistance from Christian rulers in a manner comparable to the Falasha Christians, their losses may have been even greater.[36] It appears probable that between half and two-thirds of all Beta Israel died in the famine and a larger number cannot be precluded. Craftsmen may well have been even more vulnerable to famine than agricultural laborers. Guebre Sellasie writes, "During this period, not only weavers and potters who lived by manual labor, but also [agricultural] laborers disappeared."[37] Certainly, none of the travellers who visited Ethiopia in the first part of the twentieth century estimated their number at more than fifty thousand.[38] Visitors in the mid-nineteenth century had cited figures more than twice as large.[39] Even more significant, missionary reports tend to confirm a picture of a dramatic decline in the population. When Mikael Aragawi visited the Beta Israel village of Afrebida in Atschafer in the middle of 1899 he noted, "When many years ago I visited this place with Debtera Beroo, many Falashas lived in it; but now not one, and we are told they had all died during the famine."[40] Famine and the Mahdist were similarly said to have reduced the Beta Israel population of Seqelt from thousands to a few hundred.[41] Thus, even if it is assumed that some of those who had vanished either converted or migrated, the actual loss of life must have been horrific.

Although extremely widespread, the impact of the famine was not uniform in all regions. Naturally the population tended to migrate to less affected areas in the hope of finding food.[42] Among the Beta Israel of Dambeya, migrations initially appear to have been limited to short-term absences in an attempt to escape the Mahdists.[43] As the situation continued to worsen, however, more and more inhabitants deserted their villages for extended periods. Beta Israel from Qwara are reported to have fled as far north as the Shanqella country, while those from Dambeya scattered in a variety of directions, including Wollo and Lasta to the West, Woggara and Ṣallamt in the northeast, and Macha and Dara to the south.[44] Beta Israel from Tigre and elsewhere, like many other residents of that region, fled northward to the newly established Italian colony of Eritrea.[45] Many did not return to their original homes for four or even seven years. Some settled permanently in these new regions, and thus further augmented the already decentralized character of Beta Israel organization.

In one respect, at least, the impact of the famine on the Beta Israel must be evaluated in a manner slightly different from that of the rest of the population. While members of the dominant population could migrate and so long as they remained alive still be counted as members of society, the Beta Israel, as a distinct subgroup, could lose members through both death and defection. One direct consequence of the vast

population movements engendered by the famine was a dramatic breakdown in traditional village life including customs that separated Beta
Israel from Christians. Although as we have already discussed, the rules
of *attenkugn* were not always observed with absolute strictness, the Beta
Israel appear to have been scrupulous in not eating meat with outsiders.
In the desperate conditions of the famine such discipline was, of course,
impossible. Food was consumed whenever available, regardless of the
social setting.[46] "The Falashas were scattered in all parts and they, to
save their lives, lived with Christians, ate and drank with them."[47] Even
the Beta Israel's fierce devotion to the Sabbath was at times sacrificed in
the interest of survival.[48] In the wake of this breakdown of social bar-
riers, a significant number of Beta Israel converted to Christianity.[49] In
the main, such converts passed directly into the Ethiopian Orthodox
Church rather than the Protestant mission. Their active commitment to
Christianity appears, in many cases, to have been limited and shallow,
for, as Mikael Aragawi noted, "They know nothing of true conversion
and regeneration. These people just know that they have been baptized;
many of them are proud, puffed up, and light-minded."[50] In some cases,
converts eventually returned to the Beta Israel. After a short period of
isolation and purification, they were able to rejoin the community.[51]
Although no clear evidence exists on this point, the famine converts may
well represent the original nucleus of the *Maryam Wodet* (Lovers of
Mary), a large body of Falasha Christians who many years after their
conversion still retained a distinctive identity and religious customs.[52]

The famine also appears to have, at least on a limited scale, worked
to the benefit of the Protestant mission as well. Some Beta Israel are
reported to have viewed the famine as a divine chastisement and accordingly sought immediate baptism from the missionaries.[53] The total number of these "famine converts" may not have been large in comparision
to the number who died, but converts too were lost to the Beta Israel
and thus must be considered when evaluating the famine's toll.

For the Falasha Christians the Mahdist invasions and subsequent
famine also combined to produce far-reaching changes in population
distribution. Prior to 1885 the mission converts were concentrated in
and around a relatively small number of mission stations.[54] Virtually all
were located in the region around Lake Tana. The greatest number were
at the chief mission station of Jenda in Dambeya. As conditions in this
area declined, the proselytes scattered. The previous large concentrations

of converts were frequently replaced by single families or individuals. Many were "lost" in the countryside and only rediscovered many years later.[55]

Changes in Leadership Patterns

More important, perhaps, than the absolute loss of members to the Beta Israel during the famine is the manner in which events in the years 1888–92 supplemented existing trends and in particular complemented the impact of the missions. One aspect deserving of special attention is the famine's impact on the leadership structure of both the mission converts and the unconverted Beta Israel. In early 1890, just after the onslaught of the famine, a dozen figures served in leadership roles for the London Society's mission. Most were assigned to specific regions of mission stations as follows:

Jenda: Mikael Aragawi, E. Sanbatu, Debtera Hiob Negusie, and Debtera Beroo
Alefa: Debtera Liena and Debtera Alamy
Gorgora: Debtera Fanta and Debtera Mehrat
Seqelt: Debtera Gebra Haiwat, Debtera Wondem Huning Negusie, and Debtera Goshu Belata

In addition, Fanta Dawit served as the mission's messenger and was responsible for contact with Europe through Massawa.[56] Two years later only seven of the mission's twelve agents survived. Although Debtera Beroo had died a natural death, Debtera Liena and Debtera Fanta had both starved to death. The latter's wife and five children perished as well.[57] Debtera Alamy was devoured by a leopard, and in the summer of 1892 Fanta Dawit was murdered by bandits.[58] Thus the famine transformed not only the number and geographic distribution of the "Falasha Christians" but also their roster of leaders.

Among the nonmission majority of the Beta Israel the impact of the famine on patterns of leadership was even more substantial. In the previous chapter we saw how the position of the Beta Israel monks was dealt a serious blow by the Protestant missionaries' attempts to undermine the Beta Israel's confidence in their religious leaders. For the already weakened Beta Israel monks, the *Kifu-qen* could not have come at a worse time. The unprecedented challenge to their spiritual dominance was suddenly followed by an overwhelming threat to their physical survival. As a relatively old and economically dependent segment of the population, they probably suffered disproportionately from the famine. The monks of Walqayit appear to have been especially hard hit—none survived. Other regions, while not as totally devastated, also experienced sharp losses among the monastic clergy.[59] Hohuara, the great center of Beta Israel monasticism, had about two hundred monks in the early 1860s.[60] By 1896 it had been superseded by the far more modest Amba Qwalit.[61]

Even more telling for the decline of monasticism than the immediate loss of life during the *Kifu-qen* was the dramatic change that occurred in the Beta Israel's attitude toward the institution. If prior to the famine the celibate monk was viewed as the most vivid symbol of piety and sanctity among the Beta Israel, in its wake married clergy came to the fore. In Tigre province no new monks were consecrated after the famine.[62] In other regions the number of new monks dwindled to a trickle.[63] Even more remarkably, a small number of monks and novices, perhaps in response to the desperate demographic condition of the community, left their monasteries to raise families. Abba Baruk, a confidant of Faitlovitch, and father of a future high priest of the Gondar region, had lived as a monk for several decades before a dream-vision convinced him to return to society. He married and had eight children.[64] Abba Yeshaq, a former high priest of the Tigre region, reported that his father was a fifteen-year-old novice in a Walqayit monastery at the time of the *Kifu-qen*. Following the famine, he forsook the monastic life to marry.[65]

As these and other examples indicate, the famine of 1888–92 marked the death knell for Beta Israel monasticism. Although some monks survived and a few new monks were consecrated as late as the early twentieth century, the combination of missionary pressure, physical devastation, and a demographic crises left the institution mortally wounded. In the aftermath of the enormous loss of life, the Beta Israel could no longer afford the "luxury" of a large class of celibate clerics. The ideal of the monastic holy man, while never totally superseded, gave way to the urgent need to maintain family life and perpetuate society.[66] By the middle of the twentieth century, it had all but disappeared.[67]

The famine appears to have had a similar, albeit less drastic, repercussions for another distinctive Beta Israel religious institution—sacrifice. Here too, the missionaries' attacks on an important element in the Beta

Israel religious system were followed by more practical difficulties as a result of the famine. For more than four years there were simply no animals available to be sacrificed. Nor did social and environmental conditions permit more than the most minimal of ritual performances. Thus, for the second time in less than two decades, sacrifices came to a halt.[68] As in the case of monasticism, the combination of religious criticism and practical difficulties appear to have produced permanent changes in sacrificial practice.

In particular, the occasions on which sacrifices were performed appear to have diminished considerably. Already by the first half of the nineteenth century economic decline had led to the elimination of some sacrifices.[69] The missionary critique and particularly the claim (confirmed by Halévy) that other Jewish groups no longer performed sacrifices may have accelerated this process. The ban on sacrifice from 1862 to 1868 would certainly have fostered the development of alternative patterns of worship. The *Kifu-qen* probably further enhanced this process. One need merely compare the long list of sacrificial occasions prepared by Flad to the far shorter list of Faitlovitch in the early twentieth century to gauge the cumulative impact of these events.[70]

The Kifu-qen *in Context*

Having briefly considered the causes of the *kifu-qen* and its effect on the Beta Israel, we shall conclude by attempting to place it in its wider context. What is the importance of the period 1888–92 for our general understanding of Beta Israel history?

First, while the Great Famine was, as we have noted, one of the most important events in Ethiopian history and did not select its victims on the basis of religion or ethnicity, its impact on the Beta Israel differed from that of many of their neighbors for several reasons. Because of their economic role as tenant farmers and artisans, they appear to have been particularly vulnerable to the ravages of the famine, and their loss of life may have been greater than in the population at large. Moreover, their social-economic position as a group dependent upon but separate from the dominant local population meant that they were liable to lose members through both death and defection. The latter was a problem of particular acuteness during the famine, when the traditional social order including communal sanctions against intercourse with outsiders, Sabbath observance, and taboos on sharing food with non-Beta Israel broke down. Thus, the Beta Israel's specific experience during the *Kifu-qen* can only be appreciated in the context of the particular niche they had come to fill in Ethiopian society and history.

Second, when viewed from the perspective of the great famine, their modern history and especially the impact of Protestant missionary activity can be seen with far greater clarity. As we have seen in the previous chapter, in its early years the primary impact of the London Society lay not in the number of conversions it achieved, but rather in the processes of modernization, education, and dissension it set in motion. In particular, it created a vulnerability among the Beta Israel which at the time of the Great Famine resulted in a substantial movement to the Ethiopian Church, a decline in the importance and prestige of monasticism, and a reduction in the frequency of sacrifical ritual. Thus, processes set in motion by the mission can be seen to have accelerated and come to fruition in the wake of the famine.

Third, an understanding of the period of the Great Famine is also crucial to the proper evalution of the Beta Israel's initial responses to their encounter with World Jewry. By the time Jacque (Ya'acov) Faitlovitch reached the Beta Israel in 1904, they were a weakened and wounded people. Their decline during the thirty-six years between Joseph Halévy's visit and that of his student had been dramatic and almost total. This decline can, in almost every case, be attributed either directly to the *Kifu-qen* or to the combination of the mission and the famine. Not only had their numbers dropped dramatically as a result of both death and conversion, but their religious life was in a clear state of transition. Monasticism and sacrificial rites, two of the religious features that most clearly distinquished them from World Jewry, were critically weakened. Under these circumstances, Faitlovitch's attempt to "normalize" Beta Israel religion and create a new modernized elite can be seen in a new light.[71] His relative success with his criticisms of monasticism and sacrifice appears far more related to the weakened condition in which he found these institutions than to any innate receptivity to his message on the part of the Beta Israel. Purity laws related to childbirth and menstruation, for example, which he also sought to eliminate, were staunchly defended and survived among most women until their arrival in Israel.[72] In a similar fashion, the successes and failures of Faitlovitch's attempts to replace or at lease supplement the traditional religious hierarchy with a new Western-educated leadership can only be properly evaluated against the background of the transition from a monastic to a priestly model.

Finally, the entire story of the Beta Israel encounter with World Jewry and the extreme imbalance that has characterized these relations must be attributed not only to Western ethnocentrism, but to the extreme decline in the status of the Beta Israel within Ethiopia from the middle of the eighteenth century onward. The "discovery" of the Beta Israel by World Jewry in the nineteenth century brought them into contact with neither an autonomous warrior people nor a valued class of artisans, but with a despised semi-caste group. Meaningful contact in terms of mutual visits and educational programs only began after famine had reduced the Beta Israel to what may well have been the lowest point in their history in terms of numbers, economic resources, and cultural resilience. Small wonder that the encounter came to be envisioned as not an exchange but as a form of charity, with all real benefits flowing in the direction of the backward and empoverished Ethiopian kinsmen.

Conclusions:
Before Faitlovitch

The arrival in Ethiopia of Jacques Faitlovitch in 1904 marks a turning point in the history of the Beta Israel. Faitlovitch, who dedicated his life to the cause of Ethiopian Jewry, was responsible more than any other single person for their entry into Jewish history and consciousness. Indeed, the processes he set in motion beginning with his first visit to Ethiopia can be said only now, more than eighty-five years later, to be reaching their logical conclusion with the *aliyah* of the Beta Israel community to Israel. The common thread that ran through all aspects of Faitlovitch's multi-pronged program on behalf of Ethiopian Jewry was the attempt to bring them closer to other Jewish communities. In part he sought to do this by reforming their Judaism, in part by raising their standards of education. He also sought to create a Western-educated elite capable of interacting on a more or less equal basis with their foreign Jewish counterparts. In no small part, however, he also tried to project an image of Ethiopian Jewry that would be both familiar and attractive to European and American Jewish audiences. Thus he portrayed the Beta Israel as a foreign Jewish element grossly out of place in their strange African environment. In his report from his first visit to Ethiopia to Baron Edmond de Rothschild he wrote:

When I was in Africa among the Falasha, surrounded by tribes of semi-savages, I felt an inexpressable joy in recording their energy, their intelligence, the lofty moral qualities which distinguish them. We can be proud to count among our own these noble children of Ethiopia, who, with a no less legitimate pride, boast of tracing [themselves] back to our origins, worshipping our God, practicing our cult. The eagerness with which they seek to regenerate themselves, to leave this African barbarism which envelops them and suffocates them, proves that the instinctive character of [their] race persists in them. ... How different in that from the other Abyssinians, so contemptuous towards the education, progress and civilization of the Europeans to which they naively believe themselves to be superior![1]

Faitlovitch was certainly not the first author to carefully shape the image of the Beta Israel. Medieval Hebrew authors, European travellers (most notably James Bruce), and Joseph Halévy had preceded him in this respect. He was, however, undoubtedly the most persistent and influential shaper of their image. In his lifetime and particular on the popular level, no other aspect of Faitlovitch's activities appear to have been as successful. The mythic image of the Falasha as a pre-Talmudic "Lost Tribe" that migrated to Ethiopia was accepted with remarkable readiness throughout the world and has dominated discussions of their religion, literature, culture, and history.

In this book, I have sought to correct this picture and to de-mythologize Beta Israel history; to reconstruct it from the sources rather than impose it upon them. This effort has produced an account of their past radically at odds with that commonly accepted. It has, moreover, raised important questions concerning which categories are most useful for understandng their history. It is to a summary of this history and the issue of these categories that I turn in this final chapter.

Judaism and Christianity in Ethiopia: A Unique Symbiosis

Until quite recently, virtually all attempts to explain the origins of the Beta Israel have had a number of characteristics in common. First, they have been essentially diffusionist in character. In other words, the presence in Ethiopia of a seemingly recognizable Jewish ethnic group has been explained primarily as the result of contact with members of one or another ancient Jewish community. Second (and here the voices of the scholars prior to the 1970s would appear to have been even closer to unanimity), the history of Judaism and Christianity in Ethiopia has been portrayed as the recapitulation in miniature of the history of these two faiths in the world at large: a small early Jewish population is said to have been superseded by a later Christian community with only a tiny remnant of Jews surviving.[2] The Beta Israel, it has been claimed, are essentially a fossilized survival from pre-Christian Aksum. In fact, as I have discussed above, the true story of the two faiths in Ethiopia is considerably different and far more complex. While there is clear evidence of Jewish influences in Ethiopia during the first centuries of the Common Era, these were not so much supplanted by Christianity as absorbed into it. Moreover, while there was almost certainly a portion of the population that remained more faithful to the earlier Judaized form of religion, it would be a tremendous simplification to identify the Beta Israel as their descendants or to depict Beta Israel religion as merely an archaic reminder of this early period. Assimilation, intermarriage, acculturation, and major religious upheavals all played a part in the emergence of the Beta Israel. Moreover, their "Judaism," far from being an ancient precursor of Ethiopian Christianity, developed relatively late and drew much of its inspiration from the Orthodox Church.

From a cultural perspective there appears to be little question that the Beta Israel must be understood as the product of processes that took place in Ethiopia between the fourteenth and sixteenth century. During this period a number of inchoate groups of *ayhud* living in the regions around Lake Tana coalesced into the people known as the Falasha. Their emergence as a distinctive people was the result of a variety of political, economic, and ideological factors. The rise of the so-called Solomonic dynasty in the last decades of the thirteenth century and its subsequent expansion throughout the Ethiopian highlands placed the *ayhud* of the Lake Tana region (as well as many other hitherto autonomous groups) under unprecedented pressure. From the early fourteenth century onward, a gradual process of disenfranchisement took place that eventually deprived many of the Beta Israel of their rights to own inheritable land (*rist*). Denied this crucial economic asset, they pursued a number of strategies to retain their economic viability. While some doubtless identified themselves with the dominant Christian landholders, others either departed for peripheral areas where competition for land was reduced or accepted the reduced status of tenant farmers. In both the latter cases, they probably began to supplement their income by pursuing crafts such as smithing, pottery, and weaving. Thus the vague religious and regional bases for their identification were supplemented and further defined by an occupational-economic distinction.

At the same time, revolutionary changes in their religious ideology, practice, and institutions resulted in the development of a far more clearly defined and articulated religious system. Under the influence of Ethiopian Christian monks such as Abba Sabra and Ṣagga Amlak the Beta Israel adopted the institution of monasticism. Monastic clergy emerged as the paramount religious authorities responsible for the definition and transmission of a distinctive religious tradition. Through their mediation the Beta Israel acquired a sophisticated liturgy, organized around new "national" holidays, and gained access to an important body of literature celebrating the exploits of Biblical heroes and the importance of certain central festivals (particularly the Sabbath) and religious principles. Although their religious system and communal identity continued to change and adapt throughout their history, it is to this crucial period in the fourteenth and fifteenth century (and not to an alleged ancient link with an external Jewish group) that we must look if we are to begin to solve the riddle of the identity and origins of the Beta Israel.

Closely related to the erroneous attempt to depict the Beta Israel as a Jewish remnant survivors from the period before Christianity is the equally misguided characterization of their religion as an archaic form of Judaism. The Beta Israel, it is widely claimed, have preserved not merely an early stage in the religious life of humankind, but, far more important, a glimpse of early Jewish life. The Beta Israel, we are told, have retained a *pre*-Talmudic form of Judaism, unique in its authenticity. Thus scholars and popular authors alike have frequently been misled and have assumed the avowedly biblical-Jewish *character* of many elements in the Beta Israel religious system to be proof of a direct link to a primitive form of Judaism.[3]

As we have seen above, both the Beta Israel's oral traditions and the testimony of their literature offer strong evidence that crucial elements in their religious system developed no earlier than the fourteenth or fifteenth century. Beta Israel accounts of their history trace virtually all major elements of their religion to the influence of the Abba Sabra and Ṣagga Amlak. Monasticism, purity laws, holidays, literary works, and the prayer liturgy are just a few of the features these culture heroes are credited with. While doubtless a somewhat idealized and condensed view of their role, this view finds support in other sources. With regard to the Beta Israel's *corpus* of sacred books, the majority can be shown to have reached them through the Ethiopian Church and to have been translated into Ge'ez from Arabic. Since translation from Arabic only became common in Ethiopia from the fourteenth century onward, none of these books can have reached the Beta Israel earlier than this period. At least one, *Nagara Muse,* was translated as late as the eighteenth century. Moreover, given the liturgical use of a number of these books including the *Arde'et, Mota Muse,* and the *gadlat* of Abraham, Isaac, and Jacob, several important rituals can be demonstrated to have acquired their current form only after these books came into the possession of the Beta Israel. Furthermore it must be remembered that even after the crystallization of a relatively clearly articulated set of beliefs and rituals changes continued to occur. Political, economic, and social factors continued to shape and transform the religion of the Beta Israel.

In part, at least, the tendency to depict Beta Israel religion in a static and ahistorical fashion may be connected with the general impression that the religions of so-called "primitive" peoples reflect some earlier stage in human development. More significant, in the specific case of the Beta Israel, however, appears to be the widespread inclination in Jewish studies to emphasize the theme of continuity over that of change and development.[4] As we shall discuss below, this is hardly the only case in which inappropriate conventions and categories hinder rather than help our understanding of the Beta Israel.

Judaism and Christianity: A Tyranny of Categories

In fact, our attempts to correct this distorted image of the Beta Israel as simply the survivors of a pre-Christian Aksumite Jewish community is illustrative of one of the major themes of this book. However pleasing it may be, both aesthetically and politically, to employ the categories *Jewish* and *Christian* in opposition, this usage of these terms has little if any basis in Ethiopian reality. Indeed, one of the central points that emerges from this study is that the application of this essentially external model does little to clarify and much to obfuscate the true nature of Beta Israel history. Thus, for example, while it is certainly possible to analyze the Beta Israel's religious system in terms of its links with "other" forms of Judaism and to consider the many elements it shares with Ethiopian

Christianity as foreign accretions, this form of analysis reflects neither the weight of the various elements nor the pattern of their historical development. In the context of Ethiopian religions, moreover, it makes little sense to ask whether a particular element or feature is Jewish *or* Christian. On the whole the two religious systems are remarkably similar. Rather than thinking in terms of a sharp dichotomy, we must instead consider a continuum

Hebraic ——————————————— Christian

or to the extent that common animistic beliefs are considered a triangle.

Animistic

Qemant

Beta Israel   Ethiopian Church

Hebraic ——————————————— Christian

While the religious system of the Beta Israel was certainly more to the Hebraic side, that of the Ethiopian Church more to the Christian, and that of the "Pagan-Hebraic" Qemant more to the Animistic,[5] few hard and clear distinctions divided their religious structures. In particular, among the common folk, as opposed to elite clerical groups, differences could at times be remarkably small. Overall, moreover, the religious system of the Beta Israel had far more in common with that of Ethiopian Christians than it did with that of any outside Jewish group.

In much the same manner, our study offers little support for any attempt to portray the Beta Israel's longstanding relationship and history of contact with Christian Ethiopians as exclusively confrontational in character. Several cases can be documented from the fourteenth through sixteenth century of cooperation between the Beta Israel and renegade political and religious groups. Somewhat later, in the Gondar period, Beta Israel soldiers fought alongside Christian troops, and their craftsmen worked with and even supervised artisans from other communities. Repeated decrees by the Emperor Yohannes I were only partially successful in removing them from parts of the city inhabited by Christians and Muslims. Moreover, even in later years when the "peace and welfare" enjoyed by the Beta Israel in the Gondar period had given way to the decline and stigmatization of the Era of the Princes, the picture was not completely negative. Christian clergy still travelled to visit the learned Beta Israel monk Abba Yeshaq in order to deepen their knowledge of biblical interpretation. All these examples, and many others that have appeared above, caution against a paradigm that depicts Beta Israel history exclusively in terms of Jews versus Christians.

To be sure, the overall picture was not a positive one. Numerous instances exist in which the Beta Israel fought against the Ethiopian emperors and their representatives. Furthermore, their gradual disenfranchisement and relegation to the subservient role of tenant farmers and despised craftsmen are well documented. No one could claim that the Beta Israel's lot was an easy one or that their position in Ethiopia society reflected particular respect or appreciation. Nevertheless, it remains highly questionable if the history of their relations with Christian Ethiopians can be best understood by depicting the hardships they faced as specifically connected to their status *as Jews*. Almost without exception the recurrent clashes between imperial troops and members of the Beta Israel can be demonstrated to be part of a larger pattern of center-periphery relations. Thus, their confrontations with Amda Seyon, Yeshaq, Sarsa Dengel, and Susenyos can all be most accurately interpreted in the context of wider imperial interests and concerns. In particular, the monumental campaigns of the latter two rulers can be undeniably shown to be connected to a growing imperial presence in the Lake Tana region, the general attempt to subdue the local Agaw peoples, and the repeated involvement of the Beta Israel ruler Gedewon in the succession struggles of the time. As a rule, the emperors of Ethiopia valued political loyalty far more than religious conformity and rarely went to battle on issues of faith alone. During most of Susenyos's struggles against the Beta Israel of Semien, their co-religionists in Wagara and Dambeya appear to have been unmolested and to have even benefitted from royal patronage. Only with the final defeat of Gedewon does the Emperor appear to have advocated action against all Beta Israel, and even here some distinctions were retained.

Nor do the anti-imperial forces appear to have used religious affiliation as their primary basis for recruitment and organization. In most periods, the Beta Israel were joined in battle by other (mainly Christian) disaffected parts of the Ethiopian population. Shared interests, rather than a shared creed, seem to have been the unifying factor in the majority of cases. Disaffected monks, embittered local rulers, and pretenders to the imperial throne all formed alliances with the Beta Israel against the Christian emperors. Moreover, it must also be remembered that at the same time as some Christians were willing to join the Beta Israel in their struggles, some Jews were not. The fourteenth century Emperor Yeshaq was aided in his battles against the ruler of Semien and Dambeya by his nephew and other Beta Israel. In the seventeenth century the Beta Israel of Dambeya appear to have continued to serve the Emperor Susenyos as builders and craftsmen throughout his campaigns against their brethren in Semien. We therefore see that any attempt to depict the Beta Israel's wars against the forces of the Emperor as primarily religious struggles, as simply a case of Jews versus Christians, is inaccurate, misleading, and receives little support from the sources.

The Missionary Challenge

Even the attempt to evaluate the impact of Protestant missionaries on the Beta Israel during the second half of the nineteenth century, a theme that at first glance would appear particularly ripe for discussion on the basis of a Jewish/Christian dichotomy, does not appear to appreciably benefit from such an approach. If we analyze the effect of the mission solely with regard to the number of Jews who accepted Christianity, its influence appears minimal at best. The conversion of a few hundred Beta Israel over of period of close to fifty years can hardly be said to have produced a major transformation of their society. As we have seen, however, the significance of the mission lies not in the relatively small group who moved from one community to another, but rather in the changes undergone by those who remained within the framework of their traditional society. The religious system of the Beta Israel, particularly their monastic leadership, sacrificial ritual, and purity practices, were subjected to an unprecedented degree of criticism. This criticism focused, moreover, not on the non-Christian character of these practices but on their foreignness to "normative" Judaism and in some cases biblical tradition. Thus, the very core of the Beta Israel's Hebraic self-image came under attack. At the same time, the crucial social role of families, elders, and clergy was strained as never before when young people and peripheral clergy such as the *debtera* were offered alternative avenues of achievement. Most important, perhaps, the missionaries were the first group to treat the Beta Israel as "Jews" in the universal sense. Ironically, their proselytization by the London Society for Promoting Christianity amongst the Jews marks the first time the Beta Israel shared an experience with Jewish communities elsewhere. Certainly, it was the mission's activities more than anything else in the period before Faitlovitch that created their awareness of the existence of a more universal form of Jewish identity and brought them to the attention of World Jewry.

Although not strictly within the time frame of this book, it must also be noted that the later activities of such counter-missionaries as Jacques Faitlovitch and his supporters are yet another subject frequently distorted by an analysis based on Jews versus Christians. While those Beta Israel who accepted Christianity, whether that of the Ethiopian Church or the Protestants, are clearly depicted as converts, the rest are usually said to have remained within their traditional community, even in those cases where they affiliated themselves with external forms of Judaism. In fact, the change in world view required to move from the Beta Israel religious system to that of Orthodox Christianity was, as we have noted, far less than that required by Rabbinic Judaism. It should, moreover, be noted that Faitlovitch's message was in many ways similar to that of his Protestant opponents: Abandon your monasticism, sacrifices, and purity rituals and accept the religion that is the true heir to the biblical faith you practice. At the least, to describe his students and their heirs as having remained within a single religious tradition risks underestimating the distance they were required to travel. Conversion to either rabbinic Judaism or Protestant Christianity required the Beta Israel to leave the Ethiopian milieu of Hebraic-Christian-Animistic beliefs and enter the world of European religious discourse.

The Great Famine

The imposition of the categories "Jewish" and Christian on Beta Israel history results not only in the misinterpretation of many episodes, but also in the total neglect of others. Nowhere is this clearer than in the case of the great famine of 1888–92, *Kifu-qen*. With the exception of the *aliyah* movement of the last two decades of the twentieth century, it is difficult to think of any event in Beta Israel history that had so decisive an impact in so short a time. Even the wars against Sarṣa Dengel and Susenyos extended over a much longer period and were far more varied in their effect on different groups of the population. The Great Famine produced migrations, conversions, and massive loss of life. It disrupted the social structure of the Beta Israel on the crucial level of both family and village, and produced far-reaching changes in their religious practices and institutions. In many ways it marked the culmination of processes first set in motion, but with only limited success, by the Protestant missionaries. Not surprisingly, therefore, it is vividly remembered in their oral accounts of their history. Yet, previous histories of the Beta Israel give it at best only a passing mention. (The famine of 1634–35 that devastated Wagara, Dambeya, and Semien has been similarly neglected.) While this striking imbalance may be due to a number of factors including a lack of familiarity with the relevant published sources, the fact that the Great Famine does not lend itself to analysis on the level of Jew/Christian would certainly appear to have contributed to its neglect.

From Beta Israel to Ethiopian Jews

Ultimately, however, my dissatisfaction with the use of "Jewish" and "Christian" as the principle analytical categories for reconstructing Beta Israel history goes deeper than the primarily utilitarian objections raised above. If convincing proof could be mustered that, whatever their apparent weaknesses, these terms represented the primary basis for the Beta Israel's own classification of their world, this would by itself constitute a strong justification for their usage. At the least, there would be an obvious need to discuss the contrast between their categories and those found in this book. Serious doubts must be raised, however, as to whether prior to the twentieth century "Jewish" and "Christian" were crucial categories to the Beta Israel themselves. Beyond the evidence already cited above which indicates that the Beta Israel did not organize politically on the basis of religion alone, nor automatically exclude relatives who had accepted Christianity, a number of other indicators should be borne in mind. Perhaps most important, there is little evidence to support the view that prior to their contact with external Jewish groups the Beta Israel either viewed themselves as "Jews"—that is, representatives of post-biblical Judaism—or referred to themselves as such. Almost all recorded versions of their origins that can be traced to the Beta Israel themselves identify their ancestors with Israelites from the Biblical period. It is only in Christian texts from the period after the arrival of the Portuguese that attempts are made to draw connections between them and Jewish groups from the Second Temple period. Moreover, as we have discussed in some detail in Chapter 3, it is highly unlikely that the Beta Israel at any time in their pre-modern history referred to themselves as *ayhud* (Jews), since this was almost exclusively a derogatory term. Indeed, there appears to be every reason to believe that well into the twentieth century, the Beta Israel, in common with many peoples of the Ethiopian highlands, took many of their cultural models and categories from the Ethiopian national epic, *Kebra Nagast*, including the dichotomy between "Bad Jews" and "Good Israelites." Certainly, when Joseph Halévy encountered his first Beta Israel in the mid-nineteenth century they did not respond to his identificaton of them as "Jews," but classified themselves as Israelites.

The crowd that surrounded me prevented me from entering into conversation with them, but I managed to ask them in a whisper, "Are you Jews?" They did not seem to understand my question, which I repeated under another form— "Are you Israelites?" A movement of assent, mingled with astonishment, proved to me that I had struck the right chord.[6]

Since the time of Halévy and particularly in the period since World War II, the Beta Israel's image of themselves has changed dramatically. In contrast to earlier times, today they prefer to largely disassociate themselves from their Ethiopian past and environment. Thus, they no longer connect their presence in Ethiopia with the national epic of Solomon and Sheba, but trace themselves to Egyptian Jewry or the lost tribe of Dan. Similarly, they prefer to be called Ethiopian Jews rather than either Falasha or Beta Israel. Increasingly, their accounts of their past and their religious traditions are shaped to stress the similarities, in some cases even the total identity, with those of other Jewish communities. Doubtless, all these changes are in some way necessary both for the Beta Israel to feel at home and for their acceptance in their new environment. They should, however, be appreciated for what they are—fascinating examples of a people's redefinition of its identity. This new identity should not, however, be taken as the inevitable starting point for an understanding of Beta Israel culture and history in earlier periods. For, as I have tried to show in this book, long before their encounter with World Jewry, the Beta Israel worshipped and created, struggled and fought, all within the context of the wider stream of Ethiopian history. As the focus of their history and the center of their communal life now move to a new context, it is to be hoped that the fascinating story of their emergence and survival in Ethiopia will continue to be cherished in all its richness and complexity.

Notes

Introduction

1. "An Outline of Falasha History," *Proceedings of the Third International Conference of Ethiopian Studies, Addis Ababa 1966* (Addis Ababa: Institute of Ethiopian Studies and Haile Sellassie I University, 1969), vol. 1: 99–112; "Toward a History of the Falasha," in David C. McCall, Norman R. Bennett, and John Butler, eds., *Eastern African History, Boston University Papers on Africa 3* (New York: Praeger, 1969), 107–132.
2. (London: George Allen & Unwin, 1982). Other recent works that include problematic reconstructions of Beta Israel history are Simon D. Messing, *The Story of the Falashas: "Black Jews" of Ethiopia* (Brooklyn: Balson, 1982); Louis Rappoport, *The Lost Jews: Last of the Ethiopian Falashas* (New York: Stein and Day, 1980). The last of these authors has improved his survey of Beta Israel history considerably in *Redemption Song: The Story of Operation Moses* (New York: Harcourt Brace Jovanovich, 1986).
3. I have discussed Kessler's book as well as several other recent works on the Beta Israel in two review articles: "On the Importance of Ethiopian Studies for an Understanding of the Falasha," *Pe'amim* 21 (1984):141–146 (Heb.); "The Two Zions and the Exodus from Ethiopia," *Studies in Contemporary Jewry* 7 (Oxford: Oxford University Press, 1991), 298–305.
4. Kay Kaufman Shelemay, "The Liturgical Music of the Falasha," Ph.D. dissertation, University of Michigan, 1977, published in greatly revised form as *Music, Ritual, and Falasha History* (East Lansing: Michigan State University, 1986, 1989); James Arthur Quirin, "The Beta Israel (Felasha) in Ethi-

opian History: Caste Formation and Culture Change, 1270–1868," Ph.D. dissertation, University of Minnesota, 1977.

5. See my detailed discussion and critique of this book, " 'Falasha' Religion: Ancient Judaism or Evolving Ethiopian Tradition?" *Jewish Quarterly Review* 79, 1 (July 1988): 49–65.

6. For bibliographic details concerning some of the major works by authors listed in both categories see the end of this book. For a fairly comprehensive survey of literature on the Beta Israel see Steven Kaplan and Shoshana Ben-Dor, *Ethiopian Jewry: An Annotated Bibliography* (Jerusalem: Ben Zvi Institute, 1988).

7. Comparisons both subtle and overt to the Nazi era have also been produced. Thus both the Emperor Zar'a Ya'eqob and a recent governor of the Gondar region have been compared to Hitler, deaths in the Sudan to the Holocaust, etc. Messing, *Falashas,* 25, compares the Ethiopian concept of *buda* (the evil eye) to Nazi prejudices.

8. Salo Wittmayer Baron, "Newer Emphases in Jewish History," in *History and Jewish Historians* (Philadelphia: Jewish Publication Society, 1964), 74. "Because of their minority status, the fate of the dispersed Jewish communities depended to an even larger extent on the propelling historic forces within the neighboring civilizations or even on some developments within each region or locality."

9. I have attempted for the sake of clarity to keep diacritical marks to a minimum. Thus "Beta Israel" not Bēta 'Esra'ēl; "Falasha" not Falāshā and so on.

10. Cf. the comments in Edward Ullendorff, "The *Confessio Fidei* of King Claudius of Ethiopia," *Journal of Semitic Studies* 32, 1 (Spring 1987): 170, n. 1.

11. Kaplan, " 'Falasha' Religion," 51, n. 8; "Two Zions," 305, n. 8.

1. Ethiopian Jews: Obscure Beginnings

1. No less than three books have recently been published in Hebrew on the subject of Jewish attitudes to Ethiopian Jewry: Michael Corinaldi, *Ethiopian Jewry: Identity and Tradition* (Jerusalem: Rubin Mass, 1988); David Chelouche, *The Exiled of Israel Will Be Gathered in* (Jerusalem: Ahva, 1988); Menachem Waldman, *Beyond the Rivers of Ethiopia: The Jews of Ethiopia and the Jewish People* (Tel Aviv: Ministry of Defence, 1989). For a discussion of one aspect of this controversy see my article, "The Ethiopians and the Rabbinate: Law, Politics, and Ritual," *Social Science Information* 28, 3 (September, 1988): 357–370.

2. One cannot, for example, even begin to answer the common question "Are the Beta Israel Jewish?" without first defining how the term Jewish is being used. Certainly, the Beta Israel's status as Jews under Israeli law has been recognized for over a decade. Similarly, the fact that important rabbinical authorities have affirmed their Jewishness results in a generally positive

answer from the perspective of *halacha* (Jewish religious law). From an historical perspective, the Beta Israel's identification of themselves as part of World Jewry can be clearly dated to their earliest contacts with other Jews in the mid-nineteenth century. These forms of Jewish identity notwithstanding, serious doubts still remain as to whether the Beta Israel are descendants of Jews who migrated to Ethiopia.

3. This apparent commonplace has unfortunately not been recognized by many writers on the subject. As we shall discuss below, all too often, attempts have been made to demonstrate the presence of Jews in "Ethiopia" (Greek) or "Kush" (Hebrew), rather than Aksum. Since both of these terms are commonly applied to vast unspecified areas south of Egypt and around the Nile basin, the results, even were they convincing, are not necessarily of relevance to the problem of the origins of the Beta Israel.

4. Among the most important sources on Aksum that consider these and other issues are Yuri Kobishchanov, *Axum* (University Park: Penn State University Press, 1979), and see particularly Joseph W. Michels, "Axumite Archaeology: An Introductory Essay": 1–34; Joseph W. Michels, "Regional Political Organization in the Axum-Yeha Area during the Pre-Axumite and Axumite Eras," paper presented at the 10th International Conference on Ethiopian Studies, Paris, France, August 1988; Karl W. Butzer, "Rise and Fall of Axum Ethiopia: A Geo-Archaeological Interpretation," *American Antiquity* 46, 3 (1981): 471–495; Francis Anfray, "The Civilization of Aksum from the First to the Seventh Century," in *General History of Africa*, vol. 2, ed. G. Mokhtar (London, Berkeley, Paris, Heinemann, University of California, UNESCO, 1981), 362–380; H. de Contenson, "Pre-Aksumite Culture," *General History*: 343–361.

5. "The Agaw are of crucial importance because they are the very basis on which the whole edifice of Aksumite civilization was constructed." Taddesse Tamrat, "Processes of Ethnic Interaction and Integration in Ethiopian History: The Case of the Agaw," *Journal of African History* 29 (1988): 6–7.

6. Graham Connah, *African Civilizations* (Cambridge: Cambridge University Press, 1987), 75.

7. Cf. Carlo Conti Rossini, *Storia d'Etiopia* (Bergamo: Instituto Italiano d'Arti Grafiche, 1928), 106: "La civilta etiopica non e se non un riflesso della civilta sud-arabica." Edward Ullendorff, *The Ethiopians* (London: Oxford University Press, 1973, 3rd ed.), 49, "Numerically the South Arabian leaven was not significant, but its superior quality revolutionized life in the Abyssinian highlands."

8. de Contenson, "Pre-Aksumite," 355. In the same article de Contenson suggests that the term "Ethio-Sabaean" might best convey the specific nature of this culture, which combined both foreign (South Arabian) and indigenous (predominantly Agaw) elements.

9. Ibid.; see also Abraham Johannes Drewes, *Inscriptions de l'Éthiopie antique* (Leiden: E. J. Brill, 1962).

10. Anfray, "Civilization," 364; Sergew Hable Sellassie, *Ancient and Medieval Ethiopian History to 1270* (Addis Ababa: United Printers, 1972), 81–82.

11. Anfray, "Civilization," 363.

12. Ibid., 376; see also 364.

13. On these inscriptions see Drewes, *Inscriptions;* on the history of Ethiopic (Ge'ez) see the article by Robert Hetzron and Marvin L. Bender, "The Ethio-Semitic Languages," in M. Lionel Bender et al., eds., *Language in Ethiopia* (London: Oxford University Press, 1976), 24–30.

14. According to the author of the *Periplus*, Zoscales was acquainted with Greek literature. Conti Rossini, *Storia*, 119.

15. Anfray, "Civilization," 376.

16. See my article "Ezana's Conversion Reconsidered," *Journal of Religion in Africa* 13 (1982): 101–109.

17. Edward Ullendorff, *Ethiopia and the Bible* (London: Oxford University Press, 1968), 3.

18. Ibid., 73–131; Edward Ullendorff, "Hebraic-Jewish Elements in Abyssinian (Monophysite) Christianity," *Journal of Semitic Studies* 1 (1956), 216–256; "*Confessio Fidei*"; Ernst Hammerschmidt, "Jewish Elements in the Cult of the Ethiopian Church," *Journal of Ethiopian Studies* 2 (1965), 1–12; and see the references in the notes that follow.

19. Ullendorff, *Ethiopia*, 105–108; "Hebraic-Jewish Elements," 247–250.

20. Ernst Hammerschmidt, *Stellung und Bedeutung des Sabbats in Äthiopen* (Stuttgart: Kohlhammer, 1963); Getatchew Haile, "The Forty-nine Hour Sabbath of the Ethiopian Church," *Journal of Semitic Studies* 33, 2 (1988): 233–254.

21. Ullendorff, *Ethiopia*, 100–103; "Hebraic-Jewish," 240–243.

22. Ullendorff, *Ethiopia*, 82–89; "Hebraic-Jewish," 233–236; Hammerschmidt, "Jewish Elements," 3.

23. Ullendorff, *Ethiopia*, 74–79; and see the discussion of this work below.

24. Maxime Rodinson, "Sur la question des 'influences juives' en Ethiopie," *Journal of Semitic Studies* 9 (1964): 11–19; August Dillmann, *Über die Regierung, insbesondere die Kirchenordnung des Königs Zar'a-Jacob* (Berlin: 1884); Kobishchanov, *Axum*, 234.

25. Ullendorff, *Ethiopia*, 36–62.

26. Ibid., 120–125; H. J. Polotsky, "Aramaic, Syriac, and Ge'ez," *Journal of Semitic Studies* 9 (1964): 1–10.

27. Wolf Leslau, "The Names of the Weekdays in Ethiopic," *Journal of Semitic Studies* 6, 1 (1961): 65; Getatchew, "Sabbath," 242–245, esp. 243.

28. Polotsky, "Aramaic," 10.

29. Getatchew, "Sabbath," 246.

30. Edward Ullendorff, "Hebrew, Aramaic and Greek: The Versions underlying Ethiopic Translations of Bible and Intertestamental Literature" in Gary Rendsburg et al., eds., *The Bible World: Essays in Honour of Cyrus H. Gordon* (New York: KTAV, 1980), 249–257; "Hebrew Elements in the Ethiopic Old Testament," *Jerusalem Studies in Arabic and Islam* 9 (1987): 42–50.

31. On the possibility of later revisions and for a superb survey of the current state of research on the Ethiopic Old Testament see Michael A. Knibb, "Hebrew and Syriac Elements in the Ethiopic Version of Ezekiel?" *Journal of Semitic Studies* 33, 1 (1988): 11–35.

32. Salo Wittmayer Baron, *A Social and Religious History of the Jews*, vol. 18 (New York: Columbia University Press, 1983), 588–590; Mitchell Dahood, *Psalms II: 51–100*, The Anchor Bible, vol. 17 (Garden City, NY: Doubleday, 1968), 300. "*Cush*. Biblical term for the territory south of Ethiopia, usually identified with present-day Ethiopia."

33. Ullendorff, *Ethiopia*, 5–6; and cf. E. A. Speiser, *Genesis, The Anchor Bible*, vol. 1 (Garden City, NY: Doubleday, 1964), 64–73.

34. Isaiah 37:9, 20:3–5, Ezekiel 29:10, 30:9, Nahum 29:10, etc. Oscar Wintermute, "Cush," *Interpreter's Dictionary of the Bible: Supplementary Volume* (Nashville, NY: Abingdon Press, 1976), 200. Ullendorff, *Ethiopia*, 5, states, "The Biblical term Cush is a vague term connoting the entire Nile Valley, South of Egypt, including Nubia and Abyssinia." Although his subsequent survey of the term's usage (5–9) is carried out with characteristic care and attention to detail, it is difficult to determine which if any of the references require an Abyssinian (Northern Ethiopian) location.

35. William Y. Adams, *Nubia: Corridor to Africa* (Princeton: Princeton University Press, 1977), 246–293; cf. Isaiah 37:9, 2 Kings 19:9.

36. Ullendorff, *Ethiopia*, 16.

37. Isaiah 11:11 "That day, the Lord will raise his hand once more to ransom the remnant of his people, left over from the exile of Assyria, of Egypt, of Panthros, *of Cush*."

    Zephaniah 3:10 "From beyond the banks of the rivers of Ethiopia (Heb. Cush) my supplicants will bring me offerings."

    Psalm 87:4 "I will add Egypt and Babylon to the nations that acknowledge me of Philistia, Tyre, and Ethiopia (Heb. Cush): 'Here so and so was born' men say."

38. See Adams, *passim*.

39. See our discussion of Aksumite history above. A pre-exilic community in Nubia could not, for example, be the source of Aramaic loanwords, a complete Biblical text, or any of the apocryphal works.

40. See, for example, David Kessler, *The Falashas: The Forgotten Jews of Ethiopia* (New York: Africana, 1982); Ruth Gruber, *Rescue: The Exodus of the Ethiopian Jews* (New York: Atheneum, 1987); Yossi Avner et al., eds., *The Jews of Ethiopia: A People in Transition* (Tel Aviv: Beth Hatefusoth, 1986).

41. For a comparison of these two versions see James D. Newsome Jr., *A Synoptic Harmony of Samuel, Kings and Chronicles* (Grand Rapids, Michigan: Baker Book House, 1986), 129–131.

42. See James B. Pritchard ed., *Solomon and Sheba* (London: Phaidon, 1974) for articles surveying this literature.

43. Carl Bezold, "Kebra Nagast. Die Herrlichkeit der Könige," *Abhandlugen philosophisch-philogischen Klasse der Königlich Bayerischen Akademie der*

Wissenschaften 23 (1909); E. A. Wallis Budge, *The Queen of Sheba and her only son Menylek* (London: The Medici Society, 1932).

44. Irfan Shahid, "The Kebra Nagast in the Light of Recent Research," *Le Muséon* 89 (1976): 133–178, dates the book to the sixth century. Getatchew Haile, "A New Look at Some Dates of Early Ethiopian History," *Le Muséon* 95 (1982): 319–320, agrees with Shahid in associating the book with the Ethiopian ruler Gabra Masqal, but suggests that he reigned in the ninth century. For an invaluable but unfortunately unpublished study of the *Kebra Nagast* see David A. Hubbard, "The Literary Sources of the Kebra Nagast," Ph.D. dissertation, St. Andrews University, 1956. Many of its most important findings are cited in Ullendorff, *Ethiopia*, 75–78. Hubbard, 351–357, suggests a sixth- or seventh-century date but believes the "final" version to be from the thirteenth or fourteenth century.

45. Ullendorff, *Ethiopia*, 74–79; Donald N. Levine, *Greater Ethiopia: The Evolution of a Multiethnic Society* (Chicago: University of Chicago Press, 1974), 92–112.

46. Taddesse Tamrat, *Church and State in Ethiopia 1270–1527* (Oxford: Clarendon Press, 1972), 250, especially n. 2.

47. James Bruce, *Travels to Discover the Source of the Nile* (Edinburgh, 1805, 2nd ed.), vol. 2, 406. The final section of this quote refers to the Christians' claim that the Israelites' descendants became Christians at a later date. Bruce's comment contrasts sharply with the view of the sixteenth century Portuguese visitor Manoel d'Almeida, who explicitly distinguishes between the Falasha and those who claim Solomonic descent, *Historia de Ethiopia* in C. Beccari, ed., *Rerum Aethiopicarum* (Rome: C. de Luigi, 1905–17), vol. 6, 41–42.

48. Samuel Gobat, *Journal of a Three Years' Residence in Abyssinia* (London: 1850, 2nd ed.), 467. The view that the Beta Israel are Jews who came to Ethiopia after the destruction of the Second Temple by the Romans, and not either Israelites or an indigenous people, first seems to appear in Ethiopian sources in the sixteenth century. It may well reflect the Portuguese understanding of their origin.

49. Antoine d'Abbadie, "Réponses des Falashas dit Juif d'Abyssinie aux questions faites par M. Luzzato," *Archives Israélites* 12 (1851–52): 183.

50. Kay Kaufman Shelemay, *Music, Ritual, and Falasha History* (East Lansing: Michigan State University Press, 1989, 2nd ed.), 17; Veronika Krempel, "Die Soziale und wirtschaftliche Stellung der Falascha in der christlich-amharischen Gesellschaft von Nordwest-Äthiopien," Ph.D. dissertation (Berlin: Freien Universität, 1972): 29. For a discussion of these traditions and their symbolic meaning see G. Jan Abbink, "L'énigme de l'éthnogenese des Beta Israel—Une approche anthropo-historique de leurs mytho-legendes," *Cahiers d'études africaines* (forthcoming).

51. This phenomenon would appear to be associated with a desire to stress their differences from their Christian Ethiopian compatriots, particularly when presenting themselves to a Jewish audience.

52. See note 39 above. To the elements listed there must also be added, for the period of Solomon, a clearly developed monotheistic belief system and cult.

53. Jacob M. Myers, *II Chronicles, The Anchor Bible*, vol. 13 (Garden City, NY: Doubleday, 1965), 56–57; W. A. L. Elmslie, *The First and Second Book of Chronicles, The Interpreter's Bible*, vol. 3 (Nashville, NY: Abingdon Press, 1954), 466. For two recent attempts to trace the Queen to an African, although not Aksumite setting see Ephraim Isaac and Cain Felder, "Reflections on the Origins of Ethiopian Civilization," *Proceedings of the Eighth International Conference of Ethiopian Studies* (Addis Ababa, Frankfurt: Institute of Ethiopian Studies, Frobenius Institute, 1988), vol. 1, 76–79; and Kessler, *Falashas*, 24–57. While Isaac and Felder make no attempt to associate the Queen with either Jewish influences in Ethiopia or the Beta Israel, Kessler claims the Queen came from Meroë in the time of King Hezekiah (!) and established Judaism in the region. This Meroëtic Judaism was, in his view, one the important sources of later Ethiopian Judaism.

54. For the text of this important letter see Corinaldi, *Identity*, 243–244.

55. For the text and a discussion of *Sefer Eldad* see Abraham Epstein, *Eldad Ha-dani: His Story and His Halakhot* (Pressburg: Abraham David Alkalai Press, 1891) (Hebrew); Waldman, *Ethiopian Jewry*, 17–30; Corinaldi, *Identity*, 87–94.

56. For Eldad as an Ethiopian see E. David Goitein, "Note on Eldad the Danite," *Jewish Quarterly Review* 17 (1926–27): 483.

57. Epstein, *Sefer Eldad*, 3–12.

58. Ullendorff, *Ethiopia*, 25–26; Carlo Conti Rossini, "Leggende geografiche guideche del IXe secolo (Il Sepher Eldad)," *Bolletina de Reale Soc. Geogr. Italiano* 6, 2 (1925): 163–164.

59. Waldman, *Ethiopian Jewry*, 21–26; Corinaldi, *Identity*, 87–94.

60. On Obadiah see Abraham David, "Obadiah Ben Abraham Yare Di Bertinoro," *Encyclopaedia Judaica* (Jerusalem: Keter, 1971): 4, 698–99.

61. Abraham Yaari, *Letters from the Land of Israel* (Ramat Gan: Masada, 1971, 2nd ed., Hebrew), 133. It is interesting to note that at least one manuscript of this letter lacks this crucial phrase claiming a Danite connection. It is unclear if its omission is intentional or accidental. The possibility cannot be dismissed that Obadiah asked the Jews he encountered if they were from the tribe of Dan and they then answered in the affirmative.

62. On the Radbaz (1479–1563) see Israel M. Goldman, *The Life and Times of Rabbi David Ibn Abi Zimra* (New York: Jewish Theological Seminary, 1970).

63. *Responsum* Part 7, #5 (20); cf. *Responsum* Part 4, #219 (1); Corinaldi, *Identity*, 117–128; Waldman, *Ethiopian Jewry*, 66–76.

64. Menachem Elon, "The Ethiopian Jews: A Case Study in the Functioning of the Jewish Legal System," *New York University Journal of International Law and Politics* 19 (1986–87): 535–563.

65. Corinaldi, *Identity*, 210–213; Elon, "Case Study," 558–559; Waldman, *Ethiopian Jewry*, 27–30.

66. As a rule, the sources that speculate on the Danite affiliation of the Beta Israel do not concern themselves with the larger question of the Biblical-Hebraic influences on Ethiopian culture.

67. Ignazio Guidi (*Breve*) *Storia della letteratura etiopica* (Rome: Instituto per l'Oriente, 1932), 92, n. 2; (Guidi, who stated this position as a mere footnote to other discussions, later withdrew his support for it.) Itzhak Ben Zvi, *The Exiled and the Redeemed* (Philadelphia: Jewish Publication Society, 1961, 2nd ed.), 52–53; Louis Marcus, "Notice sur l'époque de l'établissement des Juifs dans l'Abyssinie," *Journal Asiatique* 3 (1829), 409–431, 4 (1829), 51–73; Epstein, *Sefer Eldad;* but cf. Conti Rossini, *Storia,* 144; Rodinson, "Influences," 16; and Philoxene Luzzato, *Mémoire sur les Juifs Abyssinie* (Paris, 1853), 12; Ullendorff, *Ethiopia,* 16–21.

68. Kessler, *Falashas,* 42–47; Menachem Waldman, *The Jews of Ethiopia* (Jerusalem: Joint Distribution Committee, 1985), 10; Shoshana Ben-Dor, "The *Sigd* of the Beta Israel," M.A. thesis, Hebrew University of Jerusalem, 1986, 180–185; and in part Baron, *History,* 588, 593.

69. While not all proponents of the Egyptian theory would necessarily subscribe to every point in this composite summary, it does reflect the essential arguments made for this position.

70. d'Abbadie, "Réponses," 183; Abbink, "L'énigme."

71. Scholars who consider the Septuagint a significant clue to the origins of Ethiopian Judaism include Baron, *History,* 365; Kessler, *Falashas,* 19–20; Ben Zvi, *The Exiled,* 252; and Epstein, *Sefer Eldad,* 152, 184.

72. This hypothesis assumes that the Beta Israel's presence in the Lake Tana region is of great antiquity and leaves unanswered the question of why they would choose to settle in this isolated and inhospitable region rather than in a cultural or commercial center.

73. Kessler, *Falashas,* 41–47; Waldman, *The Jews,* 10. Luzzato, Marcus, and Epstein all wrote prior to the discovery of the Elephantine papyri, and thus make no reference to this community.

74. Bezalel Porten, *Archives from Elephantine* (Berkeley and Los Angeles: University of California, 1968); Albert Leopold Vincent, *La religion des judéo-arméens d'Elephantine* (Paris: P. Geuthner, 1937); Arthur Ernest Cowley, *Aramaic Papyri of the Fifth Century B.C.* (Oxford: The Clarendon Press, 1923).

75. Waldman, *The Jews,* 10.

76. Baron, *History,* 588. It should also be noted that neither of these reports can be demonstrated to refer to the Jewish garrison.

77. For more on this point see my article, "The Origins of the Beta Israel: Five Methodological Cautions," *Pe'amim* 33 (1987): 41–47 (Hebrew).

78. Deborah Lifchitz, "Un sacrifice chez les Falachas, Juifs d'Abyssinie," *La Terre et la vie* 9 (1939): 116–123. Cf. however, Waldman, *The Jews,* 10, "The Jews of Yev [Elephantine], like those of Abyssinia, built a temple and performed sacrifices."

79. Porten, *Elephantine,* 126–128.

80. Ibid., ix. It is strange to find Kessler, *Falashas*, 42, quoting this passage with approval given his claim that Elephantine practice was "remarkably reminiscent" of that of the Beta Israel.
81. Wolf Leslau, *Falasha Anthology* (New Haven: Yale University Press, 1951), xxxii, "The day celebrated in the strictest manner is the Sabbath."
82. On the dating of Jubilees see James C. Vanderkam, *Textual and Historical Studies in the Book of Jubilees* (Missoula, Montana: Scholars Press, 1977), 207–285. On the decline of the garrison at Elephantine see Porten, *Elephantine*, 296–301.
83. I am grateful to Professor Edward Ullendorff (personal communication, 28 August 1990) for clarifying this point.
84. Porten, *Elephantine*, p. 174, and see especially 151–179; Cf. Vincent, *Elephantine*, 562–680; Abraham Schalit, "Elephantine," *Encyclopaedia Judaica* 6, 608. "There is no escaping the conclusion that two goddesses dwelt alongside Yahu and were worshipped with Him in the Elephantine Temple."
85. Porten, *Elephantine*, 163.
86. Schalit, "Elephantine," 609.
87. Porten, *Elephantine*, 119–122, 289–293.
88. Norman Henry Snaith, "Bible: Canon," *Encyclopaedia Judaica* 4: 822–823.
89. Ullendorff, *Ethiopia*, 16–17.
90. Michels, "Axumite Archaeology," 23–27; Kobishchanov, *Axum*, passim.
91. Rodinson, "Influences," 16.
92. Ullendorff, *Ethiopia*, 20.
93. Josephus Flavius, *Antiquities* XV 9, 3; Strabo, *Geography*, XVI, 23.
94. *Bamidbar Rabba*, ix; *Babylonian Talmud, Rosh Hashanah*, 26a.
95. Ullendorff, *Ethiopia*, 17; Ze'ev Hirschberg, *Israel in Arabia* (Tel Aviv: Masada, 1947, Hebrew), 36–74.
96. Ullendorf, *Ethiopia*, 17–23; Leslau, *Falasha Anthology*, xliii; Carl Rathjens, *Die Juden in Abessinien* (Hamburg: M. W. Kaufman, 1921), 92; Carlo Conti Rossini, "Appunti di storia e letteratura Falascia," *Rivista degli studi orientali* 8 (1919–20): 598–609.
97. Joseph Halévy, *La Guerre de Sarsa Dengel Contre les Falachas* (Paris: 1907), 75; Itzhak Grinfeld, "The Falasha and Their Languages in the Present and the Past," *Pe'amim* 33 (1987) (Hebrew): 57, suggests that Jews arrived in two stages: (1) prior to the fourth century; (2) as prisoners in the sixth century. He views the latter as ancestors of the Falasha. For a detailed discussion of this episode see Chapter 2.

2. Speculation and Legend

1. On these legends see Acts 8:26–36 and August Dillmann, "Zur Geschichte des Axumitischen Reiches im vierten bis sechsten Jahrhundert," *Abhandlungen der Königl. Akademie der Wissenschaften zu Berlin* 1 (1880): 4–6. For two scholars who have questioned this view see Getatchew Haile, "The

Homily in Honor of St. Frumentius," *Analecta Bollandiana* 92 (1979): 309–318; Kobishchanov, *Axum*, 67–73, 85–87.

2. Getatchew, "Frumentius"; J. P. Migne, *Patrologia cursus completus: series latina* (Paris: Garnier, 1844/55) XXI, 479; *Patrologia cursus completus: series graeca* (Paris: Garnier, 1857/66), LXVII, 125, 996, LXXII, 969; Dillmann, "Zur Geschichte," 6–17.

3. Migne, *Series graeca*, XXV, 636.

4. Francis Anfray, André Caquot and Pierre Nautin, "Une nouvelle inscription grecque d'Ezana, roi d'Axoum," *Journal des Savents* (1970): 260–274.

5. Enno Littmann, *Deutsche Aksum-Expedition* (Berlin: G. Reimer, 1913), vol. 4, 32–35.

6. August Dillmann, *Lexicon Linguae aethiopicae* (Leipzig: 1865),750; on the translation of *Ecclesiasticus* see Conti Rossini, *Storia*, 223, but cf. Knibb, "Hebrew and Syriac Elements," 15, n. 15.

7. Kaplan, "Ezana's Conversion."

8. Rathjens, *Juden*, 17; Max Wurmbrand, "Falashas," *Encyclopaedia Judaica*, vol. 6, 1143. Cf. Ullendorff, *Ethiopia*, 25.

9. Taddesse, *Church and State*, 23.

10. Ullendorff, *Ethiopia*, 25. Ephraim Isaac has suggested that these elements can be traced to Jewish-Christians who played a key role in the introduction and development of early Christianity in Ethiopia. Although the suggestion is a provocative one, little of the evidence he produces requires a Jewish-Christian source. In addition, his argument rests to a considerable degree on the claim that Ezana himself converted to Jewish-Christianity and not a more normative form. This particular claim is no longer tenable since the publication in 1970 of the king's Trinitarian inscription. See Ephraim Isaac, "An Obscure Component in Ethiopian Church History," *Le Muséon*, 85 (1972): 225–259.

11. Syncretism is, admittedly, an overused and terribly imprecise term. Objectively speaking, *all* religious traditions are syncretic. The term is used here to stress that neither in this period nor perhaps in any other did Ethiopian forms of Judaism and Christianity closely conform to foreign models of the "true" faith. From the second through sixth century in particular, the distinctions between the different faiths may have been limited, especially in the eyes of the common people.

12. Dillmann, "Zur Geschichte," 26; Conti Rossini, *Storia*, 162–163; but cf. Getatchew Haile, "A New Ethiopic Version of the Acts of St. Mark," *Analecta Bollandiana* 94 (1981), 117–134; W. H. C. Frend, *The Rise of the Monophysite Movement* (Cambridge: Cambridge University Press, 1972), 305.

13. Taddesse, *Church and State*, 29.

14. Conti Rossini, *Storia*, 156–165.

15. Ullendorff, *Ethiopia*, 30–62; Knibb, "Hebrew and Syriac Elements," 11–21.

16. Ullendorff, *Ethiopia*, 27, esp. n. 4; "Hebrew, Aramaic, Greek"; "Hebrew Elements"; Theodor Nöldeke, review of Dillmann, "Über die Regierung, insbesondere die Kirchenordnung des Königs Zar'a Jacob," *Gottingische Gelehrte Anzeigen* (1884): 580–81.

17. Hirschberg, *Israel*, 75–111; Shahid, "Kebra Nagast"; "Byzantium in South Arabia," 17–22; *Dumbarton Oaks Papers* 33 (1979): 23–94; *The Martyrs of Najran: New Documents* (Bruxelles: Société des Bollandistes, 1971); Kobishchanov, *Axum*, 91–108; Sergew, *Ethiopian History*, 126–143.

18. Shahid, "Kebra Nagast," 148–149.

19. Ibid., 148.

20. Kobishchanov, *Axum*, 97; Shahid, "Byzantium," 38–66, esp. 56, "The Ethiopian victory did not simply signal the initiation of a new political supremacy in Arabia, but introduced a new culture, centered in a religion intolerant of the old order and its pagan symbols."

21. Shahid, "Kebra Nagast," esp. 135, 139–140; Getatchew, "Some Dates," 319–320.

22. Shahid, "Kebra Nagast," 137–146; Getatchew, "Some Dates," 320, follows much the same reasoning, but assigns the book to the ninth century on the basis of his redating of Gabra Masqal, hitherto believed to be a son of Kaleb. Even if one accepts his dating of this king, there is no clear evidence for an anti-Jewish reform during his reign.

23. Ethiopia is said to have provided sanctuary to the early followers of Muhammad. Its ruler is said to have been "a king under whom none are persecuted." John Spencer Trimingham, *Islam in Ethiopia* (London: Frank Cass, 1954), 44.

24. J. W. McCrindle, *The Christian Topography of Cosmas* (London: Hakluyt Society, 1898), 54–66, esp. 61–62. The association of the Samenai with the Athagau may also be significant. Cf. Littmann, *Aksum Expedition*, 19–20, 24–25 (Inscriptions 8 and 9).

25. McCrindle, *Cosmas*, 67.

26. Joseph Varenbergh, "Studien zur abessinischen Reichordnung (Šer'ata Mangešt)," *Zeitschrift für Assyriologie* 30 (1915–16): 11. In making this suggestion I am following a line of reasoning initially suggested by Getatchew Haile, "Some Dates," 319, although he connects the phrase to events in the ninth century.

27. Sergew, *Ethiopian History*, 159–161; Getatchew, "Some Dates."

28. In the main, this reconstruction is similar to that proposed by Getatchew Haile, "Some Dates," 318–320. Getatchew has, however, recently suggested that Gabra Masqal should be dated to the ninth century. In his argument, therefore, the primary indications of a Jewish-Christian conflict in this period are the *Kebra Nagast*, the "separation" of the Falasha, and the Gabra Masqal-Beta Israel rivalry. In our own argument as presented above, the Christian-Jewish conflict is well documented and the other elements are suggested as products of this conflict. Even if in agreement with Getatchew we were to date the *Kebra Nagast* and Gabra Masqal to the ninth century, our basic claim that the Kaleb-Du Nuwas conflict created a crisis for the Jews of Aksum would remain intact. Indeed, it is difficult to imagine that they could have remained unaffected by the events of the sixth century. In a similar fashion, while we have no basic argument with Ullendorff's attempt *Ethiopia*, 117, to associate the Falasha with "those elements

in the Aksumite kingdom who resisted conversion to Christianity," he underestimates the evidence for ethnic and cultural change over time. As we shall discuss below, his claim (ibid.) that their religion "may well mirror to a considerable extent the religious syncretism of the pre-Christian Aksumite kingdom" is extremely problematic.

29. Given the previously discussed biblical-Hebraic molding of Ethiopian Christianity, the dividing line between Christianized Agaw and Judaized Agaw may not have been very clear during this early period. Hebraic elements could have reached the Agaw through both Christian and Jewish channels. The various groups are probably best understood as forming a continuum with regard to their emphasis on Hebraic-biblical elements. It is doubtful if any of them possessed as fully articulated a religious system as the Beta Israel from the fifteenth century and onward. Indeed, in many respects they probably more closely resembled the "Pagan-Hebraic" Agaw people known as the Qemant. See Frederick C. Gamst, *The Qemant: A Pagan-Hebraic Peasantry of Ethiopia* (Prospect Heights, IL: Waveland Press, Inc., 1969).

30. Sergew, *Ethiopian History*, 159–175; but cf. Getatchew, "Some Dates," 318–320.

31. Conti Rossini, *Storia*, 197–201; Kobishchanov, *Axum*, 110–111.

32. Kobishchanov, *Axum*, 116–117.

33. Ibid., 118–119; Butzer, "Axum," 489; T. T. Mekouria, "The Horn of Africa," *General History of Africa*, ed. M. Elfasi (London, Berkeley, Paris: Heinemann, University of California, UNESCO, 1988) III, 563–565.

34. Kobishchanov, *Axum*, 118; Taddesse Tamrat, "Ethiopia, The Red Sea, and the Horn," *Cambridge History of Africa*, vol. 3, ed. Roland Oliver (Cambridge: Cambridge University Press, 1977), 98.

35. Francis Anfray, "Les rois d'Axoum d'après la numismatique," *Journal of Ethiopian Studies* 6 (1968): 1–5; Kobishchanov, *Axum*, 115–116.

36. Butzer, *Axum*, 485–492.

37. Michels, "Regional Political Organization," 9.

38. Taddesse, *Church and State*, 34–38.

39. A. Z. Aešcoly, *The Book of the Falasha* (Jerusalem: Rubin Mass, 1943, Hebrew), 164; Ullendorff, *Ethiopia*, 25–26; Edward Ullendorff and C. F. Beckingham, *The Hebrew Letters of Prester John* (London: Oxford University Press, 1982), 154.

40. Baron, *History*, 373; P. Borchadt, "Die Falaschajuden in Abessinien im Mittelalte," *Anthropos* 18–19 (1923–24): 261–263; Conti Rossini, "Leggende," 162–176; Kobishchanov, *Axum*, 119; Corinaldi, *Identity*, 94; Sergew, *Ethiopian History*, 212–213.

41. Borchadt, "Die Falaschajuden," 261–263.

42. Conti Rossini, "Leggende," 171–176.

43. Aešcoly, *The Book of the Falasha*, 164.

44. Cf. Conti Rossini, "Leggende," 176. On the Oromo (Galla) see Herbert S. Lewis, "The Origin of the Galla and Somali," *Journal of African History* 7 (1966): 27–46.

45. Waldman, *Ethiopian Jewry*, 26–27; but cf. Corinaldi, *Identity*, 89–94.
46. Conti Rossini, "Leggende," 177–181; Ullendorff and Beckingham, *Prester John*, esp. 155–159.
47. Azriel Shochat, "Eldad Ha-Dani," *Encyclopaedia Judaica* 6, 577. Baron, *History*, 373–374 has similar comments concerning the significance of El-dad's reports of a kingdom for other Jews, but also accepts its existence as a fact. "Discarding the legendary features, it seems likely that the Jews dominated parts of Ethiopia before the conversion of the mass of the population to Christianity in the fourth century and again at least from the ninth century on." Strangely, his note to this section (p. 593, n. 13) has no connection to the contents of the text!
48. The precise meaning of the term Hadani remains obscure. Sergew, *Ethiopian History*, 208, suggests that it means "bring up." Kobishchanov, *Axum*, 294, n. 297, believes it derives from the root hdn, "to feed," "to breastfeed," "to nourish," and translates it as "feeder," a reference to the person who fed a king, who for ritual reasons could not feed himself. Van Varenburgh, "Reichsordnung," 3, and Carlo Conti Rossini, *La langue des Kemant* (Vienna: Kaiserliche Akademie der Wisenschaften, 1912) derive it from an Agaw term that means "king." If the last of these hypotheses is correct, the replacement of the *Negus* (Ge'ez: King), by the *hadani* may be indicative of an ethnic change in the leadership. While many vocalizations render the term as *hadani* using "d" for "ḍ," the latter is the correct form, and there is no connection between this title and Eldad's alleged tribal affiliation.
49. Littmann, *Aksum Expedition*, vol. 4, 43–48 (Inscriptions 12–14).
50. Kobishchanov, *Axum*, 120. For a note of caution concerning the interpretation of these inscriptions see René Schneider, "Yuri M. Kobishchanov, *Axum*, A Review Article," *Journal of Ethiopian Studies* 17 (1984): 163.
51. Taddesse, *Church and State*, 38–41.
52. Sawirus ibn al-Mukaffa, *History of the Patriarchs of the Egyptian Church*, tr. by Yassa 'abd Al-Masih et al. (Cairo: Societe d'archéologie copte, 1943–59), vol. 2, part 2, 171; cf. E. A. W. Budge, *The Book of the Saints of the Ethiopian Church* (Cambridge: Cambridge University Press, 1928), vol. 1, 233–234; Jules Perruchon, "Notes pour l'histoire d'Éthiopie: Lettre adresée par le roi d'Ethiopie au roi Georges de Nubie sous le patriarcat de Philothee 981–1002 ou 1003," *Revue sémitique* 1 (1893): 71–76, 359–372.
53. Muhammed Ibn Haukal, *Configuration de la terre* tr. Johannes Hendrik Kramers and Gaston Wiet (Paris: G. P. Maissonneue and Larose, 1964) 56, English translation, Taddesse, *Church and State*, 39. Elsewhere, *Configuration*, 16, Ibn Haukal, who wrote ca. 977 states that the queen had reigned for thirty years.
54. Conti Rossini, *Storia*, 286, reading Beni-al-amouta for Damoutah; Taddesse, *Church and State*, 38–39; esp. 39, n. 1; O. G. S. Crawford, ed., *Ethiopian Itineraries: Circa 1400–1524* (Cambridge: Cambridge University Press, 1958), 81–82. Some Ethiopian traditions identify Yodit as an ancestor of the thirteenth-century Damoti pagan ruler Motalome.

55. See the sources cited by Taddesse, *Church and State*, 38, n. 5.

56. Bruce, *Travels*, vol. 2, 451–453. Elsewhere her name appears as Gudit, Esato (fire), Judith, Ga'wa, and Tirda Gabaz. Cf. Sergew, *Ethiopian History*, 226.

57. Cf. Richard Keïr Pankhurst, "Problems about Bruce's History of the Zagwe Dynasty," *Quardeni di Studi Etiopici* 6–7 (1985–1986): 86–92.

58. Rathjens, *Juden*, 18–24, is primarily based upon Bruce. Cf. Rene Basset, "Études sur l'histoire d'Éthiopie," *Journal asiatique* 7th series, 17 (April–May–June 1881): 428, n. 60; Perruchon, "Notes pour l'histoire," 359–372.

59. Messing, *Falashas*, 14; Rapoport, *The Lost Jews*, 135–142.

60. Sergew, *Ethiopian History*, 225–230. Even these accounts are highly legendary in character and may well reflect the interpolation of later traditions.

61. The association by marriage of Yodit with the rulers of Bugna in the Lasta region parallels similar traditions concerning the Zagwe dynasty—cf. Conti Rossini, *Storia*, 304–305; the alleged massacre of the royal (Solomonic) children in a mountain fortress may well reflect Ahmad Gragn's destruction of Amba Geshan in the sixteenth century. Taddesse, *Church and State*, 301; the claim that Judith's parents (Gedewon and Judith) ruled over the Semien appears to be the product of later "Falasha" traditions.

62. Bruce, *Travels*, vol. 2, 453.

63. The Queen of Sheba is said to have been a virgin, Judith, a prostitute; some oral traditions concerning Judith claim that she, like the Queen of Sheba, was tricked into having sexual relations against her will.

64. Taddesse, "Agaw," 9.

65. On the Zagwe see Taddesse, *Church and State*, 53–66; Conti Rossini, *Storia*, 303–321; "Appunti ed oservazioni sui re Zāguē e Takla Hāymānot," *Rendiconti della Reale Accademia dei Lincei*, ser. 5, 4 (1895): 144–159; Sergew, *Ethiopian History*, 239–287.

66. On such churches especially in Lalibala see Jules Leroy, *L'Éthiopie: Archéologie et culture* (Brussels: Deselee De Brower, 1972), 121–160; Georg Gerster, *Churches in Rock* (London: Phaidon, 1970), 85–108.

67. Steven Kaplan, *The Monastic Holy Man and the Christianization of Early Solomonic Ethiopia* (Wiesbaden: Franz Steiner, 1984), 20.

68. Taddesse, *Church and State*, 64–66.

69. Ibid., 65 (map).

70. Taddesse Tamrat, "The Abbots of Dabra Hayq: 1248–1535," *Journal of Ethiopian Studies* 8, 1 (1970): 112–113.

71. Rapoport, *The Lost Jews*, 143. There is similarly no basis for Rapoport's claim on the preceding page that "the Beta-Israel prospered under the Zagwe."

72. C. F. Beckingham, "The Achievements of Prester John," in *Between and Islam and Christendom* (London: Variorum Reprints, 1983), Chapter I, 3.

73. "There is only the most perfunctory attempt at verisimilitude. . . . There is more convincing detail in More's *Utopia* or in Butler's *Erewhon*." Ibid., 14.

74. Conti Rossini, "Leggende," 177–181; Ullendorff and Beckingham, *Prester John*, 153–159.

75. Waldman, *Ethiopian Jewry*, 31–33; Corinaldi, *Identity*, 97–101.

76. Unfortunately, nothing is known about Benjamin except those facts that can be gleaned from his travelogue. Among the many editions of this document see A. Asher, *The Itinerary of Rabbi Benjamin of Tudela* (London: A. Asher, 1840–41), 2 vols.; Eliacim Carmoly, *Notice historique sur Benjamin de Tudèle* (Bruxelles et Leipzig: Chez Kiessling et Co., 1852); Marcus Nathan Adler, *The Itinerary of Benjamin of Tudela* (London: Frowde, 1907).

77. Waldman, *Ethiopian Jewry*, 31–32; Corinaldi, *Identity*, 95–97; Borchadt, "Falascha," 259–260; Carlo Conti Rossini, "Piccoli studi etiopici. I. L'itinerario di Beniamino da Tudela e l'Etiopia," *Zeitschrift für Assyriologie* 27 (1912): 358–365; Ullendorff, *Ethiopia*, 27, n. 1.; Leslau, *Falasha Anthology*, xxxix; Salvatore Tedeschi, "L'Éthiopie dans L'itinéraire de Benjamin de Tudèle," *Proceedings of the ninth international congress of Ethiopian studies* (Moscow: USSR Academy of Sciences Africa Institute, 1988), vol. 6, 212–213.

78. Waldman, *Ethiopian Jewry*, 30.

79. Adler, *Benjamin*, 68; *Jewish Travellers* (London: G. Routledge and Sons, 1930), 371.

80. Robert I. Hess, "The Itinerary of Benjamin of Tudela: A Twelfth Century Jewish Description of Northeast Africa," *Journal of African History* 6 (1965): 18; cf. J. Lelewel, in Carmoly, *Benjamin*, 29. This identification is strengthened by the fact that several medieval Arabic authors claimed that the Beja practiced biblical customs (oral communication, Dr. Habib Tawa, June 1991).

81. Cf. Benjamin on the Jews of Khulam. Borchadt's suggestion "Falascha," 260, that the Jews of Ethiopia were not yet black is scarcely credible!

3. From Ayhud to Falasha: The Invention of a Tradition

1. Carlo Conti Rossini, "L'evangelo d'oro di Dabra Libanos," *Rendiconti della Reale Accademia dei Lincei*, ser. 5, 2 (1902): 187, 190, 192–193. See also n. 66 in Chapter 2.

2. Cf. Taddesse, *Church and State*, 60–64.

3. Ibid., 64–68.

4. Levine, *Greater Ethiopia*, 73.

5. Perruchon, "Amda Seyon," 293 [*kama 'ayhud*: like Jews]. For a discussion of the difficulties associated with identifying the *ayhud* see the discussion below.

6. Cf. Jules Perruchon, *Les chroniques de Zar'a Yâ'eqôb et de Ba'eda Mâryâm, rois d'Éthiopie de 1434 à 1478* (Paris: Librairie Émile Bouillon, 1893), 96–97, for a similar perception of these groups as lapsed Christians. Both of these passages suggest an open and very dynamic religious milieu in which a number of groups existed whose commitment to both Jewish and Christian elements fluctuated.

7. Cf. Shelemay, *Music*, 21. On the Ewostatians see Kaplan, *Holy Man*, 38–39, and Taddesse, *Church and State*, 209–219.

8. C. Conti Rossini, "Note di agiografia etiopica (Abiya-Egzi, Arkaledes e Gabra Iyesus)," *Rivista degli studi orientali* 17 (1938): 446 [*daqiqa 'ayhudni:* the sons of the Jews].

9. C. Conti Rossini, "Appunti di storia e letteratura falascia," *Rivista degli studi orientali* 8 (1920): 571; "L'agiografia etiopica e gli atti del santo Yafqiranna-Egzi," *Atti del Reale istituto veneto di scienze, lettere ed arti* 96 (1936–37): 419–420; I. Wajnberg, "Das Leben des H. L. Jāfqerana 'Egzi'," *Orientalia Christiana Analecta* 106 (1936): 50–60.

10. Conti Rossini, "Appunti," 571–573; Wajnberg, "Jafqerana 'Egzi'," 56–58 (Ge'ez: *haymanota 'ayhud:* religion of the Jews). While most scholars have taken the view that Qozmos provided the Beta Israel with additional copies of the *Orit*, as I argue below, he may well have been responsible for introducing the written text to them. For the earlier view see Kaplan, *Holy Man*, 101; Shelemay, *Music*, 21; Hess, "Toward a History," 113.

11. Although Taddesse, *Church and State*, 199, n. 3, challenges the claim that the *Kantiba* joined the rebels following his defeat, this does, in fact, appear to be the meaning of the text.

12. Wajnberg, "Jafqerana 'Egzi'," 58; Conti Rossini, "Appunti," 571–572, 576–577.

13. Conti Rossini, "Appunti," 576–577; Wajnberg, "Jafqerana 'Egzi'," 60. The rebellion occurred between the years 1380–88. According to Quirin, "The Beta Israel," 79–80, n. 12, Beta Israel tradition claims that Dawit was not successful in defeating them.

14. Rene Basset, *Études sur L'histoire d'Éthiopie* (Paris: Imprimerie Nationale, 1882), 11–12; Taddesse, *Church and State*, 200–201.

15. Quirin, "The Beta Israel," 56.

16. Ibid.; Taddesse, *Church and State*, 213–219. The Ewostatian monastic movement championed a number of traditional Ethiopian religious practices, most notably the Saturday Sabbath, in the face of opposition from the royal court and the Coptic Abuna.

17. Maqrizi quoted by Taddesse, *Church and State*, 154.

18. Carlo Conti Rossini, "Il 'Gadla Filipos' ed il 'Gadla Yohannes' di Dabra Bizan," *Memorie della Reale Accademia dei Lincei* 8 (1901): 146.

19. Taddesse, *Church and State*, 200, treats "Bet-Ajer" as a personal name. It appears more likely that this is, in fact, an official title. A praise poem in honor of Amda Ṣeyon mentions Abet Azar as an Agaw (!) leader fought by the king. Cf. Ignazio Guidi, "Le canzoni Geez-Amarina in onore di re abissini," *Rendiconti della Reale Accademia dei Lincei*, ser. 4, 5 (1889): 62. G. W. B. Huntingford, ed. and tr., *The Glorious Victories of Amda Seyon, King of Ethiopia* (Oxford: Clarendon Press, 1965), 129, and cf. 133, "Abet 'azar" was probably an Agaw title, formed perhaps from abeto "lord, master," and agar "land." See also Enno Littmann, "Altamharischen Glossar," *Rivista degli studi orientali* 20 (1943): 492. Merid Wolde Aregay, "Southern Ethiopia and the Christian Kingdom, 1508–1708, with Special Reference to the Galla Migrations and Their Consequences," Ph.D. disser-

tation, University of London, 1971, 72, suggests that "it is quite possible that the Abet Ajar of the Agaw who defied Amda Ṣeyon was a Falasha leader." He may, in fact, have led the rebels "like Jews" discussed above. This term would also appear to be further evidence of the intrinsic connection between the Beta Israel and other Agaw peoples. Getatchew Haile has suggested (oral communication, May 1990) that Beta Jar may be a tribal designation not unlike Beta Israel.

20. Taddesse, *Church and State*, 200. Cf. Basset, "Études," 11–12; Bruce, *Travels*, III, 95, for shorter accounts of this episode. Both the chronicle edited by Basset and the traditions quoted by Bruce date from several centuries after these events and identify Yeshaq's foes as Falasha.

21. Taddesse, *Church and State*, 200. Other allies of the king were rewarded as well. "The 24 elders of *Balaw Amba* are particularly referred to as having been rewarded by the king for their co-operation against the Falasha." Ibid., n. 3.

22. Ibid., 201. The text continues in a marginal note: "Since then, the Beta Israel have been called *Falashoch.*" This text has yet to be published, and Getatchew Haile (oral communication, May 1990) has expressed grave concerns about its authenticity.

23. Quirin seems to view Yeshaq's victory as the catalyst for a rapid wholesale reorganization of Beta Israel society. Cf. "The Beta Israel," 58, "For the Beta Israel, the main consequence of their defeat and loss of independence *in this war* was a fundamental reorganization and redirection of their society" (emphasis added). As we shall discuss below, the changes were probably neither as rapid nor as sweeping as he claims. In a similar fashion, several difficulties exist with attempts made by scholars to see this decree as the source for the application of the name Falasha to the Beta Israel. Cf. my article, "The Fälasha and the Stephanite: An Episode from *Gädlä Gäbrä Mäsih,*" *Bulletin of the School of Oriental and African Studies* 48, 2 (1985): 279–282, and see the discussion of this term below.

24. Basset, "Études," 12. Taddesse, *Church and State*, 200. The most famous of these churches was Yeshaq Debir in Woggara. Cf. Bruce, *Travels*, 95.

25. Carlo Conti Rossini, *Acta Sancti Abakerazun et Sancti Takla Hawaryat, Corpus Scriptorum Christianorum Orientalum* 24 (1910), 103–109. This passage is all but ignored in the discussions of Taddesse, *Church and State*, 201, n. 2; Krempel, "Falascha," 37–39; and Quirin, "The Beta Israel." See my discussion of the passage, "A Source for the History of the Beta Israel (Falasha) from the *Life* of Abuna Takla Hawaryat," *Pe'amim* 15 (1983): 124–133 (Hebrew).

26. Conti Rossini, *Takla Hawaryat*, 104.

27. Ibid., 105–106.

28. Ibid., 107–108, cf. 105. Prior to his conversion his name had been Yessahalo Egzi'abher.

29. Although the treatment of Yessahalo Krestos is in keeping with canon law and could thus be assumed to be common, many hagiographic sources

indicate that the Church often integrated new converts with surprising speed. Cf. Kaplan, *Holy Man,* 117.

30. Perruchon, "Zar'a Ya'eqob," 96–97 [*wa-konu 'ayhud:* and they became Jews]. See also Jules Perruchon, "Histoire d'Eskender, d'Amda Seyon II et de Na'od," *Journal asiatique,* ser. 9, 3 (1894): 365–366.

31. Perruchon, *Zar'a Ya'eqob,* 142–143.

32. Ibid., 142–143; Carlo Conti Rossini, *Historia Regis Sarsa Dengel (Malak Sagad): Corpus Scriptorum Christianorum Orientalium: Scriptores Aethiopic* 3 (1907), 96–97. The leaders of this rebellion are identified as Amba Nahad of Ṣallamt, Sagay of Semien, and Kantiba (of Dambeya?). According to the chronicle of Sarṣa Dengel, it took Marqos seven years to defeat the rebel. Significantly, the chronicles of Zar'a Ya'eqob and Ba'eda Maryam do not specify the ethnicity of the rebels other than the comment in the former that they had "become Jews." The chronicle of Sarṣa Dengel, written about a century later, calls them Falasha.

33. Taddesse, *Church and State,* 268–296.

34. For a more detailed consideration of this period and the sources on the Beta Israel see Chapter 4. For the present it is relevant to note that none of these sources uses the term "Falasha" or depicts the *ayhud* in a manner that differs significantly from other pre-sixteenth-century sources.

35. This is done rather haphazardly by such popular writers as Kessler and Rapoport. It is also characteristic of much of the writings of Aešcoly. More recently, Quirin, "The Beta Israel," 19, n. 1, has written, "It is the contention of this thesis, however, that the consistency, richness, and continuity of the historical traditions—in both written and oral sources—constitutes sufficient evidence to justify the association of all these terms (Ayhud, Felasha, Kayla, Beta Israel, Israel) with the same group of people at least since the fourteenth century." In fact, his citation of the sources is far more sophisticated than this quote might seem to indicate and cautiously ignores many references to *'ayhud* who are obviously not connected to the Beta Israel. See also his article "The Beta 'Esrā'ēl and *'Ayhud* in Fifteenth-Century Ethiopia: Oral and Written Traditions," *Northeast African Studies* 10, 2–3 (1988): 89–103.

36. Krempel, "Falascha," 255–256.

37. Taddesse, *Church and State,* 206–247; Dillmann, *Zar'a Jacob.* See in particular the numerous polemics against the *ayhudawi* in *Mashafa Milad.* Kurt Wendt, ed., *Das Maṣḥafa Milād (Liber Nativitatis) und Maṣḥafa Sellāsē (Liber Trinitatis) des Kaisers Zar'a Ya'qob, CSCO Script Aeth.* 41, 43.

38. Getatchew Haile, "A Preliminary Investigation of the *Ṭomara T∂sb∂'t* of Emperor Zar'a Ya'∂qob of Ethiopia," *Bulletin of the School of Oriental and African Studies* 43 (1980): 217 (tr) = 231 (tx); see also Carlo Conti Rossini, *Il libro della luce del negus Zar'a Ya'qob (Mashafa Berhan), Corpus Scriptorum Christianorum Orientalium, Scriptores Aethiopici,* 52, 74.

39. Getatchew, "Ṭomara T∂sb∂'t," 219.

40. Taddesse Tamrat, "Problems of Royal Succession in Fifteenth Century Ethiopia: A Presentation of the Documents," *IV Congresso Internazionale*

di Studi Etiopici (Rome: Accademia Nazionale dei Lincei, 1974) I, 519–525.

41. For a similar problem see the comments of Michael Heyd on the use of the designation enthusiasm. "The Reaction to Enthusiasm in the 17th Century: From Antistructure to Structure," *Religion* 15 (1985): 279, " 'Enthusiasm' was primarily a *derogatory* label, not a neutral designation of any homogeneous group in the 16th, 17th, and 18th centuries. It was applied to a broad and diversified spectrum of movements and individuals."

42. On the Stephanites see Taddesse Tamrat, "Some Notes on the Fifteenth Century Stephanite "heresy" in the Ethiopian Church," *Rassegna di Studi Etiopici* 22 (1966): 103–115; and Getatchew Haile, "The Cause of the Ǝsṭifanosites: A Fundamentalist Sect in the Church of Ethiopia," *Paideuma* 29 (1983): 93–119. For a reference to a Falasha as *ayhud* in a Stephanite text see Kaplan, "Gadla Gabra Masih," 280.

43. Conti Rossini, *Sarṣa Dengel;* cf. Perruchon, *Zar'a Ya'ecob,* 96–97, 142–143, 176–177.

44. Conti Rossini, "Gabra Iyasus," 445.

45. Conti Rossini, "Appunti," 571–573.

46. Conti Rossini, *Takla Hawaryat,* 105.

47. In acknowledging the existence of Jewish elements in the religion of the *ayhud* during this period, we are not, of course, denying the existence of other components. Cf. ibid., 104, for the usage of an Agaw term "Yadera" for God. See also our discussion of the later development and crystallization of Beta Israel religion below.

48. Even James Bruce, who perhaps more than any other writer deserves credit for popularizing the exploits of the Falasha Kings, makes no mention of a monarchy in this period. On this and other aspects of Beta Israel political organization see my article, "Leadership and Communal Organization among the Beta Israel (Falasha): An Historical Study," *Encyclopaedia Judaica Yearbook 1986–87* (Jerusalem: Keter, 1988): 154–163, esp. 155–156.

49. Quirin, "The Beta Israel," 54–67; Shelemay, *Music,* 208–216.

50. Quirin, "The Beta Israel," 58–61.

51. Kessler, *Falashas,* 94–105; Rapoport, *The Lost Jews,* 144. Cf. Quirin, "The Beta Israel," 53, "Though the new political-economic demands of the encroaching state were significant causal factors, the conflicts were expressed mainly in religious terms."

52. Kaplan, *Holy Man,* 91.

53. Although it has been claimed that Qozmos converted to Judaism, there is no evidence for this in the sources. Cf. Quirin, "The Beta Israel," 52. Given the fluidity of religious identity during this period and the lack of clear borders between different forms of Judaism/Christianity, the move from one group to another need not have necessitated any radical change or conversion.

54. Kaplan, "Gabra Masih." On the Stephanites see note 42 above. Many of the *ayhud* mentioned in the reign of Zar'a Ya'eqob were members of this dissident Christian sect.

55. Aešcoly, *Falashim,* 1; Leslau, *Anthology,* IX; Halévy, "Rapport au comité

central de l'Alliance Israélite Universelle," *Bulletin de l'Alliance Israélite Universelle* (1868): 90. Cf., however, Ullendorff, *Ethiopia*, 29, who suggests that the term dates to the sixteenth century.

56. Taddesse, *Church and State*, 201. The final bracket is in Taddesse's published translation; the previous two are my own addition. Getatchew Haile (oral communication, May 1990) has informed me that he is very sceptical of the historicity of this alleged decree. If he is correct, the "decree" may be a product of later oral traditions that associated the decline of the Falasha with Yeshaq's period. His reservations also strengthen the view that the name falasha did not originate with this decree. Dr. Getatchew has also expressed his doubts concerning the alleged derivation *falasi:falasha*, as has Professor Robert Hetzron (oral communication, October 1990).

57. Kaplan, "Gadla Gabra Masih."

58. Waldman, *Ethiopian Jewry*, 62–64. For a translation of a portion of this text see Steven Kaplan, "Some Hebrew Sources on the Beta Israel (Falasha)," *Proceedings of the Eighth International Conference of Ethiopian Studies* (Cambridge, Frankfurt: ELM, Frobenius Institute, 1988), I, 205. It is significant to note that in earlier writings (1517, 1521, 1525) that concern the Jews of Ethiopia, Ha-Levi does not use this term.

59. Quoted in Ullendorff, *Ethiopia*, 28; cf. Basset, *Futuh al-Habaša*, 342 (tr.).

60. British Library, Orient. Ms. 705, f. 149. Conti Rossini, "Gabra Iyasus," published only an Italian translation of this portion of this *gadl*.

61. André Caquot, "Les actes d'Ezrā de Gunda Gundē," *Annales d'Éthiopie* 4 (1961): 75.

62. On the Ethiopian land tenure system see, for example, Richard Pankhurst, *State and Land in Ethiopian History* (Addis Ababa: Institute of Ethiopian Studies and Oxford University Press, 1966); Alan Hoben, *Land Tenure among the Amhara of Ethiopia* (Chicago and London: University of Chicago Press, 1973).

63. Quirin, "The Beta Israel," 59–60.

64. See, for example, the reference in *Gadla Takla Hawaryat*, 104, to those who had converted because they "feared the command of the king and governors." Quirin, "The Beta Israel," 83, n. 42, views the testimony of Elijah of Ferrara concerning Ethiopians, who "make a show of Christianity," as a reference to this phenomenon. Elijah is, however, almost certainly discussing the public demonstrations of Ethiopian Christians. Corinaldi, *Tradition and Identity*, 103.

65. Quirin, "The Beta Israel," 60.

66. Ibid., 60–61. While in basic agreement with Quirin on the timing of this transformation, I find it difficult to view the evidence he marshals as conclusive. Among the earliest writers to note the association of the Beta Israel with crafts was the Portuguese Almeida, Book II, Chapter 25.

67. Wolf Leslau, "Taamrat Emmanuel's Notes on Falasha Monks and Holy Places," in *Salo Wittmayer Baron Jubilee Volume* (Jerusalem: American Academy for Jewish Research, 1974) II, 623–637; Quirin, "The Beta Is-

rael," 61–63; Shelemay, *Music,* 78–88; Kaplan, *Holy Man,* 39–41; Shoshana Ben-Dor, "The Holy Places of Ethiopian Jewry," *Pe'amim* 22 (1985): 32–52 (Hebrew).
68. The traditions vary widely as to the precise details of Abba Sabra's biography. While most claim he was originally a Christian, some view him as a Jew; his reason for fleeing the king is variously reported to have been a murder he committed, his involvement in idolatrous practices, or his position as a Beta Israel leader. Cf. Ben Dor, "Holy Places," 41–45.
69. Shelemay, *Music,* 79–80. These include sacred music, religious literature, laws of social purity, the liturgical cycle, and the architecture of the prayer house.
70. Conti Rossini, *Storia,* 156–165.
71. For a more detailed discussion of each of these movements see Taddesse, *Church and State,* 156–174, 206–220, 226; Kaplan, *Holy Man,* 36–44.
72. Several authors have claimed that Qozmos introduced monasticism to the Beta Israel in the fourteenth century, but this receives no explicit support in the sources. Cf. Hess, "History," 113; "Outline," 102; Quirin, "The Beta Israel," 62; Shelemay, *Music,* 32, 81.
73. Quirin, "The Beta Israel," 61.
74. Getatchew Haile has speculated that this may be an account of the fate of Zamika'el, a notorious heretic from the time of Zar'a Ya'eqob, who not only denied Mary, but Christ himself. As such he was one, albeit the most extreme, of numerous Christians who appear to have reacted strongly against this emperor's imposition of the cult of Mary and other religious innovations. Getatchew Haile, "The End of a Deserter of the Established Church of Ethiopia," *Sixth International Conference of Ethiopian Studies, Tel Aviv, 14–17 April 1980* (Rotterdam: A. P. Balkema, 1986): 193–203.
75. Perruchon, *Zar'a Ya'eqob,* 5, 10–13, 94–95, 98–100; Taddesse, "Succession," 518–526. One of Zar'a Ya'eqob's sons, Galawdeyos, is even accused of having become a "Jew," and while it is tempting to try to connect this to the traditions about Ṣagga Amlak, the reference almost certainly refers to his rebellious political behavior. Cf. Getatchew, *"Ṭomara T∂sb∂'t,"* 219.
76. Kaplan, *Holy Man,* 32–44.
77. "The Beta Israel," 61. Quoted in Kaplan, *Holy Man,* 40, and for a similar interpretation see also Ben-Dor, "Holy Places," 36.
78. Kaplan, " 'Falasha' Religion," 58.
79. It is, unfortunately, impossible to reconstruct the religious system of these *ayhud.* In all probability, however, their religious system was probably closer to that of the "Hebraic-pagan" Qemant than that of the later Falasha. Cf. Gamst, *Qemant.*
80. Dillmann, *Lexicon,* 1342. Cf. the prayer in the Monastic ritual, "Mawas'et za-falaseyan." This connection was, I believe, first suggested by Kay K. Shelemay, "Historical Ethnomusicology: Reconstructing Falasha Liturgical History," *Ethnomusicology* 24 (1980): 246.
81. For a detailed discussion of Beta Israel literature see my article, "The

Literature of the Beta Israel" Retrospect and Prospect," *Pe'amim* 41 (1990): 90–111 (Hebrew).

82. Leslau, *Anthology*, 11–16. Both manuscripts of *Te'ezaza Sanbat* found in the Faitlovitch collection (Tel Aviv University, Ramat Aviv, Israel) omit this section and begin with Leslau, 16, line 3. This section, which is probably a later addition to the text, shows certain similarities to the Arabic Christian, later Christian Ethiopic work known as *Qalamentos*.

83. Leslau, *Anthology*, 16–19; Steven Kaplan, *"Te'ezāza Sanbat: A Beta Israel Work Reconsidered,"* *Gilgul* (Supplements to *Numen* 50), ed. Shaul Shaked et al. (Leiden: E. J. Brill, 1987), 107–124.

84. For a summary of this complex work see Leslau, *Anthology*, 3–8.

85. One clear exception to this rule is the *Arde'et* (Disciples). The Christian version concerns Jesus and his disciples, the Beta Israel version transforms this into Moses and his disciples, i.e., the leaders of the twelve tribes. See Mordechai Wurmbrand, *The Falasha Arde'et* (Tel Aviv: Chug Nemanei Beit Faitlovitch, 1964 (Hebrew); Rene Basset, "Enseignement de Jesus Christ à ses Disciples et Prières Magiques," *Apocryphes Éthiopiens* 8 (Paris: Librarie de l'art indépendent, 1896); Enno Littmann, "The Magic Book of the Disciples," *Journal of the American Oriental Society* 25 (1904): 1–48.

86. Dillmann, *Zar'a Jacob;* Taddesse, *Church and State,* 220–231; Getatchew, "Tomara," 208, n. 14.

87. Of these works only a badly fragmented version of the *Testament of Abraham* has been published. For a more complete edition and translation of this text as well as the other two Testaments see Maurice Gaugine, "The Falasha Version of the Testaments of Abraham, Isaac, and Jacob," Ph.D. dissertation, University of Manchester, 1965. See also Kaplan, "Literature," 97–98.

88. Kaplan, *"Te'ezaza Sanbat";* Max Wurmbrand, *The Death of Aaron* (Tel Aviv: Chug Nemanei Beit Faitlovitch, 1961, Hebrew).

89. *Mota Muse, Mota Aron,* the *Gadlat* of Abraham, Isaac, and Jacob, *Dersana Abreham wa Sara, Nagara Muse.*

90. Enrico Cerulli, *Storia della letteratura etiopica* (Milan: Nuova Accademia Editrice, 1956), 31–33, 67–70.

91. Leslau, *Anthology,* 10, 96, 106; Shelemay, *Music,* 57–59; Quirin, "Beta Israel," 63–64.

92. Kaplan, "Literature," 101; "Falasha Religion," 63–64.

93. Wolf Leslau, "A Falasha Religious Dispute," *Proceedings of the American Academy of Jewish Research* 26 (1946–47): 89–95.

94. Bender, et al., eds., *Language,* 13–18.

95. See, for example, Jack Goody, ed., *Literacy in Traditional Societies* (Cambridge: Cambridge University Press, 1968); *The Logic of Writing and the Organization of Society* (Cambridge: Cambridge University Press, 1986).

4. *Resistance and Defeat: 1468–1632*

1. Merid, "Southern Ethiopia," 33.

2. Cf. Abir, *Red Sea,* 43, "The struggle of the Solomonic monarchs against

autonomous tendencies of subordinate govvernors and other centrifugal forces in their kingdon is a dominant theme in the history of mediaeval and post-medieval Ethiopia."

3. It is, of course, not my intention to argue that the failure of the Beta Israel to *assimilate* can be explained purely or even primarily as a product of geographic conditions. Rather, I seek to simply draw attention to the crucial role played by their region's rugged conditions in prolonging their military resistance. Cf. Quirin, "Beta Israel," 11–12, 37, n. 25. Although some have argued (Kessler, p. 93) that prior to their defeat by Susenyos in the seventeenth century the Beta Israel numbered as many as half a million souls, this figure appears grossly exaggerated. It is, it must be noted, based on an extrapolation from a statement of James Bruce who visited Ethiopia almost a century and a half after the final defeat of the Beta Israel. So high a figure is, moreover, greatly suspect in light of all we know about both world and Ethiopian demographics in the pre-modern period. In Ethiopia, for example, recurrent wars, epidemics, and famines must have severely limited population growth. A peak figure of about 100,000 Beta Israel appears most reasonable. See Baron, *History*, 379–382.

4. Of course, the development of a unique Beta Israel identity and the manipulation of elements of Christian Ethiopian culture as discussed in the previous chapter was crucial to the survival of the group.

5. Perruchon, *Zar'a Ya'eqob*, 111.

6. Taddesse, *Church and State*, 286–291.

7. The noted rabbi and talmudic scholar Obadiah of Bertinoro reports on these wars in both 1488 and 1489. In the former letter he notes that the conflict has been going on for four years. Cf. Corinaldi, *Identity*, 106–107; Waldman, *Ethiopian Jewry*, 41–44.

8. Getatchew, "Deserter," 194. Getatchew does not view this as a reference to the "Falasha" who were "too far from the central administration to be a threat." Even if we concede this point, the Hebrew sources from this period offer clear indications of continued clashes between the Beta Israel and the Christian rulers.

9. Waldman, *Ethiopian Jewry*, 60–61; Corinaldi, *Identity*, 109–115. This is in a letter from 1517. A more detailed version appears in a letter from 1525.

10. Waldman, *Ethiopian Jewry*, 36–92; Corinaldi, *Identity and Tradition*, 102–128. Although concerned with the religious practices of the Beta Israel, these sources are generally so determined to place these within the context of contemporary debates between Rabbinates and Karaites that they ignore all other features. Thus, no mention is made of monasticism, purity laws, sacrifices, and other important features of Beta Israel religion.

11. For a brief discussion and English translation of some of these documents see Kaplan, "Hebrew Sources," 199–208.

12. On Ba'eda Maryam's defeat in 1474 and its consequences as well as Eskender's similar difficulties see Perruchon, *Zar'a Ya'eqob*, 180–182; "Histoire d'Eskender, d'Amda-Seyon II et de Na'od, rois d'Éthiopie," *Journal asiatique*, ser. 9, 3 (1894): 343–345; Taddesse, *Church and State*, 295–296.

13. Lebna Dengel had an older brother who was passed over as "unsuitable for the position." Cf. Abir, *Red Sea,* 70. Other minors to be crowned emperor during this period include, Eskender, Amda Ṣeyon II, and Ya'eqob (1596–1603, 1605–1607). Ya'eqob clearly appears to have been chosen in preference to an older and more able candidate.

14. Taddesse, *Church and State,* 287–289. Helena's period of influence began in the reign of Ba'eda Maryam and although interrupted by Eskender, did not conclude until Lebna Dengal assumed power ca. 1516.

15. Alvarez, I, 276–279.

16. According to the aforementioned Abraham Halevi, the Falasha rebelled yet again in 1520 and enjoyed considerable success. "And in the year 5280 [1519-20] the Jews were strengthened and they raised up a banner and broke the yoke of the Gentiles from upon them and succeeded against them in their wars." No other support exists for this claim. Corinaldi, *Identity and Tradition,* 113; Waldman, *Ethiopian Jewry,* 61.

17. Abir, *Red Sea,* 77–88; Joseph Cuoq, *L'Islam en Éthiopie des origines au XVIe siècle* (Paris: Nouvelles Editions Latines, 1981): 218–223.

18. See *Futūh al-Habasha,* tr. and ed. Rene Basset (Paris: Ernst Leroux, 1897–1901).

19. Taddesse, *Church and State,* 302.

20. Basset, *Futuh,* 455–460 (tr.); Cf. however, Bruce, *Travels,* III, 188, who claims that they only allied themselves with Gragn after a long period of resistance. Hess, "Toward a History," 114. For evidence of the assistance rendered to the Muslims by predominantly pagan Agaw see Enrico Cerulli, "Gli atti di Tekle Alfa," *Annali* II (1943): 37.

21. R. S. Whiteway, *The Portuguese Expedition to Abyssinia in 1541–1543* (London: Hakluy Society, 1902), 56–65, esp. 57–60, and see the important discussion of this episode by C. F. Beckingham, "A Note on the Topography of Ahmad Gragn's Campaigns in 1542," *Journal of Semitic Studies* 4 (1959): 362–373.

22. Basset, "Etudes," 19; Beckingham, "Topography," 368.

23. Quirin, "Beta Israel," 70.

24. Quirin, ibid., 71, suggests this may also have been due to Galawdewos' need for Beta Israel workers to rebuild churches and other buildings and his overriding need for internal peace. On Galawdewos' reign see William Conzelman, ed. and tr., *Chronique de Galawdewos (Claudius) roi d'Éthiopie* (Paris: Bouillon, 1895). For an important and extremely positive reevaluation of Galawdewos see Merid, "Southern Ethiopia," 107–118, 159–194, 230ff.

25. Another brother, Ya'eqob, the childless Galawdewos's presumptive heir, had died in 1555.

26. Richard K. Pankhurst, *A History of Ethiopian Towns* (Wiesbaden: Franz Steiner Verlag, 1982): I, 94; Quirin, "Beta Israel," 73.

27. Already in the reign of Galawdewos the Beta Israel of Wagara "were growing restless, probably because they were unwilling to pay taxes." Gon-

çala Rodrigues, letter of February 3, 1556, quoted by Merid, "Southern Ethiopia," 165; see also 177–178.

28. Taddesse, "Agaw," 12–13.

29. Ibid., 13–15.

30. Letter of Fulgenico Freire to Nunes Barreto, August 12, 1560. Beccari, *Rerum*, X, 105.

31. Kropp, *Geschichte*, 54–55; Francisco Maria Esteves Pereira, *Historia de Minas, Rei de Ethiopia* (Lisbon: 1888), 28, 45–46; P. Petri Paez S.I., *Historia da Etiopia*, Livro III, Capitulo VI, in Becarri, *Rerum*, II, 54–55; Jules Perruchon, "Notes pour l'histoire d'Éthiopie. Le règne de Minas ou Admas-Sagad (1559–1663)," *Revue sémitique* 4 (1896): 283; Conti Rossini, *Sarṣa Dengel*, 86; Merid, "Southern Ethiopia," 178.

32. Merid, "Southern Ethiopia," 230–232, and see the following pages until 287 for details. Quirin, "The Beta Israel," 91, n. 97, and Mordechai Abir, *Ethiopia and the Red Sea* (London: Frank Cass, 1980), 167–170, largely follow Merid in their evaluation of Sarṣa Dengel's rule.

33. For this chronology see Merid, "Southern Ethiopia," 285–287 and Quirin, "The Beta Israel," 92, n. 107. Carlo Conti Rossini, *Sarṣa Dengel;* Halévy, *Sarṣa-Dengel.* Popular authors, particularly those who have relied on Halévy's excerpted version of Sarṣa Dengel's chronicle rather than Conti Rossini's complete edition, have generally failed to view these battles in the general context of this emperor's policies, and have overestimated the role the king's alleged anti-Jewish animus played in provoking these clashes. Cf. Kessler, *The Falashas*, 98–100, who also incorrectly states on p. 127 that the original text is in Amharic.

34. "The Beta Israel," 73.

35. Abir, *Red Sea*, 167, "Serse Dingils's decision in 1579 to consolidate his government in the Falasha provinces rather than to confront the Galla [Oromo] could be considered the turning point of his reign, if not a watershed of Ethiopian history. This disastrous decision, part of the emperor's misguided policy, opened the plateau to Galla migration and sparked off a chain reaction which led to the final decline of the Solomonic kingdom."

36. Pankhurst, *Towns*, 94–96.

37. Ibid., 96.

38. Although they date from a much later period, the words of the clergy to the Emperor Tewodros II are probably applicable to our period. "Stay four months in Gondar and eat Armacheho, Segeded, Welqayit, Simen, Tegre; stay four months at Aringo and eat Begemdir, Last, Yehu, Werehimano, Wello, Shewa, stay four months at Tibaba and eat Mecha, Agew, Damot, Gojjam as of yore," Sven Rubenson, *King of Kings, Tewodros of Ethiopia* (Addis Ababa, 1966), 69.

39. Conti Rossini, *Sarṣa Dengel*, 96–97; Halévy, "Sarṣa Dengel," 392. See also Paez, *Historia*, Livro III, Capitulo XIV, in Beccari, *Rerum*, vol. II, 141–144, for a Portuguese account that closely follows that of the royal chronicles.

40. Conti Rossini, *Sarṣa Dengel*, 112–113; Halévy, "Sarṣa Dengel," 412. Both

Radai's decision to rename the mountains and his choice of names appear significant. The act of renaming itself may be seen as a symbolic statement of his sovereignty over the region. His choice of names may have been intended as a challenge to Sarṣa Dengel's claim to be an Israelite (Solomonic) ruler. Sarṣa Dengel is also said to have been motivated by his desire to avenge an earlier victory (in the reign of Minas) by Radai over Harbo, who commanded troops from Tigre. According to traditions recorded by Quirin, "The Beta Israel," 74, 92, n. 108, a Beta Israel *azmach* at Sarṣa Dengel's court incurred his wrath by (1) insulting his wife or (2) refusing to convert to Christianity.

41. Conti Rossini, *Sarṣa Dengel,* 95–96, 98–99; Halévy, "Sarṣa Dengel," 406, 411. The chronicler makes special mention of the meager property possessed by the Beta Israel leader, Radai.

42. Conti Rossini, *Sarṣa Dengel,* 88, 107; Halévy, "Sarṣa Dengel," 405. In one crucial episode the Beta Israel on the *amba* (plateau) are said to have panicked and failed to roll four enormous stones down upon the Christian troops.

43. Conti Rossini, *Sarṣa Dengel,* 95; Halévy, "Sarṣa Dengel," 406; Perruchon, "Sarṣa Dengel," 180.

44. Conti Rossini, *Sarṣa Dengel,* 88–89, see also 110; Halévy, "Sarṣa Dengel," 399; Paez, *Historia,* Livro III, Capitulo XIV, in Beccari, *Rerum* II, 141.

45. Merid, "Southern Ethiopia," 287.

46. In the chronicle of Sarṣa Dengel, Conti Rossini, 93–100; Halévy, 399–414, the campaigns against Kalef and Radai are intermingled. Hess, "History," 115, and "Outline," 104, treats these as a single episode. The shorter royal chronicles (cf. Perruchon, "Sarṣa Dengel," 180), however, clearly distinguish between these two installments of the Beta Israel-imperial struggle.

47. Conti Rossini, *Sarṣa Dengel,* 100–106, esp. 106; Halévy, "Sarṣa Dengel," 414–421, esp. 421; Paez, *Historia,* 143–144.

48. Roger W. Cowley, *The Traditional Interpretation of the Apocalypse of St. John in the Ethiopian Church* (Cambridge: Cambridge University Press, 1983), 314.

49. Bruce, *Travels,* III, 251, dates Gushen's defeat to January 19, 1594 (sic), and claims that four thousand Beta Israel soldiers died at the time. Cf. Conti Rossini, *Sarṣa Dengel,* 106–112; Halévy, "Sarṣa Dengel," 423; Paez, *Historia,* Livro III, Capitulo XIV, in Beccari, *Rerum,* 144.

50. Conti Rossini, *Sarṣa Dengel,* 108; Halévy, "Sarṣa Dengel," 423–424; Paez, *Historia,* Livro III, Capitulo XIV, in Becarri, *Rerum,* 144. Although Hess, "History," 116; "Outline," 105; and Kessler, *The Falashas,* 100, claim that Gedewon and his followers eventually committed suicide this does not appear to be the sense of either the Ge'ez or Portuguese sources. Gedewon, moreover, reappears almost immediately as the royal appointed governor of Semien and the brother of Sarṣa Dengel's mistress Harago. The chronicle of Susenyos explicitly mentions that Gedewon opposed four Ethiopian rulers, Sarṣa Dengel, Ya'eqob, Zadengel, and Susenyos. F. M. Esteves Pereira, *Chronica de Susenyos, Rei de Ethiopia* (Lisbon: Imprensa Nacional, 1892)

I, 282. The Ṣarṣa Dengel's chronicler's need to convince his readers that Gedewon escaped by chance rather than as a result of an intentional decision to let him pass may be, at least in part, connected with his sister's prominent position and his own later rise to power. The precise relationship between the various Beta Israel rulers remains unclear. Rada'i and Kalef were brothers. Merid, "Southern Ethiopia," 356, n. 2, suggests that Gushan and Gedewon were their brothers as well, and that a fifth sibling—their sister Harago—was the mistress of Ṣarṣa Dengel. Quirin, "The Beta Israel," 92, n. 109, suggests that there may have been two pairs of brothers (Kalef and Radai/Gushan and Gedewon).

51. Merid, "Southern Ethiopia," 356–360; Almeida, *Historia*, 41–42. Besides Zamaryam and Ya'eqob, Harago had two other sons, Kefla Maryam and Matako; both were probably also sons of Ṣarṣa Dengel and were killed by Susenyos when he came to power.

52. Jules Perruchon, "Notes pour l'histoire de'Éthiopie: Règnes de Ya'qob et Za-Dengel (1597–1607)," *Revue sémitique* 4 (1896): 356–361.

53. Basset, *Études*, 124.

54. Ibid.; Merid, "Southern Ethiopia," 361–370. Girma and Merid, *Luso-Ethiopian Relations*, 70–71; Esteves Pereira, *Susenyos*, I, 49.

55. Esteves Pereira, *Susenyos*, I, 50–53; Merid, "Southern Ethiopia," 371–387; Girma and Merid, *Luso-Ethiopian Relations*, 71–73. For a far more negative evaluation of Zadengel see Abir, *Red Sea*, 181–184. Cf. Perruchon, "Ya'qob," 359–362.

56. Esteves Pereira, *Susenyos*, I, 53–94; Perruchon, "Ya'qob," 360–363; Abir, *Red Sea*, 184–185; Merid, "Southern Ethiopia," 388–394; Girma and Merid, *Luso-Ethiopian Relations*, 73–75.

57. Esteves Pereira, *Susenyos*, 110–132; Jules Perruchon, "Notes pour l'histoire d'Éthiopie: Règne de Susenyos ou Seltan-Segad (1607–1632), *Revue sémitique* 5 (1897): 79.

58. Perruchon, "Susenyos," 79; Esteves Pereira, *Susenyos*, 132–141.

59. Esteves Pereira, *Susenyos*, I, 150; Bruce, *Travels*, III, 304–306; Perruchon, "Susenyos," 173–174.

60. Esteves Pereira, *Susenyos*, 150–151; Bruce, *Travels*, 305–306; Segenet was the name of one of Gedewon's major strongholds.

61. Bruce, *Travels*, III, 306; Perruchon, "Susenyos," 174; Esteves Pereira, *Susenyos*, I, 151–153; Basset, *Études*, 26. Quirin, "Beta Israel," 76, states that Takluy was hung, but this appears to be a misunderstanding of the texts.

62. Bruce, *Travels*, 307–308; Esteves Periera, *Susenyos*, I, 155. Those who escaped are said to have fled to Phineas, a Beta Israel leader. Hess, "History," 117; "Outline," 105, claims that Phineas replaced Gedewon, but this appears to be based on Bruce's mistaken report of Gedewon's death at this time.

63. Perruchon, "Susenyos," 173; Esteves Pereira, *Susenyos*, I, 155–156; cf. Pankhurst, *Towns*, 102. Some chronological difficulties exist with regard to the precise timing of this episode.

64. Esteves Pereira, *Susenyos*, I, 155–156; Bruce, *Travels*, III, 308.

65. While Wagara and Janfekera are easily recognizable among the areas mentioned, other regions are more difficult to identify. Cf. Quirin, "Beta Israel," 93, n. 114.

66. Girma and Merid, *Luso-Ethiopian*, 72, 86.

67. Although Susenyos did not receive the sacraments and publicly convert until March 1622, he is said to have secretly converted as early as 1618. Perruchon, "Susenyos," 174; Girma and Merid, *Luso-Ethiopian*, 88.

68. Girma and Merid, *Luso-Ethiopian*, 84.

69. Esteves Pereira, *Susenyos*, I, 190.

70. Girma and Merid, *Luso-Ethiopian*, 94–95.

71. Ibid., 97–104.

72. Esteves Pereira, *Susenyos*, 221–222. Malk'ea Krestos, who commanded the imperial troops, had previously played a crucial role in subduing the rebellion of Yona'el.

73. Esteves Pereira, *Susenyos*, I, 271–272, 278–279, 280–284; Perruchon, "Susenyos," 177. Rather surprisingly, Hess makes no mention of this episode in either of his surveys. Throughout the Susenyos' chronicle this claiment to the throne is referred to as "the son of Arzo," with no personal name given. The shorter chronicle identifies him as Za-Manfas Qeddus.

74. Giacome Barrati, *The Late Travels of S. Giacome Baratti, an Italian Gentleman*, tr. G.D. (London: Benjamin Billingsly, 1670), 108–109; Esteves Pereira, *Susenyos*, I, 154–156; Almeida, *History*, 54–55; Quirin, "Beta Israel," 93, n. 114.

75. Almeida, *Historia*, Ch. 12, 54–55.

76. Quirin, "Beta Israel," 181, n. 12.

77. Esteves Pereira, *Susenyos*, I, 155–156.

5. Glory and Decline: 1632–1855

1. Almeida quoted in Richard Pankhurst, *The History of Famine and Epidemics in Ethiopia* (Relief and Rehabilitation Commission: Addis Ababa, 1985), 45; see also 46–47.

2. Leslau, "A Falasha Religious Dispute," *Proceedings of the American Academy for Jewish Research* 16 (1947): 80.

3. Pankhurst, *Towns*, 41–48, 94–112; Ronald J. Horvath, "The Wandering Capitals of Ethiopia," *Journal of African History* 10 (1969): 205–219.

4. Pankhurst, *Towns*, 94–100, and see 100–112 for a discussion of other such sites in the region.

5. Ibid., 117–121.

6. Jules Perruchon, "Notes pour l'histoire d'Éthiopie: Le règne de Fasiladas (Alam-Sagad) de 1632 a 1667," *Revue sémitique* 5 (1897): 363f, 366, 6 (1898): 86, 88.

7. E. Van Donzel, *A Yemenite Embassy to Ethiopia 1647–1649. Al-Haymi's Sirat al-Habasha. Newly Introduced, Translated and Annotated* (Wiesbaden: Franz Steiner, 1986).

8. Pankhurst, *Towns*, 122–125.

9. Pankhurst, *Towns*, 168.

10. See Jules Leroy, "Ethiopian Painting in the Middle Ages," in G. Gerster, ed., *Churches*, 66–67. Stanislav Chojnacki, *Major Themes in Ethiopian Painting* (Athiopische Forshungen 10) (Franz Steiner: Wiesbaden, 1983), 134, disagrees with Leroy's analysis, but still comments on the important stylistic developments of this period.

11. See Cowley, *Interpretation*, 23–34. The history of Ethiopian chant is the subject of an important study by Kay Kaufman Shelemay and Peter Jeffries, *Ethiopian Christian Chant: An Anthology*, 3 vols. (Madison, WI: A-R Editions, Inc., in press).

12. For a useful analysis of this period see Laverle Bennette Berry, "The Solomonic Monarchy at Gondar 1630–1755: An Institutional Analysis of Kingship in the Christian Kingdom of Ethiopia," Ph.D. dissertation, Boston University, 1976.

13. Both smiths and potters were suspected of magic because of their ability to transform objects by placing them in fire. Alvarez reported (*Prester John* II, 442–444, that in the sixteenth-century royal camps smiths resided in the area of the prostitutes and strangers. Ludolf was told [*A New History of Ethiopia, Being a Full and Accurate Description of the Kingdom of Abessinia* (London: J. P. Gent, 1682), 390–391)] that "The silly vulgar people could not endure Smiths as being a sort of Mortals, that spit fire, and were bred up in Hell." For a fuller discussion of such beliefs see the end of this chapter.

14. Quirin, "Beta Israel," 165–167.

15. This is remembered in a folktale in which one Beta Israel soldier is said to be worth one hundred Christians.

16. Ludolf, *History*, 390; Quirin, "Beta Israel," 166.

17. Ludolf, *History*, 390–391; Almeida, 54–55.

18. Balthazar Telles, *The Travels of the Jesuits in Ethiopia*, tr. (London: J. Knapton, 1710), 206. Although no explicit mention is made here of the Beta Israel, their own traditions associate them with work as builders in the time of Susenyos. Given their role as smiths, they would certainly have been among those whom Paes taught to make tools and would logically have been involved in the other aspects of the work.

19. Quirin, "Beta Israel," 166, 169–172. Although the contemporary sources usually make no specific mention of the role played by the Beta Israel, their own traditions and later sources a quite explicit concerning their role. For a discussion of the political significance of the castles and churches of this period see Berry, "Gondar," 174–183, 192–199.

20. Bruce, *Travels*, II, 633–634.

21. Taddesse, *Church and State*, 91; Berry, "Gondar," 260.

22. Merid, "Southern Ethiopia," 565. This process may have already begun in the time of Susenyos himself, but it is more likely that it occurred only in the reign of his son Fasiladas, who appears to have cancelled his father's harshest decrees against the Beta Israel.

23. Ignazio Guidi, *Annales Iohannis I, Iyasu I et Bakaffa, Corpus Scriptorum*

Christianorum Orientalum Script. Aeth. 5 (Paris: 1903), 21. Earlier the same king had mediated a violent conflict between the "Kayla" and the Tulama on the Wallo-Begemder border. Of all the names used for the Beta Israel *Kayla* is by far the most puzzling. According to Abba Yeshaq, a nineteenth-century Beta Israel monk and high priest, the name refers to those who "did not cross the sea" when Menelik I and his men crossed the sea on Saturday (d'Abbadie, "Réponses," 240; cf. also the curious statement, ibid., 268, "Je respecterai le sabbat jusqu'à la mer"). Since this Agaw term does not appear as a designation of the group prior to the seventeenth century, its derivation from so early an event is as doubtful as for the previously discussed Falasha. The term could perhaps be related to the Beta Israel practice of not crossing a river on the Sabbath (cf. Leslau, *Anthology,* xi), but this too is not certain.

24. d'Abbadie, quoted by Quirin, "The Beta Israel," 167.
25. Quirin, "Beta Israel," 172–177.
26. See, for example, the apparent reference to a Beta Israel official in the royal chronicles as *Bajerond* Isayyas, the chief of the carpenters who served during the reign of Iyasu II. Ignazio Guidi, *Annales Regum 'Iyasu II et 'Iyo'as, Corpus Scriptorum Christianorum Orientalium,* 67 (Louvain: Imprimerie Orientaliste, 1954), 91.
27. Quirin, "Beta Israel," 176.
28. Kaplan, "Leadership," 157; Quirin, "Beta Israel," 176, reports a tradition that the *bajerond* was chosen by his fellow workers but had to receive royal confirmation. For an interesting discussion of the role of externally created middlemen in a modern Ethiopian case see Uri Almagor, "Institutionalizing a Fringe Periphery: Dassanetch-Amhara Relations," in Donald Donham and Wendy James, eds., *The Southern Marches of Imperial Ethiopia* (Cambridge: Cambridge University Press, 1986), 96–115.
29. Quirin, "Beta Israel," 168–172.
30. Ibid., 169. Pankhurst, however, appears to connect the existence of Kayla Meda with a later separation of the Beta Israel. See *Towns,* 127.
31. These were, in fact, standard characteristics of urban centers and were found to a lesser extent in Ethiopia's "wandering capitals" as well.
32. The Beta Israel laws of social purity known as *attenkugn* (don't touch me) are attributed to the fifteenth-century monastic leader Abba Sabra. (See Chapter 3.) Given the tendency in oral traditions to date virtually all important religious institutions to his time, some caution must be exercised in dating these laws. It is difficult to discern any period in which they could have been observed strictly by all Beta Israel. Indeed, tenant farmers, soldiers, and craftsmen would all have found them an onerous burden. In all probability such laws represent an ideal for behavior practiced in reality primarily by only the monastic clergy.
33. Guidi, *Iohannis I,* 9; trans. Pankhurst, *Towns,* 127 (emphasis added).
34. Ibid., 36. See, however, Berry, "Gondar," 16, who claims that following the earlier decree the Beta Israel and others were forcibly resettled.
35. Ludolf, *History,* 390–391.

36. Quirin, "Beta Israel," 178–179. Such traditions must be viewed with more than a little skepticism particularly in light of contemporary reports of conversions.

37. Baratti, 109–110.

38. d'Abbadie, "Réponses," 235.

39. For the Beta Israel version of this text see, Steven Kaplan, *Les Falashas*, 97–105. For the Christian version see Lazarus Goldschmidt, *Die abessinischen Handschriften der Stadtbiobliothek zu Frankfurt am Main* (Berlin: S. Calvary and Co., 1897), 91–101.

40. On the Syriac version see I. H. Hall, "The Colloquy of Moses on Mt. Sinai," *Hebraica*, 7, 3 (1881): 161–177.

41. Two manuscripts in the Faitlovitch collection date the work to the years 1757/58; the text published by Goldschmidt dates the translation to 1754/55.

42. Kaplan, " 'Falasha' Religion."

43. Shelemay, *Music*, 199–203. It is important to note that the Beta Israel do not appear to have incorporated many of the changes that entered the Christian liturgy in the Gondar period, most notably the Ethiopian Christian system of musical notation. Oral communication, Shelemay, August 1990.

44. Mordechai Abir, "Ethiopia and the Horn of Africa," *The Cambridge History of Africa* IV, ed. Richard Gray (Cambridge: Cambridge University Press, 1975), 564–571; Berry, "Gondar," 49–56.

45. Guidi, *Iyasu I,* 170. Of course, some allowance should be made for the stereotyped panegyric tone of the chronicler.

46. For a description of Gondar and its court during this period see V. Nerssian, tr., and Richard Pankhurst, ed. and annot., "The visit to Ethiopia of Yohannes T'ovmacean, an Armenian Jeweller in 1764–66," *Journal of Ethiopian Studies* 15 (1982): 79–104.

47. So called because it resembled the biblical period of the Judges when "There was no king in Israel: every man did what was right in his own eyes" (Jud. 17:6). In recent historiography it has been common to call this period the "Era of the Princes" because effective power rested with various local military leaders and chiefs. Mordechai Abir, *Ethiopia: The Era of the Princes* (London: Longman, 1968), xxiii, but cf. his comments in *Cambridge History*, 571.

48. Sven Rubenson, "Ethiopia and the Horn," in *The Cambridge History of Africa*, V, ed. John E. Flint (Cambridge: Cambridge University Press, 1976), 57.

49. Ibid., 70; cf. Abir, *Cambridge History*, 573–574.

50. Ullendorff, *Ethiopians*, 12–14.

51. These include Henry Salt, Samuel Gobat, and Antoine d'Abbadie. Ibid., 14–20; Rubenson, *Survival*, 16–20; on the French explorers see Georges Malécot, *Les voyageurs français et les relations entre la France et l'Abyssinie de 1835 à 1870* (Paris: Librairie Orientaliste Paul Geunther, 1972).

52. Pankhurst, *Towns*, 178–179.

53. Ibid., 179. Salomon II (1777–79); Takla Giyorgis (1779–84, etc.).

54. Pankhurst, *Towns*, 254.

55. *Travels*, II, 622–623; 3, 380; 4, 112.

56. Nathaniel Pearce, *The Life and Times of Nathaniel Pearce* (London: Colburn and Bentley, 1831), I, 234; Eduard Rüppel, *Reise in Abyssinien* (Frankfurt am Main: Schmerber, 1835–1840), II, 91, both claim that it was no longer in use. Gobat, *Journal*, 90, however, found three large rooms and some smaller ones in good condition except for dust and filth, and claimed that the Emperor still used one of them.

57. Of Gondar's churches, popularly numbered as forty-four but probably greater in number, nearly half (Pearce, *Life*, II, 234), perhaps as few as nineteen (d'Abbadie, *Journal*, 160) were still in use.

58. Pearce, *Life*, I, 244 (best builders); Gobat, *Journal*, 468.

59. On the decline in the population of Gondar see Pankhurst, *Towns*, 257.

60. Ibid., 173–179, 147–245. Cf. Gobat, *Journal*, 112, who while visiting Gondar reported that the Etchege (an important Church official) "made many excuses for not being able to furnish me with everything that I want, because the armies, passing and repassing this year, have ruined his fields."

61. Rubenson, *Cambridge History*, 70.

62. Quirin, "Beta Israel," 205–206. See, for example, the purchase by a Tigrean noble of twenty-five (and not five as appears in Huntingford, *Land Charters*, 67) parcels of Falasha land or in Falasha territory. Conti Rossini, *Liber Axumae, Corpus Scriptorum Christianorum Orientalum Script. Aeth.* 24 (Louvain: 1962): 53.

63. *Travels*, V, 13; cf. Hess, "Outline," 107; "History," 119.

64. *Journal*, 122.

65. For example, Edmond Combes and Maurice Tamisier, *Voyage en Abyssinie, dans le pays des Galla, de Choa et D'Ifat, 1835–1837* (Paris: Desessart, 1838), I: 350; Gobat, *Journal*, 310; Henry Dufton, *Narrative of a Journey Through Abyssinia in 1862–63* (London: Chapman & Hall, 1867), 165, 169–171.

66. Quirin, "Beta Israel," 212–219. Although Quirin seeks to argue for a historical process whereby the term was increasingly identified with the Beta Israel (see esp. 214), the evidence for this sort of evolution is not totally supported by the sources. Interestingly, a similar development from a term designating a particular status, to one almost exclusively associated with a single group does appear to have occurred with the name *Falasha*. For a further discussion of the designation of *buda* and its implications, see the final section of this chapter.

67. Gobat, *Journal*, 122, 310.

68. d'Abbadie, "Réponses," 264.

69. Leslau, "Dispute," 80.

70. *Ras* Ali I a Yejju Galla emerged as kingmaker and founder of a dynasty in the 1770s. Among his successors were *Ras* Gugsa (ca. 1803–25) and *Ras* Marye (1828–31). Cf. Quirin, "Beta Israel," 220.

71. *Voyage,* I, 349.
72. Aešcoly, "Notes," 100–101.
73. Leslau, "Religious Dispute," 81.
74. Ibid., 235. Whether this reform was ever enforced must be questioned in light of Flad's testimony that in the mid-nineteenth century the Beta Israel and Christians celebrated St. Michael's feast on the same day. *The Falashas (Jews) of Abyssinia* (London: William Macintosh, 1869), 50.
75. *Journal,* 120.
76. "Réponses," 239. See 268, where a learned Beta Israel mentions his knowledge of "le nouveau Testament des Chretiens."
77. On Language see Grinfeld, "Languages," 50–73.
78. Although the Beta Israel were not the only group identified as *buda,* by the nineteenth century the complex equations that associated *buda,* blacksmiths, and the Beta Israel were firmly entrenched. Gobat met a Beta Israel woman who was considered to be the "Queen of the boudas" (*Journal,* 176–177). Plowden reports somewhat later that "Fellashas or Jews are also universally said to be Bouddhas." Walter Plowden, *Travels in Abyssinia and the Galla Country with an Account of a Mission to Ras Ali in 1848* (London: Longmans, 1868), 121. Among the many modern discussions of the *buda* complex see Quirin, "Beta Israel," 212–218; J. Abbink, "A Socio-Structural Analysis of the Beta Esra'el as an 'Infamous Group' in Traditional Ethiopia," *Sociologus* 37, 2 (1987): 140–154; Ronald A. Reminick, "The Evil Eye among the Amhara," in C. Maloney, ed., *The Evil Eye* (New York: Columbia University Press, 1976), 85–101.
79. Cf. Messing, "Falashas," 24–26. The connection between these two sets of beliefs is made more explicit in Abbink, "Infamous Group," and particularly in Quirin, "Beta Israel," 212–232.
80. These beliefs as well as many other aspects of Beta Israel-Christian relations are the subject of a doctoral dissertation currently being researched by Ms. Hagar Salamon of the Hebrew University. For a similar case of negative stereotypes "centred on similar spheres and (used) similar images and idioms" see Almagor, "Dassanetch," 106–112. In the Beta Israel case, of course, the duration and intensity of the contacts as well as the obvious cultural similarities are far greater than that of the Dassanetch, a southern Ethiopian people. More generally, see James A. Boon, *Other Tribes, Other Scribes* (Cambridge: Cambridge University Press, 1982), 112–114, esp. 114, "Cultures produce beliefs in cultural others."
81. Plowden *Travels,* 121, states that "Many have assured me that they have killed or seen killed hyaenas with an earring in their ears, the inference being that they are females who have forgotten to take them out on assuming the brute form."
82. Gobat, *Journal,* 178; Dufton, *Narrative,* 169–170, cites Parkyns' account of a woman changed into an ass.
83. *Travels,* 123.
84. Gobat, *Journal,* 181.

85. Examples of this mocking of Christian beliefs as idolatrous appears in reports of the missionaries [Cf. *Jewish Missionary Intelligence* (September 1908): 133], and in modern testimonies of informants. Oral communication Hagar Salamon.

86. Ironically, the Beta Israel themselves seem to have shared many of the Christians' ideas about the transformative capacity of immersion in water, whether as baptism or for the sake of purity. It is also interesting to note that this belief has continued in Israel where the Beta Israel feared that the Israeli rabbinate would trick them into accepting ritual immersion.

87. Gobat, *Journal*, 178.

88. Plowden, *Travels*, 117, 120. Toward the close of his discussion of the *buda*, Plowden notes that "The bloodstone is considered a great cure for haemorrhage." It is unclear if this is related specifically in the context of the *buda* or more generally.

89. Krempel, "Falascha," 141; Abbink, "Infamous Group," 150.

90. *Jewish Missionary Intelligence* (September 1933), 108.

91. *Annual Report* (LSPCJ) (1903): 96.

92. Cf. from a later period the Beta Israel who argued, "We shall never accept a religion which eats men's flesh and drinks men's blood," *Jewish Intelligence* (November 1899): 170.

93. Flad, *Falashas*, 18; Halévy, "Travels," 219. Cf. Almagor, "Dassanetch," 108.

94. Ibid., 16, emphasis added.

95. Modern informants voice disgust at the Christian (and modern Jewish) failure to isolate a woman when she bleeds. This interpretation departs from that of Abbink, "Infamous Group," 147, who views this custom as an internal purity rule, irrelevant to Christian-Beta Israel relations. In part at least the difference from my interpretation lies with his emphasis on the functional, as opposed to mine on the symbolic.

96. Abbink, "Infamous Group," 147. As with most of their major institutions, the Beta Israel attributed this pattern of behavior to the fifteenth century and the figures of Abba Sabra and Sagga Amlak. In fact, they may well have developed in a much later period.

97. Almagor, "Dassanetch," 109.

6. A Mission to the Jews

1. Rubenson, *Survival*, 173–174; *Tewodros*, 15–45.

2. For this and much of what follows see Crummey, *Priests*, 10–13, 29ff.

3. On Gobat, including his later tenure as Anglican Bishop of Jerusalem, see Samuel Gobat, *Journal*, and *Samuel Gobat, Bishop of Jerusalem* (London: 1884).

4. On Gobat's successors, most notably C. W. Isenberg and J. L. Krapf, see Crummey, *Priests*, 40–57; Rubenson, *Independence*, 71–76, 150–159, 176–178. Flad originally travelled to Ethiopia in 1855 with Krapf.

5. Crummey, *Priests*, 122–129.

6. Max Warren, *The Missionary Movement from Britain in Modern History* (London: S.C.M. Press, 1965).

7. See the discussion in Crummey, *Priests*, 2–6.

8. On the beginning of mission activity see *Jewish Intelligence* (hereafter: *JI*) (1 November 1860): 358–360; (1 June 1869): 141; (1 September 1869): 218–219; W. T. Gidney, *The History of the London Society for Promoting Christianity amongst the Jews* (London: London Society for Promoting Christianity amongst the Jews, 1908), 370.

9. *JI* (1 November 1860): 360.

10. *JI* (April 1861): 89.

11. Stern initially describes the permission as "unqualified," but this contrasts with his own statements concerning the Abuna's concerns as well as with other missionaries' statements and actions. Cf. *JI* (1 September 1869): 218. The London Society faced similar difficulties in much of North Africa and the Middle East where work among local Muslims was prohibited.

12. *JI* (1 July 1961): 202.

13. *Jewish Review* (hereafter *JR*) (January 1862): 2–3; cf. *JR* (November 1874): 143; *JI* (1 May 1864): 105.

14. "The Abyssinian Church and the Difficulties to Effect a Reform," *JI* (1 February 1868): 25–33, esp. 32. "Fifty individuals formed into a nucleus for a future Reformed Church in the heart of Abyssinia. Here was a band of believers baptized into a fallen Church, and yet not absorbed into that Church—virtually adherents to the creed of the Protestants, and yet nominally attached that of the Abyssinians—avowedly followers of our infallible and Divine Revelation, and yet apparently leaning to erroneous error and human traditions." "English Protestants," *JR* (May 1871): 19; "Flad's Children," *Annual Report* (hereafter *AR*) (1885): 121–122; cf. *JI* (1 May 1866): 112; *JR* (June 1881):24.

15. F. G. (Eric) Payne, *Ethiopian Jews: The Story of a Mission* (London: Olive Press, 1972) and Kessler, *Falashas*, 106–120. While adopting greatly differing perspectives to the mission, both neglect the native agents. Useful biographies of these figures are scattered throughout the mission literature, for example, *JI* (October 1893): 154–155; *JI* (December 1873), 288–294. In Ethiopia, as elsewhere, many of the London Society's missionaries were themselves Jewish converts. Cf. Robert Michael Smith, "The London Jews' Society and Patterns of Jewish Conversion in England, 1801–1859," *Jewish Social Studies* 43, 3–4 (Summer–Fall 1981): 276–286.

16. This episode, one of the most discussed in Ethiopian history, will not detain us here, since its direct relevance to the study of the Beta Israel is limited. From the vast literature on this incident see Rubenson, *Tewodros*, 67–89; Crummey, *Priests and Politicians*, 115–144.

17. See J. Martin Flad, *60–Jahre-in-der-Mission-unter-den-Falachas-in-Abessinien* (Giessen: Brunnen Verlag, 1922), 252–255; (1874), 264–296; (1881), 320–350.

18. Flad died on 1 April 1915; his autobiography (*60–Jahre*) was published posthumously.

19. *JI* (1 October 1869): 244; *AR* (1880): 127; cf. Rapoport, *The Lost Jews*, 168–169. The claim of forced tattooing of crosses on Ethiopian Jews resurfaced in the *Jewish Chronicle* (London) in early 1985, but was later retracted.
20. *JR* (April–May 1863): 15–16; *JI* (July 1880): 184.
21. *JR* (May 1871): 18; *JR* (April 1878): 15–16.
22. *JR* (April–May 1863): 15.
23. *JI* (1 October 1869): 244; *JR* (May 1871): 19; *AR* (1889): 121.
24. *JR* (November 1874): 45; *AR* (1876): 107; *AR* (1883): 117, 119.
25. *JR* (January 1862): 19; *JI* (1 September 1869): 220; *JR* (February 1881): 7. Cf. M. Louise Pirouet, *Black Evangelists* (London: Collings, 1978): 23, "Evangelicals have always been characterized by a horror of what they describe as 'nominal' Christianity."
26. *JI* (February 1900): 184.
27. *JI* (July 1880): 185. Of course, their opposition to such moves was based in large part on the realization that once converted the Beta Israel would not be fair game for the Protestant mission.
28. *JR* (April–May 1863): 15–16; *JR* (November 1874): 48.
29. *JR* (April–May 1863): 15.
30. *JI* (1 May 1866): 113; *JR* (April 1878): 15–16. In the early twentieth century the missionaries remarked pointedly on the Jewish counter-missionary Faitlovitch's propensity to distribute large sums of money. *JI* (July 1906): 107.
31. *JI* (1 March 1863): 67.
32. On this crucial episode in Beta Israel history see the next chapter.
33. *JR* (May 1871): 18–19. Cf. *JR* (November 1863), where Stern suggests paying native agents 5 pounds each per year including clothing—a total expenditure of 20 pounds; cf. *JI* (September 1899): 130.
34. *JI* (April 1871): 81; *AR* (1870): 76.
35. *JI* (December 1873): 290–291.
36. Ibid., 289–290.
37. *JI* (October 1893): 154–155.
38. *JI* (1 November 1863): 280; *JR* (November 1874): 46. On the London Society's concern for the "temporal distress" of Jews, see Smith, "London Jews' Society," 276, 283.
39. *JI* (February 1983): 23, "Many Abyssinian Christians believed that the Falashas are Budas, but they have given it up now, seeing so many Falashas becoming good Christians." *JI* (January 1901): 8, "We were baptized because we wished to avoid the shame of being called Falashas." But see *JI* (February 1893): 26, "Formerly you were Falashas, now you are 'Budas'."
40. *JI* (December 1900): 185.
41. *JR* (April–May 1863): 17.
42. *JR* (January 1862): 3.
43. *JR* (1 July 1861): 177–178.
44. *JI* (1 March 1863): 67; *JI* (1 July 1861): 181.

45. *JI* (1 July 1861): 188. Stern continues by describing Abba Mahari's haggard appearance and his fanatic gaze; the overall impression is, nevertheless, that he was much impressed by this monk. On Abba Mahari, see Shoshana Ben-Dor, "The Journey to Eretz Israel: The Story of Abba Mahari," *Pe'amim* 33 (1987): 5–31 (Hebrew).

46. *JI* (1 July 1861): 189.

47. Ibid., 190–191; *JI* (1 November 1860): 358; *JI* (1 July 1861): 175–176, 182, 202.

48. *JR* (April–May 1863): 18; *JI* (1 November 1863): 296.

49. *JI* (April 1898): 53.

50. *JR* (January 1862): 2.

51. *JR* (April–May 1863): 17.

52. *JI* (1 November 1869): 358; *JR* (May 1871): 18; *JR* (November 1871): 18; *JR* (November 1874): 41, 43; Ya'acov Faitlovitch, *Journey to the Falasha* (Tel Aviv: Devir, 1959): 88 (Hebrew).

53. *JI* (1 July 1861): 179, 186, 194, 195. See, however, the comments below on one major literate group, the *debtera*.

54. *JI* (1 March 1863): 67; *JR* (April–May 1863): 15; *JI* (1 November 1863): 276.

55. Cf. Charles Pelham Groves, "Missionary and Humanitarian Aspects of Imperialism from 1870 to 1914," in *Colonialism in Africa 1870–1960*, L. H. Gann and Peter Duignan, eds. (Cambridge: Cambridge University Press, 1969) I, 462–496.

56. Cf. Eric Fenn, "The Bible and the Missionary," in *Cambridge History of the Bible*, Stanley Lawrence Greenslade, ed. (Cambridge: Cambridge University Press, 1963) III, 383–407; Lamin Sanneh, *Translating the Word* (Maryknoll, NY: Orbis, 1989).

57. Ullendorff, *Ethiopia*, 62–72. According to Gidney, *History*, 480, Flad completed a new translation of the Bible in 1888. The Society's Hebrew New Testament (Smith, "London Jews' Society," 283) was, of course, of no use in Ethiopia.

58. See, for example, *JI* (1 November 1863): 276–277. On the London Society's schools, see Smith, "London Jews' Society," 276, and Yehoshua Ben-Arieh, *Jerusalem in the 19th Century* (New York, Jerusalem: St. Martin's Press, Ben Zvi Institute, 1984), 335–336.

59. Gidney, *History*, 616, estimates these as numbering only two to three hundred, but this appears to be an unrealistically low figure, especially for the period after 1888.

60. In July 1862, twenty-two "inquirers" were baptised. A further nineteen followed shortly after. *JR* (April–May 1863): 15; *JI* (1 October 1969): 244.

61. *JI* (1 October 1869): 245; *JI* (June 1894): 85. Gidney, *History*, 616, claims a figure of 1513 converts by 1908. Payne, *Ethiopian Jews*, 68, cites a figure of 1600 by 1909. Even these figures must be viewed with considerable suspicion. While the missionaries quote 1470 converts by 1894 (an average of about forty-three baptisms a year for thirty-four years), it is difficult to

find even a single year in which that many adult baptisms are reported. Gidney, *History,* reports only forty-three baptisms from 1900 to 1909.
62. *AR* (1885): 122.
63. *JI* (November 1893): 163; *JI* (April 1898): 53–55; *JI* (November 1899): 169–170; *AR* (1904): 122. In the last of these cases, the native agent, Sanbato Daniel, reported discovering three to four hundred previously unreported converts!
64. *JI* (1 October 1869): 245; Gidney, *Sites,* 20.
65. Cf. *AR* (1878): 119; *AR* (1879): 124.
66. *JR* (May 1871): 19; *JR* (November 1874): 47; *JR* (1882): 42.
67. Cf. Leslau, *Anthology,* xxiii.
68. Joseph Halévy, "Travels in Abyssinia," tr. James Picciotto in *Miscellany of Hebrew Literature,* ed. A. Lowy (London: Wertheimer, Lea, and Co., 1877), 79.
69. Donald N. Levine, *Wax and Gold* (Chicago: University of Chicago Press, 1965), 171–173.
70. On the involvement of Beta Israel *debterotch* in magic see Halévy, "Travels," 47.
71. Johann M. Flad, *The Falashas (Jews) of Abyssinia,* tr. S.P. Goodhart (London: William Macintosh, 1869), 32.
72. *JI* (1 May 1864): 101, 110; *JR* (November 1882): 42; *AR* (1876): 108; *AR* (1877): 108; and cf. the list in *JI* (March 1891): 33.
73. *JR* (November 1874): 44, 46, 47.
74. *AR* (1876): 108; *JI* (September 1884): 239.
75. *JR* (May 1871): 19, but cf. on his wife, *JR* (November 1974): 43,47.
76. *JI* (September 1884): 239.
77. Cf. however, *JI* (July 1880): 183; *JR* (May 1884): 19, for instances of Beta Israel who claimed that they could not convert lest they sever their relationship with family members. Both patterns clearly indicate the centrality of kinship ties among the Beta Israel, who lacked any formal political or communal organization.
78. *JR* (April–May 1863): 16–20; on sacrifice among the Beta Israel see Deborah Lifchitz, "Un sacrifice chez les falachas, juifs d'Abyssinie," *La terre et la vie* 9 (1939): 116–123.
79. Cf. Bonar A. Gow, *Madagascar and the Protestant Impact* (London: Africana Publishing Co., 1979), 95; E. Ilogu, *Christianity and Ibo Culture* (Leiden: E. J. Brill, 1974), 65; Felix K. Ekechi, *Missionary Enterprise and Rivalry in Iboland* (London: Frank Cass, 1972): 37–41.
80. Cf. Edward Ullendorff, *The Ethiopians* (London: Oxford University Press, 1973, 3rd. ed.), 178–180, esp. 178, n. 1.
81. *JR* (April–May 1863): 14.
82. Ibid., 18–20; *JI* (1 October 1869): 245; Leslau, "Dispute," 71–95. Oral traditions concerning this episode have been collected and prepared for publication by Ms. Shoshana Ben-Dor.
83. Cf. *JR* (April–May 1863): 14. The Beta Israel reluctance to emphasize the

issue of sacrifice probably reflects their later recognition that even in Jewish eyes this practice was unique and problematic.

84. For some of the differing versions concerning the outcome of the case see Leslau, "Dispute," 82; Halévy, "Travels," 72–73; JR (April–May 1863): 18–20.

85. On the threat of a renewed ban on sacrifices cf. JR (May 1871): 19.

86. JR (April–May 1863): 15.

87. JI (1 November 1863): 284.

88. AR (1883): 117. Cf. AR (1878): 119; AR (1892): 150.

89. AR (1872): 92; JR (November 1874): 43; JR (April 1878): 15–16. This phenomenon was even further intensified in the early twentieth century following the visit of the European Jewish counter-missionary Jacques (Ya'acov) Faitlovitch in 1904. Cf. JI (August 1906): 118; (October 1906): 155; (July 1908): 107; (September 1908): 133, etc.

90. G. O. M. Tasie, *Christian Missionary Enterprise in the Niger Delta* (Leiden: E. J. Brill, 1978), 44; Elizabeth Isichei, *Varieties of Christian Experience in Nigeria* (London: Macmillan, 1982), 64, 67; Ekechi, *Iboland*, 37.

91. Matthew Schoeffeleers and Ian Linden, "The Resistance of the *Nyau* Societies to Roman Catholic Missions in Colonial Malawi," in Terence O. Ranger and Isaria N. Kimambo, eds., *The Historical Study of African Religion* (Berkeley: University of California, 1974), 268; Tasie, *Niger Delta*, 61.

92. JR (April–May 1863): 15–16; JR (April 1878): 15.

93. Ben-Arieh, *Jerusalem*, 335.

94. Kaplan, "Leadership": 157–159.

95. JR (April–May 1863): 14; cf. JR (May 1884): 19; JI (July 1880): 183–184; AR (1885): 121.

96. JR (April–May 1863): 15; cf. AR (1878): 119; AR (1879): 124; AR (1885): 120.

97. JI (July 1880): 183; JR (May 1884): 19; AR (1885): 121.

98. AR (1883): 117–118.

99. JR (May 1884): 17–19. See also AR (1884): 121. On the *Seged* see Ben-Dor, "Seged," and Shelemay, *Music*, 48–50.

100. JR (November 1874): 47; JI (July 1889): 105–106; JI (April 1898): 55; JI (June 1900): 12; JI (January 1901): 9; JI (March 1901): 44. Also representative of this trend is the development of mixed housing with Falasha Christians and Jews side by side. Cf. JR (November 1882): 41.

101. In part, at least, the failure to exclude the missionaries may have been due to a fear that they would attempt to renew the ban of sacrifices. Cf. JR (May 1871): 19.

102. Thus, the European Jew Halévy was treated as more of an outsider than some Beta Israel converts.

103. For a detailed discussion of these episodes see Ben-Dor, "Abba Mahari."

104. Ibid.; cf. Flad, *Falashas*, 37–38; Halévy, "Travels," 72–73.

105. Halévy, "Travels," 72.

106. See Quirin, "Beta Israel," 225; but cf. Ben-Dor, "Abba Mahari," 18–26.

107. Hermann Zotenberg, "Un document sur les Falachas," *Journal asiatique,* sixieme series, 9 (1867): 265–268. Waldman, *Ethiopian Jewry,* 127–128; Corinaldi, *Identity and Tradition,* 146–148.

108. Ben-Dor, "Abba Mahari," 26. On Ethiopian traditions concerning a messiah named Tewodros, see Herbert Weld-Bludell, *The Royal Chronicle of Abyssinia 1769–1840* (Cambridge: Cambridge University Press, 1922): 515–517.

109. *JI* (November 1874): 292.

110. *AR* (1877): 119.

111. *AR* (1880): 127. This migration may, at least in part, have been a response to the religious policies of the Emperor Yohannes IV.

112. In particular, the migration of 1862 is commonly depicted as a second attempt to reach the Holy Land via the Red Sea. Cf. Flad, *Falashas,* 37–38.

113. See the reports of Eliezer Sinai Kirschbaum, Solomon Judah Rapoport, and Louis Marcus excerpted in Waldman, *Ethiopian Jewry,* 104–108; Mordecai Eliav, "The Awakening of West-European Jewry to the Assistance of the Falashas," *Tarbiz* 35, 1 (1965): 66 (Hebrew). In part, at least, these authors may have been misled by Bruce's claim that kings and queens still ruled the Falasha.

114. Luzzato, "Falashas"; d'Abbadie, "Réponses"; Waldman, *Ethiopian Jewry,* 109–116.

115. Waldman, *Ethiopian Jewry,* 130–132; Eliav, "Awakening," 66–67.

116. Corinaldi, *Identity and Tradition,* 144–145; Waldman, *Ethiopian Jewry,* 125.

117. *Der Israelit,* 26, September 26, 1864; *Jewish Chronicle,* September 26, 1864. Schwartz had earlier been an important supporter of attempts to send an emissary to the Jews of Ethiopia.

118. Waldman, *Ethiopian Jewry,* 127.

119. Zotenberg, "Un document"; Waldman, *Ethiopian Jewry,* 127–128; Corinaldi, *Identity and Tradition,* 146–148.

120. Among the early travellers were Israel Joseph Benjamin and Dr. Yehezkel Asche. Cf. Waldman, *Ethiopian Jewry,* 120–122, 132–138; Eliav, "Awakening," 66–69.

121. Waldman, *Ethiopian Jewry,* 138–139; Eliav, "Awakening," 69–70. At the same time, he wrote to Rabbi Solomon Judah Rapoport of Prague.

122. Eliav, "Awakening," 70–73 esp. n. 71; Corinaldi, *Identity and Tradition,* 154–155; Waldman, *Ethiopian Jewry,* 144–148, and particularly 144–146 for the text of this proclamation.

123. Eliav, "Awakening," 71–73; Waldman, *Ethiopian Jewry,* 144–156; Corinaldi, *Identity and Tradition,* 155–158. The response was not, however, unanimous. Of particular note were the article by Rabbi Joseph Schwartz of Jerusalem, who argued that the Beta Israel were not Jews (cf. Waldman, *Ethiopian Jewry,* 140–143) and the decision not to fund a mission taken

by the *Alliance Israélite Universelle* on October 10, 1864, the day before Hildesheimer composed his letter.

124. The letter appeared on February 8, 1865, in the Jewish paper *Hamagid.* Waldman, *Ethiopian Jewry,* 156–160.

125. Halévy's account of his journey appeared in numerous versions and languages. The best known are "Travels" and "Excursion," but see Steven Kaplan and Shoshana Ben-Dor, *Ethiopian Jewry: An Annotated Bibliography* (Jerusalem: Ben Zvi Institute, 1988), 73–76, for a more complete listing.

126. See, for example, Rubenson, *Survival; Tewodros,* Crummey, *Priests.*

127. Halévy initially identified himself as a "white Falasha," "Travels," 39, not knowing that Henry Aaron Stern had used a similar form of introduction.

128. See "Travels," 47, where Halévy criticizes Beta Israel practice by refusing the offer of a protective amulet offered by a *debtera.* An example of Halévy's shaping of his account are his attempts to downplay the importance of Beta Israel monks.

129. Cf. "Rapport," 101–102.

130. Waldman, *Ethiopian Jewry,* 166. In 1908 the *Alliance* responded to the successful mission by Halévy's student, Jacques (Ya'acov) Faitlovitch, by organizing a counter-mission by Rabbi Haim Nahoum, who delivered an overwhelmingly negative report on the Beta Israel. Cf. ibid, 189–197.

7. Kifu-qen: *The Great Famine of 1888–92*

1. Richard Pankhurst, "The Great Famine of 1888–1892," in *The History of Famine and Epidemics in Ethiopia prior to the Twentieth Century* (Addis Ababa: Relief and Rehabilitation Commission, n.d.), 57; Richard Pankhurst and Douglas H. Johnson, "The Great Drought and Famine of 1888–92 in Northeast Africa," in Douglas H. Johnson and David M. Anderson, eds., *The Ecology of Survival: Case Studies from North African History* (London: Lester Crook Academic Publishing, 1988), 48, 67.

2. Pankhurst and Johnson, "Famine," 51.

3. *JI* (July 1889): 107.

4. *JI* (September 1892): 148.

5. Interview, Webe Akala, 9 December 1986.

6. Interviews, Qes Yemanu, 25 November 1987; Mika'el Adamas 18 December 1987. Informants from Tigre (Adamas, Abba Yeshaq Iyasu, 18 December 1987) tended to stress the importance of Yohannes's death. Those from other regions put a greater emphasis on the Mahdists.

7. *JMI* (February 1893): 22, 28; *JMI* (November 1893): 164; *JMI* (May 1894): 66. During at least part of this period, the Mahdist army's purpose was probably a search for food, rather than an attempt to achieve any major political objectives. Cf. Pankhurst and Johnson, "Famine," 60–61.

8. In this respect, at least, these regions appear to more closely resemble the Sudan, where political factors played a larger role in the development of the

famine than other areas of Ethiopia. Cf. Pankhurst and Johnson, "Famine," 67–68. Guebre Sellassie, *Chronique du règne de Menelik II* (Paris: Masionneuve Freres, 1930–31), II, 487, notes that Bagemder and Semien were badly misgoverned during the period after Yohannes.

9. Pankhurst, "Famine," 58–59.
10. Cited in Pankhurst, "Famine," 62; Pankhurst and Johnson, "Famine," 50.
11. *Chronique* II, 487. He also notes that the sounds of neither fowl nor dogs were heard.
12. Interview, Abba Yeshaq, 18 December 1987.
13. *JI* (April 1901): 50; Cf. Alaqa Lamma Haylu quoted by Pankhurst, "Famine," 67–68; Pankhurst and Johnson, "Famine," 50, "The chief cause of the famine was the death of cattle, because people could not plough they left their land fallow."
14. Flad, *60 Jahre*, 405. (Translation, Pankhurst, "Famine," 69.)
15. *JI* (April 1891): 50; *JMI* (November 1893): 164; *JMI* (February 1893): 27.
16. *JMI* (January 1893): 3. Cf. Pankhurst, "Famine," 70–74; Pankhurst and Johnson, "Famine," 51, report the grain price rose by 1 to 200 percent and that of cattle between thirty to forty times.
17. Interview, Qes Hadana, 5 February 1988.
18. To this day certain roots are remembered by the Beta Israel for the lifesaving role they filled during the famine. Virtually all informants mentioned the search for these roots.
19. *JMI* (February 1893).
20. Pankhurst, "Famine," 86–87; Pankhurst and Johnson, "Famine," 53.
21. *AR* (1892): 148.
22. *JMI* (February 1893): 23; interviews, Mikael Adamas, 18 December 1987; Alazar, 14 January 1988.
23. Interviews, Alazar, 14 June 1988; Mikael Adamas, 18 December 1987.
24. *JMI* (February 1893): 27. Guebre Sellassie, *Chronique,* II, 487, reports that the vultures thrived on human flesh.
25. Interviews, Qes Yemanu, 25 November 1987; Alazar, 14 January 1988.
26. *JI* (November 1892): 178; *JMI* (January 1893): 3.
27. *JI* (November 1892): 178.
28. Pankhurst, "Famine," 88–90; Pankhurst and Johnson, "Famine," 54.
29. Salimbeni, an Italian observer, quoted in Pankhurst and Johnson, "Famine," 54, and cf. 60–61.
30. Guebre-Sellassie *Chronique,* II, 487–488. Among these, potters are specifically mentioned.
31. *AR* (1885): 122.
32. *JI* (July 1890): 107.
33. *JMI* (May 1884): 66.
34. *JI* (March 1891): 33.
35. *JI* (February 1892): 20; *JMI* (1894): 84.
36. *JI* (February 1892): 20; *JMI* (February 1893): 27; *JMI* (November 1893): 163. Cf. Guebre Sellassie, *Chronique,* II, 488, on royal assistance to Christian nobles from Bagemder and Semien.

37. *Chronique,* II, 487. He also notes (488) that following the famine potters had to been imported into the region.
38. Jacques Faitlovitch, *Quer durch Abessinien. Meine zweite Reise zu den Falaschas* (Berlin: Poppelaur, 1910).
39. Halévy, "Travels," 98; Flad, *Falasha,* 14; Stern, *Wanderings,* 194.
40. *JMI* (December 1900): 185.
41. *JMI* (July 1903): 108.
42. Pankhurst, "Famine," 93–98; Pankhurst and Johnson, "Famine," 52–53.
43. *JI* (June 1889): 82; *JI* (September 1892): 149.
44. *AR* (1892): 148, 149; *JI* May (1891): 65. Several of the areas mentioned by Flad, *Falashas,* 11, as places of refuge during the famine of 1863 recur in both oral traditions and missionary sources concerning the Great Famine. This may be an indication that the flight of refugees was not random, but rather followed certain traditional patterns.
45. Interview, Abba Yeshaq, 18 December 1987. Pankhurst, "Famine," 93–97; Pankhurst and Johnson, "Famine," 53.
46. Interview, Qes Hadana, 5 February 1988.
47. *JMI* (December 1900): 84.
48. *JMI* (February 1893): 24; interview, Abba Yeshaq, 18 December 1987.
49. *JMI* (December 1900): 184 and all informants. Some oral traditions also report a number of conversions to Islam.
50. *JMI* (December 1900): 184.
51. Interviews, Alazar, 14 January 1988; Qes Hadana, 5 February 1988.
52. Messing, *Story,* 93–99. Messing traces the origin of the *Maryam Wodet* to forced conversions during the reign of Yohannes IV (1871–1889). Contemporary evidence, however, offers little indication that large-scale conversions of the Beta Israel took place at this time (*AR* 1880: 127). Alazar (interview, 14 January 1988) stated that the *Maryam Wodet* were converts from the time of the famine. Qes Hadana (interview, 5 February 1988), however, claimed that they had existed even earlier.
53. *AR* (1891): 139; *AR* (1892): 151.
54. *AR* (1890): 131.
55. *AR* (1891): 139; *JMI* (November 1899): 169–170; *JMI* (January 1901): 8–10.
56. *JI* (July 1890): 104; *AR* (1890): 134.
57. *AR* (1891): 139–140; *AR* (1892): 151.
58. *JI* (November 1892); *JMI* (February 1893): 23.
59. Interviews, Abba Yeshaq, 18 December 1987; Qes Hadana, 5 February 1988.
60. Flad, *Falasha,* 29.
61. *JMI* (July 1896): 84. d'Abbadie was told that only twenty monks resided at Horhawa ("Réponses," 261). In 1908 Faitlovitch reported that eight monks resided at Gouraba. Leslau found only three.
62. Interview, Abba Yeshaq, 18 December 1987.
63. Interviews, Alazar, 14 January 1988; Qes Hadana, 5 February 1988.
64. Interviews, Qes Yemanu, 2 December 1987; Qes Hadana, 5 February 1988.

65. Interview, 18 December 1987.
66. Cf. the testimony of Abba Gette, 17 November 1986, "In the *Kifu-qen* many died. So they had no wives, husbands were also scarce. So they would come, they would come to us [to Chelga] ... to look for a wife, a man would look for a wife."
67. Leslau, *Anthology,* xxvi; Shelemay, *Music,* 87.
68. The previous halt from 1862–68 came about as the result of the ban on sacrifices initiated by the missionaries, which was discussed in the previous chapter.
69. d'Abbadie, "Réponses," 264. On the relationship between the frequency of sacrifice and the quantity of potential sacrificial victims see Raymond Firth, "Offering and Sacrifice: Problems of Organization," *Journal of the Royal Anthropological Institute* 92 (1963): 12–24.
70. Flad, *Falasha,* 52–54, Jacques Faitlovtich, *Notes d'un Voyage chez les Falachas (Juifs d'Abyssinie)* (Paris: Ernest Leroux, 1905), 2; cf. Emanuela Trevisan Semi, "Le Sriet: Un rite d'investiture sacredotale chez les Beta Esrae'ël (Falashas)," *Revue des études Juives* 141 (1987): 101–124.
71. In additon to Faitlovitch's own accounts of his journeys see Itzhak Grinfeld, "Jacques Faitlovitch—'Father' of the Falashas," in Yossi Avner et al., eds., *The Jews of Ethiopia—A Community in Transition* (Tel Aviv: Beth Hate-futsoth, 1986), 30–35; "Taamrat Emanuel—Harbinger of the Renascence of Ethiopian Jewry," *Pe'amim* 22 (1985): 59–74; Messing, *Falashas,* 62–79.
72. Emanuela Trevisan Semi, "The Beta Israel (Falashas): From Purity to Impurity," *Jewish Journal of Sociology* 25 (1985): 103–114.

Conclusions: Before Faitlovich

1. "Notes," 27. For a similar quote from Faitlovitch see Shelemay, *Music,* 26.
2. More recently, of course, the popular writing of Beta Israel history has been largely focused upon the modern Jewish themes of "exile" and "return," with the arrival in Israel depicted as the culmination of a universal Jewish vision.
3. Cf. Kaplan, " 'Falasha' Religion," for a detailed refutation of this view, as well as Chapter 3.
4. Shelemay has noted this tendency in the study of synagogue music, for example. "Discussions of synagogue music in the past have often been preoc-cupied with tracing continuity, while ignoring or disparaging change." "Music in the American Synagogue: A Case Study from Houston," in Jack Werth-eimer, ed., *The American Synagogue. A Sanctuary Transformed* (Cambridge: Cambridge University Press, 1987), 411.
5. On the Qemant see Gamst, *Qemant.*
6. Halévy, "Travels," 37.

Bibliography

Books and Articles

Abbadie, Antoine d'. "Réponses des Falashas dit Juif d'Abyssinie aux questions faites par M. Luzzato," *Archives Israélites* 12 (1851–52): 179–185, 234–240, 259–269.

Abbink, G. Jan. "A Socio-Structural Analysis of the Beta Esrae'l as an 'Infamous Group' in Traditional Ethiopia," *Sociologus* 37, 2 (1987): 140–154.

———. "L'énigme de l'éthnogenese des Beta Israel—Une approche anthropo-historique de leurs mytho-legendes," *Cahiers d'études africaines* (forthcoming).

Abir, Mordechai. *Ethiopia: The Era of the Princes.* London: Longman, 1968.

———. "Ethiopia and the Horn of Africa," in Richard Gray, *Cambridge History of Africa*, 4th ed. Cambridge: Cambridge University Press, 1975.

———. *Ethiopia and the Red Sea.* London: Frank Cass, 1980.

Adams, William Y. *Nubia: Corridor to Africa.* Princeton: Princeton University Press, 1977.

Adler, Marcus Nathan. *The Itinerary of Benjamin of Tudela.* London: Frowde 1907.

———. *Jewish Travellers.* London: G. Routledge and Sons, 1930.

Aešcoly, A. Z. *The Book of the Falasha.* Tel Aviv: Masada, 1943 (Hebrew).

———. "Notices sur les Falachas ou Juifs d'Abyssinie d'après le 'journal de voyage' d'Antoine d'Abbadie," *Cahiers d'études africaines* 2, 1 (1961).

Almagor, Uri. "Institutionalizing of a Fringe Periphery: Dassenetch-Amhara Relations," in Wendy James and Donald Donham, eds., *The Southern Marches of Imperial Ethiopia*. Cambridge: Cambridge University Press, 1987, 96–115.

Anfray, Francis. "Les rois d'Axoum d'après la numismatique," *Journal of Ethiopian Studies* 6 (1968): 1–5.

——. "The Civilization of Aksum from the First to the Seventh Century," *General History of Africa*, ed. G. Mokhtar. London, Berkeley, Paris: Heinemann, University of California, UNESCO, 1981, II, 362–380.

Anfray, Francis, André Caquot, and Pierre Nautin. "Une nouvelle inscription grecque d'Ezana, roi d'Axoum," *Journal des Savents* (October–December 1970): 260–274.

Arab Faqih [Chihab Eddin Ahmed b. 'Abdel Qadar]. *Futūh al Habasha*, tr. René Basset. Paris: Ernst Leroux, 1897–1901.

Asher, A. *The Intinerary of Rabbi Benjamin of Tudela*. 2 vols. London: A. Asher, 1840–41.

Avner, Yossi, et al., eds. *The Jews of Ethiopia: A People in Transition*. Tel Aviv: Beth Hatefusoth, 1986.

Baratti, Giacomo. *The Late Travels of S . . . , an Italian Gentleman in the Remote Countries of the Abissins or of Ethiopia Interior*, trans. by G. D. London: Benjamin Billingsley, 1650.

Baron, Salo Wittmayer. "Newer Emphases in Jewish History," *History and Jewish Historians*. Philadelphia: Jewish Publication Society, 1965.

——. *A Social and Religious History of the Jews*, vol. 18. New York: Columbia University Press, 1983.

Basset, René. *Études sur l'histoire d'Éthiopie*. Paris: Imprimerie Nationale, 1882.

——. "Enseignement de Jesus Christ à ses Disciples et Prières Magiques," *Apocryphes Éthiopiens* 6. Paris: Librarie de l'art indépendant, 1896.

Beccari, C., ed. *Rerum Aethiopiarum*. Rome: C. De Luigi, 1905–17.

Beckingham, C. F. "A Note on the Topography of Ahmad Gran's Campaigns in 1542," *Journal of Semitic Studies* 4 (1959): 362–373.

——. *Between Islam and Christendon*. London: Variorum Reprints, 1983.

Ben-Arieh, Yehoshua. *Jerusalem in the 19th Century*. New York, Jerusalem: St. Martin's Press, Ben Zvi Institute, 1984.

Bender, M. Lionel, et al. *Language in Ethiopia*. London: Oxford University Press, 1976.

Ben-Dor, Shoshana. "The Holy Places of Ethiopian Jewry," *Pe'amim* 22 (1985): 32–52 (Hebrew).

——. "The *Sigd* of the Beta Israel," M.A. thesis, Hebrew University of Jerusalem, 1986 (Hebrew).

——. "The Journey to Eretz Israel: the Story of Abba Mahari," *Pe'amim* 33 (1987): 5–31 (Hebrew).

Ben Zvi, Itzhak. *The Exiled and the Redeemed*. Philadelphia: Jewish Publication Society, 1961.

Berry, Laverle Bennette. "The Solomonic Monarchy of Gondar 1630–1755: An Institutional Analysis of Kingship in Christian Ethiopia," Ph.D dissertation, Boston University, 1976.

Bezold, Carl. "Kebra Nagašt. Die Herrlichkeit der Könige," *Abhandlugen phi-*

losophisch-philogischen Klasse der Königlich Bayerischen Akademie der Wisenschaften 23 (1909).

Boon, James A. *Other Tribes, Other Scribes.* Cambridge: Cambridge University Press, 1982.

Borchadt, P. "Die Falascha juden in Abessinien im Mittelalten," *Anthropos* 18–19 (1923–24): 258–266.

Bruce, James. *Travels to Discover the Source of the Nile,* 2nd ed. Edinburgh: A. Constable, 1805.

Budge, E. A. W. *The Book of the Saints of the Ethiopian Church.* Cambridge: Cambridge University Press, 1928.

Butzer, Karl W. "Rise and Fall of Axum, Ethiopia: A Geo-Archaeological Interpretation," *American Antiquity* 46, 3 (1981): 471–495.

Caquot, André. "Les actes d'Ezrā de Gunda-Gundē," *Annales d'Ethiopie* 4 (1961): 69–121.

Carmoly, Eliacim. *Notice historique sur Benjamin de Tudèle.* Bruxelles et Leip zig: Chez Kiessling et Co., 1852.

Cerulli, Enrico. "Gli atti di Tekle Alfa," *Annali* 2 (1943): 1–89.

———. *Storia della letteratura etiopica.* Milano: Nuova Accademia Editrice, 1956.

Chelouche, David. *The Exiled of Israel Will Be Gathered.* Jerusalem: Ahva, 1988.

Chojnacki, Stansislav. *Major Themes in Ethiopian Painting* (Äthiopische Forshungen 10). Wiesbaden: Franz Steiner, 1983.

Combes, Edmund, and Maurice Tamisier. *Voyage en Abyssinie, dans le pays des Galla, de Choa et d'Ifat, 1835–1837.* Paris: Desessart, 1838.

Connah, Graham. *African Civilizations.* Cambridge: Cambridge University Press, 1987.

Contenson, H. de. "Pre-Aksumite Culture," *General History of Africa,* ed. G. Mokhtar. London, Berkeley, Paris: Heinemann, University of California, UNESCO, 198l, II, 343–361.

Conti Rossini, Carlo. "Appunti ed oservazioni sui re Zague e Takla Haymanot," *Rendiconti della Reale Accademia dei Lincei* ser. 5, 4 (1895): 144–159.

———. "Il 'Gadla Filipos' ed il 'Gadla Yohannes' di Dabra Bizan," *Memorie della Reale Accademia dei Lincei* 8 (1901): 61–170.

———. *Historia Regis Sarsa Dengel (Malak Sagad), Corpus Scriptorum Christianorum Orientalium* Script. Aeth. 3 (1907).

———. *Acta Sancti Abakerazūn et Sancti Takla Hāwaryāt, Corpus Scriptorum Christianorum Orientalium.* Script. Aeth. 24, 1910.

———. "Piccoli studi etiopici. I. L'itinerario di Beniamino da Tudela e l'Etiopia," *Zeitschrift für Assyriologie* 27 (1912): 358–365.

———. *La langue des Kemant.* Vienna: Kaiserliche Akademie der Wissenschaften, 1912.

———. "Appunti di Storia e letteratura Falascià," *Rivista degli studi orientali* 8 (1919–20): 563–610.

———. "Leggende geografiche guideche del IXe secolo (Il Sepher Eldad)," *Bolletino d. Reale Soc. Geogr. Italiano* 6, 2 (1925): 162–176.

Conti Rossini, Carlo. *Storia d'Etiopia*. Bergamo, Instituto Italiano d'Arti Grafiche, 1928.

———. "L'agiografia etiopica e gli atti del santo Yafqiranna-Egzi (secolo XIV)," *Atti del Reale Istituto Veneto 96*, 2 (1937): 403–433.

———. "Note di agiografia etiopica" (Abiya-Egzi, Arkaledes e Gabra Iyesus), *Rivista degli studi orientali* 17 (1938): 409–452.

———. *Liber Axumae, Corpus Scriptorum Christianorum Orientalum Script. Aeth.* 24. Louvain: Imprimerie Orientaliste, 1962.

Conti Rossini, Carlo, and Lanfranco Ricci. *Maṣḥafa Birhān, Corpus Scriptorum Christianorum Orientalum* Script. Aeth. 47, 48, 51, 52. Louvain: Imprimerie Orientaliste, 1964/65

Conzelman, William E. *Chronique de Gālawdēwos (Claudius) roi d'Éthiopie.* Paris: E. Bouillon, 1895.

Corinaldi, Michael. *Ethiopian Jewry: Identity and Tradition.* Jerusalem: Rubin Mass, 1988 (Hebrew).

Cowley, Arthur Ernest. *Aramaic Papyri of the Fifth Century B.C.* Oxford: Clarendon Press, 1923.

Cowley, Roger W. *The Traditional Interpretation of the Apocalypse of St. John in the Ethiopian Orthodox Church.* Cambridge: Cambridge University Press, 1983.

Crawford, O. G. S., ed. *Ethiopian Intineraries: Circa 1400–1524.* Cambridge: Cambridge University Press, 1958.

Crummey, Donald. *Priests and Politicians: Protestant and Catholic Missions in Orthodox Ethiopia 1839–1868.* Oxford: Clarendon Press, 1972.

Cuoq, Joseph. *L'Islam en Éthiopie des origines au XVIe siècle.* Paris: Nouvelles Editions Latines, 1981.

Dahood, Mitchell. *Psalms II: 51–100, The Anchor Bible,* vol. 17. Garden City, NY: Doubleday, 1968.

David, Abraham. "Obadiah Ben Abraham Yare Di Bertinoro," *Encyclopaedia Judaica,* Jerusalem, IV, 698–699.

de Contenson, H. "Pre-Aksumite Culture," *General History of Africa,* ed. G. Mokhtar. London, Berkeley, Paris: Heinemann, University of California, UNESCO, 1981, II, 343–361.

Dillmann, August. *Lexicon Linguae aethiopicae.* Leipzig: Weigel, 1865.

———. "Zur Geschichte des Axumitischen Reiches im vierten bis sechsten Jahrhundert," *Abhandlugen der Königl. Akad. d. Wissenschaften zur Berlin* 1 (1880): 1–51.

———. *Über die Regierung insbesondere die Kirchenordnung des Königs Zar'a-Jacob.* Berlin: Verlag der Koniglichen Akademie der Wissenschaften, 1884.

Donzel, E. van. *A Yeminite Embassy to Ethiopia 1647–1649. Al-Haymi's Sirat al-Habasha. Newly Introduced, Translated and Annotated.* Wiesbaden: Franz Steiner, 1986.

Drewes, Abraham Johannes. *Inscriptions de l'Éthiopie antique.* Leiden: E. J. Brill, 1962.

Dufton, Henry. *Narrative of a Journey Through Abyssinia in 1862–3.* London: Chapman & Hall, 1867.

Ekechi, Felix K. *Missionary Enterprise and Rivalry in Iboland.* London: Frank Cass, 1972.

Elmslie, W. A. L. *The First and Second Books of Chronicles: The Interpreter's Bible,* vol. 3. Nashville, NY: Abingdon Press, 1954.

Elon, Menachem. "The Ethiopian Jews: A Case Study in the Functioning of the Jewish Legal System," *New York University Journal of International Law and Politics* 19 (1986–87): 535–563.

Epstein, Abraham. *Eldad Ha-Dani: His Story and His Halakhot.* Pressburg: Abraham David Alkalai Press, 1891 (Hebrew).

Esteves Pereira, Francisco Maria. *Chronica de Susenyos, Rei de Ethiopia.* Lisbon: Imprensa Nacional, 1892.

——. *Historia de Minas, Rei de Ethiopia.* Lisbon: Imprensa Nacional, 1888.

Faitlovitch, Ya'acov (Jacques). *Notes d'un Voyage chez les Falachas (Juifs d'Abyssinie).* Paris: Leroux, 1905.

——. *Quer durch Abessinien. Meine Zweite Reise zu den Falaschas.* Berlin: Poppelauer, 1910.

——. *Journey to the Falasha.* Tel Aviv: Devir, 1959 (Hebrew).

Fenn, Eric. "The Bible and the Missionary," in Stanley Lawrence Greenslade, ed., *Cambridge History of the Bible.* Cambridge: Cambridge University Press, 1963, III: 383–407.

Firth, Raymond. "Offering and Sacrifice: Problems of Organization," *Journal of the Royal Anthropological Institute* 92 (1963): 12–24.

Flad, Johann Martin. *The Falashas (Jews) of Abyssinia,* tr. S. P. Goodhart. London: William Macintosh, 1869.

——. *60-Jahre-in-der-Mission-unter-den-Falachas-in Abessinien.* Giesen: Brunnen Verlag, 1922.

Frend, W. H. C. *The Rise of the Monophysite Movement.* Cambridge: Cambridge University Press, 1972.

Gaguine, Maurice. "The Falasha Version of the Testaments of Abraham, Isaac, and Jacob," Ph.D. dissertation, University of Manchester, 1965.

Gamst, Frederick C. *The Qemant: A Pagan-Hebraic Peasantry of Ethiopia.* Prospect Heights, IL: Waveland Press, 1969.

Gerster, Georg. *Churches in Rock.* London: Phaidon, 1970.

Getatchew Haile. "The Homily in Honor of St. Frumentius," *Analecta Bollandiana* 92 (1979): 309–318.

——. "A Preliminary Investigation of the *Tomarä Täsbä't* of Emperor Zär'a Ya'ə qob of Ethiopia," *Bulletin of the School of Oriental and African Studies* 43 (1980): 207–234.

——. "A New Ethiopic Version of the Acts of St. Mark," *Analecta Bollandiana* 94 (1981): 117–134.

——. "A New Look at some Dates of Early Ethiopian History," *Le Muséon* 95 (1982): 311–322.

——. "The Cause of the Ǝsṭifanosites: A Fundamentalist Sect in the Church of Ethiopia," *Paideuma* 29 (1983): 93–119.

——. "The End of a Deserter of the Established Church of Ethiopia," *Sixth*

International Conference of Ethiopian Studies, Tel Aviv, 14–17 April 1980. Rotterdam: A. P. Balkema, 1986, 193–203.

———. "The Forty-nine Hour Sabbath of the Ethiopian Church," *Journal of Semitic Studies* 33, 2 (1988): 233–254.

Gidney, W. T. *Sites and Scenes.* London: London Society for Promoting Christianity amongst the Jews, 1898.

———. *The History of the London Society for Promoting Christianity amongst the Jews.* London: London Society for Promoting Christianity amongst the Jews, 1908.

Girma, Beshah, and Merid Wolde Aregay. *The Question of the Union of the Churches in Luso-Ethiopian Relations (1500–1632).* Lisbon: Junta De Investigacoes do Ultramar and Centro de Estudos Historicos Ultramarinos, 1964.

Gobat, Samuel. *Journal of a Three Years' Residence in Abyssinia,* 2nd ed. London: 1850.

———. *Samuel Gobat, Bishop of Jerusalem his Life and Work.* London: 1884.

Goitein, E. David. "Note on Eldad the Danite," *Jewish Quarterly Review* 17 (1926–27): 483.

Goldman, Israel M. *The Life and Times of Rabbi David Ibn Abi Zimra.* New York: Jewish Theological Seminary, 1970.

Goldschmidt, Lazarus. *Die Abessinischen Handschriften der Stadtbibliothek zu Frankfurt am Main.* Berlin: S. Calvary and Co., 1897.

Goody, Jack, ed. *Literacy in Traditional Societies.* Cambridge: Cambridge University Press, 1968.

———. *The Logic of Writing and the Organization of Society.* Cambridge: Cambridge University Press, 1986.

Gow, Bonar A. *Madagascar and the Protestant Impact.* London: Africana Publishing, 1979.

Grinfeld, Itzhak. "Ta'amrat Emmanuel—Harbinger of the Renascence of Ethiopian Jewry," *Pe'amim* 22 (1985): 59–74 (Hebrew).

———. "Jacques Faitlovitch—'Father' of the Falashas," in Yossi Avner, et al., eds., *The Jews of Ethiopia—A Community in Transition.* Tel Aviv: Bet Hatefutsoth, 1986, 30–35.

———. "The Falasha and their Languages in the Present and the Past," *Pe'amim* 33 (1987): 50–73 (Hebrew).

Groves, Charles Pelham. "Missionary and Humanitarian Aspects of Imperialism from 1870 to 1914," in L. H. Gann and Peter Duignan, eds., *Colonialism in African 1870–1960.* Cambridge: Cambridge University Press, 1969, I, 462–496.

Gruber, Ruth. *Rescue: The Exodus of the Ethiopian Jews.* New York: Atheneum, 1987.

Guebre, Sellassie. *Chronique du règne du Ménélik II,* ed. M. de Coppet. Paris: Masionneuves Frères, 1930–31.

Guidi, Ignazio. "Le canzoni Ge'ez-Amarina in onore di re abissini," *Rendiconti della Reale Accademia dei Lincei* ser. 4, 5 (1889): 53–66.

———. *Annales Iohannis I, Iyasu I, Bakaffa. Corpus Scriptorum Christianorum Orientalium Script. Aeth.* 5, Paris: 1903.

———. *Annales Regum Iyasu II et Iyo'as. Corpus Scriptorum Orientalium Script. Aeth.* 67. Louvain: Imprimerie Orientaliste, 1954.

———. *(Breve) Storia della letterature etiopica.* Rome: Instituto per l'Oriente, 1932.

Halévy, Joseph. "Rapport au comité central de l'Alliance Israélite Universelle," *Bulletin de l'Alliance Israélite Universelle* (1868): 85–102.

———. "Travels in Abyssinia," tr. James Picciotto, in A. Lowy, ed., *Miscellany of Hebrew Literature.* London: Wertheimer, Lea, and Co., 1877.

———. "La guerre de Sarṣa-Dengel contre les Falasha, extrait des Annales de Sarṣa-Dengel," *Revue sémitique* 14 (1906): 392–427; 15 (1906): 119–163, 263–287. Reprinted separately, Paris: E. Leroux, 1907.

Hall, I. H. "The Colloquy of Moses on Mt. Sinai," *Hebraica*, 7, 3 (1881): 161–177.

Hammerschmidt, Ernst. *Stellung und Bedeutung des Sabbats in Äthiopen.* Stuttgart: W. Kohlhammer, 1963.

———. "Jewish Elements in the Cult of the Ethiopian Church," *Journal of Ethiopian Studies* 2 (1965): 1–12.

Hess, Robert, I. "The Itinerary of Benjamin of Tudela: A Twelfth Century Jewish Description of Northeast Africa," *Journal of African History* 6 (1965): 15–24.

———. "An Outline of Falasha History," *Proceedings of the Third International Conference of Ethiopian Studies.* Addis Ababa: Institute of Ethiopian Studies, 1969, vol. 1, 101–106.

———. "Toward a History of the Falasha," in *Eastern African History,* eds. Daniel F. McCall, Norman R. Bennett, and Jeffrey Butler. Boston University Papers on Africa, vol. 3. New York: Frederick A. Praeger, 1969: 107–132.

Hetzron, Robert. "Agew," *Afroasiatic Liguistics,* 3, 3 (1976): 1–45.

Hetzron, Robert, and Marvin L. Bender. "The Ethio-Semitic Languages," in M. Lionel Bender et al., eds., *Language in Ethiopia.* London: Oxford University Press, 1976, 24–30.

Heyd, Michael. "The Reaction to Enthusiasm in the 17th Century: From Anti-structure to Structure," *Religion* 15 (1985): 279–289.

Hirschberg, Ze'ev. *Israel in Arabia.* Tel Aviv: Masada, 1947 (Hebrew).

Hoben, Allan. *Land Tenure among the Amhara of Ethiopia.* Chicago: University of Chicago Press, 1973.

Horvath, Ronald J. "The Wandering Capitals of Ethiopia," *Journal of African History* 10 (1969): 205–219.

Hubbard, David A. "The Literary Sources of the *Kebra Nagašt*," Ph.D. dissertation, St. Andrews University, 1956.

Huntingford, G. W. B., ed. and tr. *The Glorious Victories of Amda Seyon, King of Ethiopia.* Oxford: Clarendon Press, 1965.

———. ed. and tr. *The Land Charters of Northern Ethiopia.* Addis Ababa: Haile Sellassie I University with Oxford University Press, 1965.

Ibn Haukal, Muhammed. *Configuration de la terre,* tr. Johannes Hendrik Kramers and Gaston Weit. Paris: G. P. Maissonneue and Larose, 1964.

Ilogu, E. *Christianity and Ibo Culture.* Leiden: E. J. Brill, 1974.

Isaac, Ephraim. "An Obscure Component in Ethiopian Church History," *Le Muséon* 85 (1972): 225–258.

Isaac, Ephraim, and Cain Felder. "Reflections on the Origins of Ethiopian Civilization," *Proceedings of the Eighth International Conference of Ethiopian Studies.* Addis Ababa, Frankfurt: Institute of Ethiopian Studies, Frobenius Institut, 1988, 71–83.

Isichei, Elizabeth. *Varieties of Christian Experience in Nigeria.* London: Macmillan, 1982.

Kaplan, Steven. "Ezana's Conversion Reconsidered," *Journal of Religion in Africa* 13 (1982): 101–109.

———. "A Source for the History of the Beta Israel (Falasha) from the *Life* of Abuna Takla Hawaryat," *Pe'amim* 15 (1983): 124–133 (Hebrew).

———. *The Monastic Holy Man and the Christianization of Early Solomonic Ethiopia.* Wiesbaden: Franz Steiner, 1984.

———. "On the Importance of Ethiopian Studies for the Study of the Falasha," *Pe'amim* 21 (1984): 141–146 (Hebrew).

———. "The Fälasha and the Stephanite: An Episode from *Gädlä Gäbrä Mäsih*," *Bulletin of the School of Oriental and African Studies* 48, 2 (1985): 279–282.

———. "The Origins of the Beta Israel: Five Methodological Cautions," *Pe'amim* 33 (1987): 33–49 (Hebrew).

———. "The Beta Israel (Falasha) Encounter with Protestant Missionaries: 1860–1905," *Jewish Social Studies* 49, 1 (Winter 1987): 27–42.

———. "The Beta Israel and the Rabbinate: Law, Politics, and Ritual," *Social Science Information* 28, 3 (September 1988): 357–370.

———. "Some Hebrew Sources on the Beta Israel (Falasha)," *Proceedings of the Eighth International Conference of Ethiopian Studies.* Cambridge, Frankfurt: Institute of Ethiopian Studies, Frobenius Institute, 1988, I, 199–208.

———. "Leadership and Communal Organization among the Beta Israel (Falasha): An Historical Study," *Encyclopaedia Judaica Yearbook 1986–7.* Jerusalem: Keter, 1988, 154–163.

———. " 'Falasha' Religion: Ancient Judaism or Evolving Ethiopian Tradition? A Review Article," *Jewish Quarterly Review* 79, 1 (July 1988): 49–65.

———. "The Literature of the Beta Israel: Retrospect and Prospect," *Pe'amim* 41 (1990): 90–111 (Hebrew).

———. "The Two Zions and the Exodus from Ethiopia," *Studies in Contemporary Jewry* 7 (1991): 298–305. (Review article.)

———. *Les Falāshās.* Turnhout, Belgium: Brepols, 1990.

Kaplan, Steven, and Shoshana Ben-Dor, *Ethiopian Jewry: An Annotated Bibliography.* Jerusalem: Ben-Zvi Institute, 1988.

Kessler, David. *The Falashas: The Forgotten Jews of Ethiopia.* New York: Africana, 1982.

Knibb, Michael A. "Hebrew and Syriac Elements in the Ethiopic Version of Ezekial?" *Journal of Semitic Studies* 33, 1 (1988): 11–35.

Kobishchanov, Yuri. *Axum.* University Park: Pennsylvania State University Press, 1979.

Krempel, Veronika. "Die Soziale und wirtschaftliche Stellung der Falascha in der christlich-amharischen wirtschaftliche von Nordwest-Äthiopien," Ph.D. dissertation, Frein Universitat, Berlin, 1972.

Kropp, Manfred. *Die Geschichte des Lebna Dengel, Claudius, und Minas.* CSCO Script. Aeth. 83–84. Louvain: E. Peeters, 1988.

Leroy, Jules. *L'Éthiopie: Archéologie et culture.* Brussells: Desele De Brower, 1973.

Leslau, Wolf. "A Falasha Religious Dispute," *Proceedings of the American Academy for Jewish Research* 16 (1947): 71–95.

———. *Falasha Anthology.* New Haven: Yale University Press, 195l.

———. "The Names of the Weekdays in Ethiopic," *Journal of Semitic Studies* 6 (1961): 62–70.

———. "Taamarat Emmanuel's Notes on Falasha Monks and Holy Places," in *Salo Wittmayer Baron Jubilee Volume.* Jerusalem: American Academy for Jewish Research, 1974, II, 623–637.

Levine, Donald N. *Wax and Gold.* Chicago: University of Chicago Press, 1965.

———. *Greater Ethiopia: The Evolution of a Multiethnic Society.* Chicago: University of Chicago Press, 1974.

Lewis, Herbert S. "The Origin of the Galla and Somali," *Journal of African History* 7 (1966): 27–46.

Lifchitz, Deborah. "Un sacrifice chez les Falachas, Juifs d'Abyssinie," *La Terre et la vie* 9 (1939): 116–123.

Littmann, Enno. "The Magic Book of the Disciples," *Journal of the American Oriental Society* 25 (1904): 1–48.

———. *Deutsche Aksum-Expedition,* vol. 4. Berlin: G. Reimer, 1913.

———. "Altamharischen Glossar," *Rivista degli studie orientali* 20 (1943): 473–505.

London Society for Promoting Christianity amongst the Jews (Journals)
Annual Report
Jewish Intelligence
Jewish Missionary Intelligence
Jewish Records

Ludolphus, Job. *A New History of Ethiopia, Being a Full and Accurate Description of the Kingdom of Abessinia.* London: J. P. Gent, 1682.

Luzzato, Philoxene. *Mémoire sur les Juifs d'Abyssinie ou Falashas.* Paris: Extrait des Archives Israélites, 1853.

Malécot, G. *Les voyageurs français et les relations entre la France et l'Abyssinie des 1835 à 1870.* Paris: Librairie Orientaliste Paul Geunther, 1972.

McCrindle, J. W. *The Christian Topography of Cosmas.* London: Hakluyt Society, 1898.

Marcus, Louis. "Notice sur l'époque de l'établissement des Juifs dan l'Abyssinie," *Journal asiatique* 3 (1829): 409–431 4 (1829): 51–73.

Mekouria, T. T. "The Horn of Africa," *General History of Africa,* ed. M. Elfasi. London, Berkeley, Paris: Heinemann, University of California, UNESCO, 1988: III, 558–574,

Merid, Wolde Aregay. "Southern Ethiopia and the Christian Kingdom, 1508–

1708, with Special Reference to the Galla Migrations and their Consequences," Ph.D. dissertation, University of London, 1971.

————. "Society and Technology in Ethiopia 1500–1800," *Journal of Ethiopian Studies* 17 (1984): 127–147.

Messing, Simon D. *The Story of the Falashas: "Black Jews" of Ethiopia*. Brooklyn: Balshon Printing and Offset, 1982.

Michels, Joseph W. "Axumite Archaeology: An Introductory Essay," in Yuri Kobishchanov, *Axum*. University Park: Pennsylvania State University Press, 1979, 1–34.

————. "Regional Political Organization in the Axum-Yeha Area During the Pre-Axumite and Axumite Eras," paper presented at the 10th International Conference on Ethiopian Studies, Paris, France, August 1988.

Migne, J. P. *Patrologia cursus completus: series latina*. Paris: Garnier, 1844/55.

————. *Patrologia cursus completus: series graeca*. Paris: Garnier, 1857/66.

Myers, Jacob M. *II Chronicles The Anchor Bible*, vol. 13. Garden City, NY: Doubleday, 1965.

Nerssian V., tr., and Richard Pankhurst, ed. and annot. "The Visit to Ethiopia of Yohannes T'ovmacean, an Armenian Jeweller in 1764–66," *Journal of Ethiopian Studies* 15 (1982): 79–104.

Newsome, James D., Jr. *A Synoptic Harmony of Samuel, Kings and Chronicles*. Grand Rapids, MI: Baker Book House, 1986.

Nöldeke, Theodor. Review of Dillmann, "Über die Regierung, insbesondere die Kirchenordnung des Königs Zar'a Jacob," *Göttingische Gelehrte Anzeigen* (1884): 577–581.

Pankhurst, Richard K. *A History of Ethiopian Towns* I. Wiesbaden: Franz Steiner Verlag, 1982.

————. *State and Land in Ethiopian History*. Addis Ababa: Institute of Ethiopian Studies and Oxford University Press, 1966.

————. *The History of Famine and Epidemics in Ethiopia Prior to the Twentieth Century*. Addis Ababa: Relief and Rehabilitation Commission, 1985.

————. "Problems about Bruce's History of the Zagwe Dynasty," *Quardeni di Studi Etiopici* 6–7 (1985–1986): 86–92.

Pankhurst, Richard K., and Douglas H. Johnson. "The Great Drought and Famine of 1888–92 in Northeast Africa," in Douglas H. Johnson and David M. Anderson, eds., *The Ecology of Survival: Case Studies from North African History*. London: Lester Crook Academic Publishing, 1988, 47–70.

Payne, F. G. (Eric). *Ethiopian Jews: The Story of a Mission*. London: Olive Press, 1972.

Pearce, Nathaniel. *The Life and Adventures of Nathaniel Pearce* .... London: Colburn and Bentley, 1831.

Perruchon, Jules. "Histoire de guerres d'Amda Seyon, roi d'Éthiopie," *Journal asiatique*, ser. 8, 14 (1889): 271–363, 381–493.

————. "Notes pour l'histoire d'Éthiopie: Lettre adressée par le roi d'Éthiopie au roi Georges de Nubie sous le patriarcat de Philothée (981–1002 ou 1003," *Revue sémitique* 1 (1893): 71–76, 359–372.

————. "Histoire d'Eskender, d'Amda Seyon II et de Na'od, rois d'Éthiopie," *Journal asiatique*, ser. 9, 3 (1894): 319–366.

————. *Les Chroniques de Zar'a Yâ'eqôb et de Ba'eda Mâryâm*. Paris: Librairie Émile Bouillon, 1892.

————. "Notes pour l'histoire d'Éthiopie: Le règne de Galawdeows (Claudius) ou Asnaf-Sagad," *Revue sémitique* 2 (1894): 155–166,263–278.

————. "Notes pour l'histoire d'Éthiopie: Le règne de Minas ou Admas-Sagad (1559–1563)," *Revue sémitique* 4 (1896): 87–90.

————. "Notes pour l'histoire d'Éthiopie: Regne de Sarṣa-Dengel ou Malak-Sagad Ier (1563–1597)," *Revue sémitique* 4 (1896): 177–185, 273–278.

————. "Notes pour l'histoire d'Éthiopie: Règnes de Yaqob et Za-Dengel (1597–1607)," *Revue sémitique* 4 (1896): 355–363.

————. "Notes pour l'histoire d'Éthiopie: Règne de Susenyos ou Seltan-Sagad (1607–1632)," *Revue sémitique* 5 (1897): 75–80, 173–189.

————. Notes pour l'histoire d'Ethiopie: La règne de Fasiladas (Alam Sagad), de 1632 a 1667," *Revue sémitique* 5 (1897), 360–372; 6 (1898): 84–92.

Pirouet, M. Louise. *Black Evangelists*. London: Collings, 1978.

Plowden, Walter. *Travels in Abyssinia and Galla Country, with an Account of a Mission to Ras Ali in 1848*. London: Longmans, 1868.

Polotsky, H. J. "Aramaic, Syriac, and Ge'ez," *Journal of Semitic Studies* 9 (1964): 1–10.

Porten, Bezalel. *Archives from Elephantine*. Berkeley and Los Angeles: University of California Press, 1968.

Pritchard, James B., ed. *Solomon and Sheba*. London: Phaidon, 1974.

Quirin, James. "The Beta Israel (Felasha) in Ethiopian History: Caste Formation and Culture Change 1270–1868," Ph.D. dissertation, University of Minnesota, 1977.

————. "The Beta 'Esrā'ēl (Falāshā) and 'Ayhud in Fifteenth-Century Ethiopia: Oral and Written Traditions," *Northeast African Studies* 10, 2–3 (1988): 89–103.

Rapoport, Louis. *The Lost Jews: Last of the Ethiopian Falashas*. New York: Stein and Day, 1981.

————. *Redemption Song: The Story of Operation Moses*. New York: Harcourt Brace Jovanovich, 1985.

Rathjens, Carl. *Die Juden in Abessinien*. Hamburg: M. W. Kaufman, 1921.

Reminick, Ronald A. "The Evil Eye among the Amhara," in C. Maloney, ed., *The Evil Eye*. New York: Columbia University Press, 1979, 85–101.

Rodinson, Maxime. "Sur la question des 'influences juives' en Ethiopie," *Journal of Semitic Studies* 9 (1964): 11–19.

Rubenson, Sven. *King of Kings: Tewodros of Ethiopia*. Addis Ababa and Nairobi: Oxford University Press, 1966.

————. "Ethiopia and the Horn," in *The Cambridge History of Africa*, V, ed. John E. Flint. Cambridge: Cambridge University Press, 1976, 51–98.

————. *The Survival of Ethiopian Independence*. London: Heinneman, 1978.

Rüppell, Eduard. *Reise in Abyssinien*. 2 vols. Frankfurt: Schmerber, 1835–1840.

Sanneh, Lamin. *Translating the Word*. Maryknoll, NY: Orbis, 1989.

Sawirus (ibn al-Mukaffa). *History of the Patriarchs of the Egyptian Church*, tr. Yassa 'abd Al-Masaih et al. Cairo: Société d'archéologie copte, 1943–59.

Schalit, Abraham. "Elephantine," *Encyclopaedia Judaica*, VI, 603–610.

Schneider, René. "Yuri M. Kobishchanov, *Axum, A Review Article*," *Journal of Ethiopian Studies* 17 (1984): 79–104.

Schoeffelers, Matthew, and Ian Linden. "The Resistance of the *Nyau* Societies to Roman Catholic Missions in Colonial Malawi," in Terence O. Ranger and Isaria. N. Kimambo, eds., *The Historical Study of African Religions*. Berkeley: University of California Press, 1974, 252–276.

Schohat, Azriel. "Eldad Ha-Dani," *Encyclopaedia Judaica*, VI, 577.

Sergew Hable Sellassie. *Ancient and Medieval Ethiopian History to 1270*. Addis Ababa: United Printers, 1972.

Shahid, Irfan. *The Martyrs of Najran: New Documents*. Bruxelles: Société des Bollandistes, 1971.

———. "The Kebra Nagašt in the Light of Recent Research," *Le Muséon* 89 (1976): 133–178.

———. "Byzantium in South Arabia," *Dumbarton Oaks Papers* 33 (1979): 23–94.

Shelemay, Kay Kaufman. *Music, Ritual, and Falasha History*, 2nd ed. East Lansing: Michigan State University Press, 1989.

———. "Historical Ethnomusicology: Reconstructing Falasha Liturgical History," *Ethnomusicology* 24 (1980): 233–258.

———. "Music in the American Synagogue: A Case Study from Houston," in Jack Wertheimer, ed., *The American Synagogue: A Sanctuary Transformed*. Cambridge: Cambridge University Press, 1987.

Shelemay, Kay Kaufman, and Peter Jeffries. *Ethiopian Christian Chant: An Anthology*. 3 vols. Madison, WI: A-R Editions, Inc., in press.

Smith, Robert Michael. "The London Jews' Society and Patterns of Jewish Conversion in England, 1801–1859," *Jewish Social Studies* 43, 3–4 (Summer–Fall 1981): 276–286.

Snaith, Norman Henry. "Bible: Canon," *Encyclopaedia Judaica*, IV, 822–823.

Speiser, E. A. *Genesis, The Anchor Bible* I. Garden City, NY: Doubleday, 1964.

Stern, Henry Aaron. *Wanderings among the Falashas in Abyssinia*, 2nd ed. London: Frank Cass, 1968.

Taddesse Tamrat. "Some Notes on the Fifteenth-Century Stephanite 'Heresy' in the Ethiopian Church," *Rassegna di studi etiopici* 22 (1966): 103–115.

———. "The Abbots of Dabra Hayq: 1248–1535," *Journal of Ethiopian Studies* 8, 1 (1970): 87–117.

———. *Church and State in Ethiopia 1270–1527*. Oxford: Clarendon Press, 1972.

———. "Problems of Royal Succession in Fifteenth Century Ethiopia: A Presentation of the Documents," *IV Congresso Internazionale di Studi Etiopici*. Rome: Accademia Nazionale dei Lincei, 1974, I, 501–535.

————. "Ethiopia, the Red Sea and the Horn," *Cambridge History of Africa,* vol. 3, ed. Roland Oliver. Cambridge: Cambridge University Press, 1977, 98–182.

————. "Processes of Ethnic Interaction and Integration in Ethiopian History: The Case of the Agaw," *Journal of African History* 29 (1988): 5–18.

Tasie, G. O. M. *Christian Missionary Enterprise in the Niger Delta.* Leiden: E. J. Brill, 1978.

Tedeschi, Salvatore. "L'Éthiopie dans L'itineraire de Benjamin de Tudèle," *Proceedings of the Ninth International Congress of Ethiopian Studies,* vol. 6. Moscow: USSR Academy of Sciences, Africa Institute, 1988, 207–221.

Telles, Balthazar. *The Travels of the Jesuits in Ethiopia.* London: J. Knapton, 1710.

Trevisan Semi, Emanuela. "The Beta Israel (Falashas): From Purity to Impurity," *Jewish Journal of Sociology* 25 (1985): 103–114.

————. "Le Sriet: Un rite d'investiture sacredotale chez les Beta Esra'ēl (Falashas)," *Revue des études Juives* 146 (1987): 101–124.

Trimingham, John Spencer. *Islam in Ethiopia.* London: Frank Cass, 1965.

Ullendorff, Edward. "Hebraic-Jewish Elements in Abyssinian (Monophysite) Christianity," *Journal of Semitic Studies* 1 (1956): 216–256.

————. *Ethiopia and the Bible.* London: Oxford University Press, 1968.

————. *The Ethiopians,* 3rd ed. London: Oxford University Press, 1973.

————. "Hebrew, Aramaic, and Greek: The Versions underlying Ethiopic Translations of Bible and Intertestamental Literature," in Gary Rendsburg, et al., eds., *The Bible World: Essays in Honour of Cyrus H. Gordon.* New York: KTAV, 1980, 249–257.

————. "Hebrew Elements in the Ethiopic Old Testament," *Jerusalem Studies in Arabic and Islam* 9 (1987): 42–50.

————. "The *Confessio Fidei* of King Claudius of Ethiopia," *Journal of Semitic Studies* 32, 1 (Spring 1987): 159–176.

Ullendorff, Edward, and C. F. Beckingham. *The Hebrew Letters of Prester John.* London: Oxford University Press, 1982.

Vanderkam, James C. *Textual and Historical Studies in the Book of Jubilees.* Missoula, Montana: Scholars Press, 1977.

Varenbergh, Joseph. "Studien zur abessinischen Reichordnung (Šer'ata Mangešt)," *Zeitschrift für Assyriologie* 30 (1915–16): 1–45.

Vincent, Leopold. *La religion des judéo-arméens d'Elephantine.* Paris: P. Geuthner, 1937.

Waldman, Menachem. *The Jews of Ethiopia.* Jerusalem: Joint Distribution Committee, 1985.

————. *Beyond the Rivers of Ethiopia: The Jews of Ethiopia and the Jewish People.* Tel Aviv: Ministry of Defence, 1989 (Hebrew).

Wajnberg, I. "Das Leben des hl. Jāfqerena' 'Egzi'," *Orientalia Christiana Analecta* 106. 1936.

Warren, Max. *The Missionary Movement from Britian in Modern History.* London: S. C. M. Press, 1965.

Wendt, Kurt, ed. *Das Maṣḥafa Milād und Maṣḥafa Sellāsē des Kaisers Zar'a Ya'qob. CSCO Script. Aeth.* 41 and 43.

Wintermute, Oscar. "Cush," *Interpreter's Dictionary of the Bible: Supplementary Volume.* Nashville: Abingdon, 1976.

Whiteway, R. S. *The Portuguese Expedition to Abyssinia in 1541–1543.* London: Hakluyt Society, 1902.

Wurmbrand, Max. "Falashas," *Encyclopaedia Judaica,* VI, 1143–1154.

———. *The Death of Aaron.* Tel Aviv: Hug Ne'mene bet Faitlovitz, 1961 (Hebrew).

———. *The Falasha Arde'et.* Tel Aviv: Hug Ne'mena bet Faitlovitz, 1964 (Hebrew).

Yaari, Abraham. *Letters from the Land of Israel,* 2nd ed. Ramat Gan: Masada, 1971 (Hebrew).

Zimra, David Ibn Abi (RadBaz). *Responsa.* Venice.

Zotenberg, Hermann. "Un document sur les Falachas," *Journal asiatique,* sixieme series, 9 (1867): 265–268.

Oral Sources

Interviews with Ethiopian immigrants were conducted by Shoshana Ben-Dor in 1986, and by me and Dr. Chaim Rosen in 1987–88. Copies and transcripts of the Kaplan-Rosen interviews have been deposited at the Institute of Contemporary Jewry, Hebrew University of Jerusalem.

Abba Gette Asress, interviewed by Shoshana Ben-Dor, November 17, 1986.

Ato Wube Akale, interviewed by Shoshana Ben-Dor, September 12, 1986.

Qes Qasata Menasse, interviewed by Shoshana Ben-Dor, December 22, 1986.

Qes Yimanu Tamayt, interviewed by Steven Kaplan and Chaim Rosen on November 25, 1987, and December 2, 1987.

Abba Yishaq Iyasu, interviewed by Steven Kaplan and Chaim Rosen on December 18, 1987.

Ato Mikael Adamas, interviewed by Steven Kaplan and Chaim Rosen on December 18, 1987.

Ato Mucheneh Alazar interviewed by Steven Kaplan and Chaim Rosen on January 14, 1988.

Qes Hadana Tekuyo interviewed by Steven Kaplan and Chaim Rosen on February 5, 1988.

Index